IRREGULAR REGULAR

IRREGULAR REGULAR

David Smiley

MICHAEL RUSSELL

FOR MY GRANDSONS
BEN & ADAM

By the same author

ARABIAN ASSIGNMENT
ALBANIAN ASSIGNMENT

© David Smiley 1994

First published in Great Britain 1994
by Michael Russell (Publishing) Ltd
Wilby Hall, Wilby, Norwich NR16 2JP

Reprinted 1994

Typeset in Sabon by The Typesetting Bureau
6 Church Street, Wimborne, Dorset
Printed and bound in Great Britain
by Biddles Ltd, Guildford and King's Lynn

ISBN 0 85955 202 0

Contents

Acknowledgements   vi

PART ONE Household Cavalry

1   England   3
2   Palestine   13
3   Commandos   13
4   Iraq   40
5   Syria and Persia   52
6   Western Desert   62

PART TWO Albania

7   MO4 and Parachute to Greece   77
8   Albanian Partisans   84
9   Return to Albania   100

PART THREE Thailand

10   Briefing and Training in India and Ceylon   115
11   Reception, Activities and Evacuation   131
12   Return to Thailand   149
13   Incidents in Thailand and French Indo-China   164

PART FOUR Albania Again

14   1949   187
15   1992   194

Index   209

Acknowledgements

All my thanks to my wife Moy, who with great patience read the draft of this book, offered advice, corrected errors and helped with the indexing. I am grateful also to my publisher, Michael Russell, for his editing and advice.

PART ONE
Household Cavalry

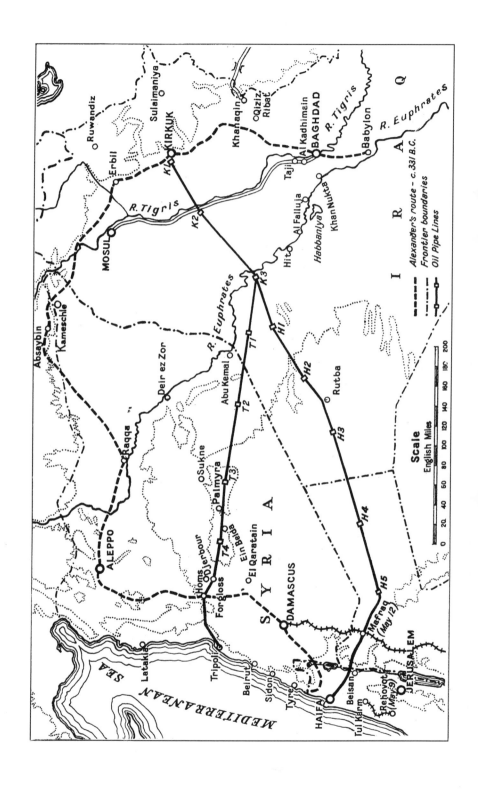

I

England

I was not expecting to enjoy my interview with the colonel, and I didn't. 'You will go back to the Riding School until I consider you are fit to ride in public again.' After passing out of the Riding School I had been detailed for my first sovereign's escort – the occasion was the state visit of the King of the Belgians. A sovereign's escort consists of seven officers and one hundred and nine other ranks, two divisions in front of the sovereign's carriage, two divisions in the rear of the carriage, the senior officers of the escort on either side of the carriage and the standard carried immediately behind.

Before the escort moved out of Hyde Park Barracks there was a detailed inspection by the adjutant. You look ugly when riding in jackboots with your stirrup leathers too short, so I had lengthened mine as long as possible. What I did not know was that the adjutant invariably gave the order 'Down two holes'. Being a new boy I did not dare to remonstrate. A trooper lengthened my stirrup leathers and the soles of my boots lost contact with my stirrups. Within a few minutes we were trotting up to Victoria Station.

I had little control over my horse and I was dreading that I might make a fool of myself and fall off. My feet were right out of the stirrups; the problem was how to get them back again. A jackboot is too thick to allow you to feel with your toe, and if you looked down, your helmet and plume could easily slip forward and then you couldn't see. So I jogged on.

The ride was a misery. Fortunately on the return there was a brief check at Hyde Park Corner and I asked one of the policemen lining the street to shove my feet back into the stirrups. He obliged but here I was unlucky. Standing in the crowd observing the unhappy incident was – the colonel. Hence my interview.

In September 1936 I had arrived at Hyde Park Barracks, Knightsbridge, commissioned a 2nd lieutenant (cornet) in the Royal Horse Guards (The Blues). At Sandhurst I had lost six months' seniority by 'dropping a term' after a crashing fall in a point-to-point which put me in hospital for six months. My only academic achievements at Sandhurst were passing out top in map reading and bottom in economics.

Rules in the Household Brigade were strict, even off parade. I was soon to find this out when I was awarded fourteen extra orderlies – an officer's equivalent to CB (confined to barracks) – for dancing downstairs in the Café de Paris in a dinner jacket. If you chose to dance downstairs in the Café de Paris you had to wear a white tie and tails; in a dinner jacket you had to confine yourself to dancing on the less conspicuous balcony upstairs. White tie and tails were also *de rigueur* at the theatre and I was once reprimanded for being seen in a party at the theatre wearing a dinner jacket – at my hostess's request.

I accepted these rather strange rules and customs, chiefly because life as a cornet in the Blues was, in most ways, idyllic. Like our sister regiment The Life Guards, we were a very small unit, almost a kind of club. The peacetime strength in 1936 was 14 officers, 419 men and 250 horses. Our only motorised transport was about a dozen Austin Sevens and a few motor cycles used by the signals troop.

Each regiment was stationed for a year in London, and then at Windsor. At the time of the change-over in October, the regiment leaving London was sometimes described by officers from other regiments as 'going on foreign service across the Serpentine'. It needed a war to get me overseas. Duties in London were mainly ceremonial; at Windsor we were supposed to do serious training, but the Army estimates at the time were so restricted that it was completely unrealistic. Officers were equipped with a sword and a .38 pistol. We were each allotted eighteen rounds per year for practice. We fired six from the ground standing, six from a horse walking, and six from a horse trotting. Later in the war my pistol shooting improved, but at this stage I seldom hit the target.

On manoeuvres a cavalry troop was supposed to be armed with a light machine-gun and an anti-tank rifle. As we hadn't any, these weapons were represented by flags, usually green and white, with a rattle to represent machine-gun fire. The Army was so under strength and ill-equipped that on most manoeuvres there were far more imaginary troops on the ground than real ones. Then, just before the war, we were issued with Bren guns. Our men liked them very much, but as soon as the war started our new toys were taken away from us and sent to the BEF in France. There weren't enough to go round.

Everything in a young officer's life depended on his NCO. We had no experience; many of the NCOs had served ten to twenty years. They knew all the tricks of the trade and the characters of our senior officers. A good NCO was one part nanny, one part coach, and one part poacher turned gamekeeper. I was lucky to have an excellent corporal of horse (sergeant).

Soldiering, however, played only a small part in our lives. Officers were encouraged to seek adventure on leave. Bob Laycock* sailed home from Australia in a windjammer. Others went on big game safaris to Kenya. Some did a stint as ADCs, usually to the Viceroy of India or Governor-General of Canada. Hunting, shooting, polo and steeplechasing were regarded as duty; in other words they didn't count against one's leave. Before the war leave was the same as it is today – six weeks in the year; but adding to it the days spent away hunting, and weekends, it must have amounted to three or four months. In those days we were informed that leave was a privilege and never a right. All my army life I failed to understand the logic of this, but I did find that the higher you climbed the ladder of promotion, the less leave you seemed to get.

The Munich crisis caused a flap. I was orderly officer and had to telephone every officer who was on leave recalling him to barracks. This did not make me very popular. We dug slit trenches and weapon pits in the sports fields in Hyde Park just opposite the barracks. To the delight of the more insubordinate, so many sandbags were piled on the roof of the Orderly Room block, which included the colonel's and the adjutant's offices, that the roof collapsed.

I was sent to the War Office in Whitehall to help with the reserve officers reporting for duty, and others volunteering. The queue stretched from the War Office as far as Trafalgar Square. This was encouraging. The Munich Agreement was then signed. My only reaction was one of relief that we were no longer confined to barracks and that night some of us celebrated with a night out, ending up at the Bag of Nails. This was our favourite night club, where we could make assignations with attractive young ladies.

* Later Major-General Sir Robert Laycock, Chief of Combined Operations and after the war Governor of Malta.

[5]

Presiding over it was the legendary Millie, a motherly and jolly woman of middle age. She treated us all as 'her boys' and saw to it that we were never robbed or blackmailed. Millie was very generous and was known not to present bills to some of her clients when she knew they were down on their luck. One could hardly say a visit to the Bag of Nails was a duty but it was certainly part of our education.

After this particular visit to the Bag of Nails I awoke with an appalling hangover. This was not in itself surprising, but when the symptoms continued for a second day I reported sick to our medical officer. It turned out that I had typhoid. The time factor indicated that it was caused by a bad oyster I had eaten in Inverness.

When I was extremely ill in the London Clinic my mother was warned that I was likely to die, and was asked if a new drug might be used on me. She agreed. It was known as M & B 693, which had never been used on a typhoid case before. Horace Evans, who had been looking after me, later wrote an article in *The Lancet* describing the success of this experiment in which I was the guinea-pig. Meanwhile, I spent the best part of three months convalescing in Nassau and Palm Beach. During my illness my weight had gone down to under six stone and I looked like a skeleton, but with plenty of swimming, daiquiris and pretty girls around I soon revived.

While abroad I had the feeling that war could not be far off. Accordingly I decided to dispose of various possessions that I thought would be an encumbrance in wartime. On rejoining my regiment I first parted with my racehorse Diabutsu, after riding him to win a selling race at Towcester. A big 18-hand tubed horse, he had provided me with a great deal of sport, including a number of winning rides when he stood up, and as many crashing falls when he didn't. I also had another horse, Shanter, whom I had hoped to ride in the Grand National, but my hopes were dashed first by my attack of typhoid, then, in 1940, by Hitler.

Next I sold my aeroplane – a Miles Whitney Straight. It had been fun flipping across to Le Touquet when I was stationed at Hythe. Yet I parted from it with relief. It had given me some nasty frights, including two forced landings. At the end of the war I took up flying again but I never really felt confident as a pilot.

I was taking part in the annual manoeuvres on Salisbury Plain when the Germans attacked Poland. We were recalled to Windsor and rode back in thirty-six hours – a distance of about sixty-four miles – which was considered fairly fast for troop horses. Back in Windsor it fell to the Household Cavalry to barricade Windsor Castle with sandbags. Initially this was not a great success. One of my brother officers had the bright idea of painting the sandbags with a form of liquid cement. After a short while the paint rotted the sandbags so we had to do the job all over again.

The Household Cavalry now took over from the Foot Guards, I believe for the first time, the duties of guarding the sovereign at Windsor Castle. My experiences as the officer on guard were not very happy. On 3 September one of the equerries asked me into his quarters to hear Neville Chamberlain's speech on the wireless, announcing that as from 11 a.m. we were at war with Germany. My feelings were of relief that at last a decision had been made. I hoped that the new life that lay ahead of me would be abroad and full of adventure.

The next morning I was asleep in bed when I was roughly shaken by an irate equerry. He demanded to know why I was not at my post when the air raid warning had gone. He added that the sentries were still standing in front of their sentry boxes, instead of taking cover in slit trenches as laid down in the orders. I replied rather lamely that I had not heard the siren, and furthermore my servant had not called me. He gave me an old-fashioned look and left, after which I hurriedly dressed. This was, I later heard, the second air raid warning of the war and turned out to be a false alarm.

The next time I was on guard I had to visit all the sentries at midnight, accompanied by the duty corporal-major. We reached the Terrace without being challenged. This struck us as odd until we found that the sentry had propped up his rifle and was stretched out fast asleep half in and half out of his sentry box – unusual behaviour, not merely because it was a gross breach of military discipline, but because sentries on the Terrace were normally doubly alert, expecting at any moment to be confronted by the ghost of Herne the Hunter who was reputed to walk there at night. The man was later charged. I was rather taken aback when his squadron leader only gave him seven days CB, which I regarded as very lenient, being under the impression that sentries who went to sleep in wartime were usually shot.

[7]

My last duty was even worse. I received a message to say that His Majesty, who was staying at the castle at the time, was very displeased to notice that smoke was issuing from one of the sentry boxes. I hurried round with the corporal-major and caught the culprit red-handed, his sentry box littered with cigarette stubs. This sentry was also put under close arrest, charged, and sentenced to twenty-eight days' detention. I could not help feeling that it was no bad thing when the Foot Guards relieved us.

On 3 September the King paid us a farewell visit. He inspected the regiment, now made up of the Life Guards and the Blues augmented by our reservists, which was drawn up on the green in front of the barracks. We were all in service dress: for the troopers this consisted of a steel helmet, khaki jacket buttoned up to the neck, over which was a leather bandolier and a gas mask; cord breeches, puttees, boots and spurs completed the uniform. The officers wore service dress tunics, Sam Brownes, a pistol holster, breeches, field boots and spurs. All swords had by now been sharpened, and the hilts painted grey so as not to reflect the sun.

Before we left Windsor there was much speculation as to where we would be sent overseas. We all suspected it would be Palestine, where the only two other horsed cavalry regiments, the Royals and the Greys, were already stationed. This was confirmed when one of our officers was put under close arrest for being so indiscreet as to say so. The younger officers thought this punishment was quite unnecessary. We suspected that it was instigated by a staff officer wanting a scapegoat to serve as an example to others for a breach of security. The point was lost shortly afterwards when a very senior and distinguished officer, who used to ride from Hyde Park Barracks, asked in a loud voice in front of a number of officers and men, 'Well, and when are you off to Palestine?'

In November the 1st Household Cavalry Regiment left Windsor for the Midlands, where the 1st Cavalry Division, of which we were to form a part, was concentrating prior to going overseas. We entrained at Windsor in the very early hours of the morning, parading in the dark with our horses. Out of the entire population of Windsor only one turned up to see us off – Canon Crawley, the Dean of Windsor, a staunch friend of the Household Cavalry. The band was not allowed to play for fear of waking the inhabitants.

This departure was in marked contrast to the return of the Blues to

Windsor in 1953, after an interval of over thirteen years' continuous service abroad. Then we were greeted by cheering crowds and a formidable array of VIPs. We marched back to the barracks with the band playing at our head. Of those who had marched out with the regiment in 1939 only fifteen returned in 1953. Two were officers – Charles Firth, the quartermaster, and myself commanding the regiment. Twelve were NCOs. There was one trooper – Darby. He had been in my troop when we left in 1939 and was now the oldest soldier in the Blues – a character of irrepressible humour and today a Chelsea Pensioner.

We detrained at Newark and marched to our quarters. Our squadron had its HQ at Kelham House, about five miles from Newark. I was the only unmarried officer in the squadron, so I lived there; the married ones lived locally with their wives in private houses or hotels. My troop by this time had reached its wartime establishment and I was in command of thirty-six men and forty horses. It was billeted in two farms, one on either side of the A1 – the Great North Road. Luckily in those days there was not much traffic.

The owners of Kelham House had no cause to welcome our stay. The first two weeks were marred by mishaps. On the first day one of our lorries crashed into the front gate and knocked down a wall. A few days later an officer's car killed one of their dogs in the drive. Later one of the mess cooks cut down a fine magnolia tree in their garden for firewood. Finally my soldier servant left on an iron, which set fire to the attic. They must have been thankful to see us go. A sequel to our stay at Kelham House occurred six years later. After the end of the war Household Cavalry HQ sent all former surviving officers from our squadron an account for their telephone calls made from Kelham House in 1940, with orders for prompt payment.

We spent about ten weeks of the so-called 'phoney war' in the Midlands before going abroad. During this time our chief task was to get our men trained and our horses fit. It was at this stage that our Bren guns were removed from us and sent to the BEF in France, where most of them were lost in the Allied defeat. In their place we were issued with Hotchkiss guns, which were museum pieces that had been lying in grease in Woolwich Arsenal since the end of the 1914-18 war. They were heavier than the Bren, more difficult to handle, and jammed repeatedly. Nobody had any confidence in them. In addition to the Hotchkiss gun each troop was equipped with the Boys anti-tank rifle. Later in the war this weapon proved incapable of penetrating German armour – but in 1940 we were happily unaware of its shortcomings.

In January 1940 I was given my final embarkation leave. I paid farewell visits to my family and dumped all unwanted baggage. My mother's large garage was already full, so to make space for my Bentley I persuaded her to dispose of the old family Rolls-Royce – a 1909 saloon. She kept the body as a chicken house and sold the chassis to a local garage for £100. Today that car would fetch over £100,000.

My worst parting was having to have my beloved Dandie Dinmont terrier, Dizzy, put down – he was then over twelve. I felt sure I would never see him again if I left him with anyone as he always pined without me. I must confess that this was the only time during the whole war that I was reduced to tears. It was a small and selfish matter; later I realised how lucky I was then not to be married. I buried Dizzy in the dogs' cemetery at Champion Lodge, the home of my uncle Crawley de Crespigny. He also kindly agreed to keep my two remaining hunters, one with a foal. I never saw them again as my uncle died during the war and the horses were sold without my knowledge.

We left England early in February. For the move the squadron was divided into two parties – horses and men. At the start only one man accompanied every four horses, the rest sailed direct to Palestine on a troopship. Major Henry Abel Smith, the squadron leader, the medical officer and myself were the only officers to go with the horses; for the journey I was appointed train and ship's adjutant.

Our overworked farriers were responsible for loading the horses, which was a difficult job. In the British standard railway cattle-waggon the animals stood at right angles to the railway line, eight in a waggon. This, with those big black horses, was a tight fit; getting the last one squeezed into the waggon was physically demanding as well as a test of the farriers' patience. As it was, on the train journey from Newark to Dover we had several delays from horses falling down in the waggons. One had been so badly kicked that its jaw was broken and one eye blinded. It was shot on the spot.

At Dover our waggons were shunted on to the ferry, where we were joined by two squadrons of the North Somerset Yeomanry, with whom we continued the rest of our journey to Palestine. The

Channel was choppy and it rained the whole way over. Although we manned machine-guns against possible enemy air attack, the only visual excitements were three mines, one wreck and a corpse.

In the late afternoon we docked at Dunkirk where the horses were taken out of the waggons, no doubt to their great relief. After a short walk to enable them to stretch their legs, they were reloaded into French cattle-waggons. The reloading took place in the dark, hampered by cold, rain and the effects of sea-sickness. The French trucks were much more practical than the British ones. Four horses stood at each end, parallel to the railway line and with their heads facing the centre; here two soldiers were seated on bales of straw whose duty it was to look after the horses.

After a two-day journey across France we arrived in the grounds of Château de la Reynarde, some twelve miles from Marseilles. The camp was memorable for its cold, squalid discomfort and filth. The troops were under canvas in temperatures of sometimes more than fifteen degrees of frost, caused by the bitter mistral that blew without respite from the north, chilling the Rhône valley in which we were camped.

The officers fared little better, being packed ten to a room in the château, which had just been vacated by Algerian troops. It was lucky that none of the windows had any glass. The stench was appalling thanks to the sanitary habits of the Algerians. They had defecated almost anywhere except in the lavatories, which in any case did not work. The place was riddled with lice and fleas.

After the first night a number of us decided to move into one of the hotels in Marseilles, without appreciating that they were already filled to capacity with staff officers. We compromised by spending our nights at the local brothels, a solution both practical and congenial. I stayed for three nights at 'Miss Lucy's', returning to the château in time for duty.

The horses were tethered out of doors on lines in the bitter cold. In spite of being covered with the maximum number of blankets, quite a few went down with pneumonia. The rumour went round that in one of the Yeomanry regiments a horse had been found dead one morning frozen stiff and still standing up.

In Marseilles we were joined for one night by the party travelling on the troopship *Dilwara* from England to Palestine. We had an excellent dinner with delicious bouillabaisse. Three of their officers were transferred to our horsed group for the rest of the journey. We were very shorthanded and, as the journey later proved, needed extra officers.

We were not sorry to see the last of the château. We led our horses to the Marseilles docks, leaving behind nine with pneumonia, and embarked on a cargo boat, the *Rhona*, that had been converted for carrying mules from Argentine to Europe. On board we had over 500 horses and, though the weather was fine, they contracted a great deal of sickness. They suffered from a form of fever caused by lack of ventilation, which gave them a high temperature that gradually developed into a type of pneumonia. During the five-day journey all the officers were employed almost continually in giving oxygen to the worst cases. This was done by pushing a rubber tube connected to an oxygen cylinder up the horses' nostrils. They obviously enjoyed the relief it gave them when they were distressed, and quickly recovered after a few minutes' dose. I gave myself a dose now and then, and found it most stimulating.

During the voyage three horses died. They were thrown overboard and we watched them floating in the sea with their legs sticking up until they were out of view – a macabre sight. Added to my duties as ship's adjutant I spent a number of hours taking down in longhand the summary of evidence for the court-martial of a yeomanry farrier who was charged with 'malingering to avoid being sent abroad by stating that he had piles, when in fact he had not had piles'.

We arrived at Haifa in the pouring rain. The low clouds enveloping the top of Mount Carmel, the streams of water running down the streets, and the dripping buildings and inhabitants gave a gloomy first impression of the Holy Land. After the men and horses had disembarked we loaded the horses into cattle-waggons. Then a three-hour train journey down the coastal plain, passing villages with white houses and orange groves, took us to Tulkarm, our first camp in Palestine.

2
Palestine

Tulkarm, built on the lower slopes of rocky barren foothills, was a typical Arab town of white houses lining dusty streets. An isolated Arab village with terraces of olives, and the occasional boy with his herd of goats were our only neighbours. Looking westwards you could see the blue waters of the Mediterranean in the far distance. In the foreground was the coastal plain – flat and fertile – with Arab villages near the hills and Jewish settlements nearer the sea. Running down the plain, parallel to the coast, was the railway that connected Turkey, through Syria and Palestine, to Egypt to the south.

Hostilities betwen the Arabs and the Jews had, by mutual consent, died down since the start of the war with Germany. The situation was still tense, however, and when we arrived in Palestine security precautions were extensive. Our tented camp in the grounds of the agricultural college was completely surrounded by a wide barbed wire fence. Sentries were permanently posted on all exits and there were prowler guards at night. Outside the camp everybody had to go about in armed parties. If an officer left the camp to do some shopping in Tulkarm, he had to have an escort of six armed troopers.

Our predecessors in Tulkarm had been an infantry battalion, who were decidedly unpopular with the local Arabs. From the time of the Arab rebellion in 1937 until the outbreak of the 1939 war British troops had been engaged in small-scale actions against the rebels. Our regiment had not been involved, which probably accounted for the friendly relations that were soon established between the local Arabs and our newly arrived British soldiers. Neither had old scores to settle. I also think that the Arab had a greater respect for, or even fear of, the cavalryman compared with his infantry counterpart.

At Tulkarm the 1st Household Cavalry Regiment was together as a complete unit for the first time. In England we had always been billeted by squadrons in different villages. This was the first chance for many Blues and Life Guards to get to know each other. Several officers I had barely met before, including Miles Graham, who had served in the Life Guards in the First World War and had retired afterwards to become a stockbroker. Considerably older than the other officers, he held the rank of captain and, apart from Colonel Jack Speed, was the only officer to wear any 1914-18 war medals. Later he took a staff job in Cairo, where he eventually attracted General Montgomery's attention. He finished the war as a major-general with a string of decorations from a knighthood downwards, having been responsible for the total administration of 21 Army Group during and after the landings in Normandy.

Another somewhat unusual officer was Bill Allen, who in prewar days had been connected with the Fascist movement. It was alleged that he and Hitler had been co-godparents to one of Oswald Mosley's children. It was furthermore strongly rumoured that Bill had joined the Life Guards just in time to avoid internment under the notorious section 18B. Extremely intelligent, well travelled, an expert in a number of strange languages, he had a dry sense of humour and was a most entertaining companion. He was also very popular with the troops, and on one occasion during a regimental boxing tournament he gave an exhibition bout with Miles Graham – no mean feat for probably the two oldest officers in the regiment. Eventually Bill left the regiment and was next heard of in Abyssinia serving with guerrillas behind the Italian lines. Later he took part in a number of cloak and dagger operations and survived the war with distinction.

Our first months in Palestine followed normal peacetime routine. Training was concentrated mainly on horsed cavalry tactics. As a welcome change, however, we carried out a number of patrols into the hills to show the flag in Arab villages. At other times we worked with the Palestine Police, making raids on Arab villages to round up suspected bandits. I managed to get attached to their patrols when I got the chance, and though I was never involved in any violent action, it was more exciting than normal duty and it also gave me an insight into some of their methods.

On my first patrol with the Palestine Police the object was to capture two Arabs wanted for murder. An informer had reported that they were spending the night in a certain house in the middle of an orange grove. He led our party, consisting of a British officer and ten

Arab policemen, to a point from where we could see the house in the moonlight. We crept up and posted ourselves round it at various strategic points. I was given a corner and one window to watch and told to shoot on sight anyone attempting to escape. At that distance I felt very doubtful of being able to hit a running Arab in the dark with a pistol. At a given signal three Arab policemen with torches rushed into the house where they found three very frightened Arabs. They were known to the police but were not the ones we were after.

The informer, a shifty-looking Arab who had all this time remained at a discreet distance under the watchful eye of a policeman, now volunteered the information that he knew a house in a nearby village where they might be hiding. We went there but again failed to find the men we wanted. The police strongly suspected that the occupants knew more about their whereabouts than they cared to divulge. The women and children were sent out of the room and the three men were detained.

The first man was seized by two Arab policemen and held upside down while his feet were placed between a rifle and its sling. He was then kept in this position while policeman took turns to beat the soles of his feet with a leather belt, with short pauses for questioning. After a time he agreed to talk, and the beating ceased. The second man talked after the application of a lighted cigarette to his testicles, but the third seemed to be the leader and more truculent. In a flash the Arab sergeant flew at him and hit him in the face until both his eyes were closed, blood was flowing and a number of teeth were spewed out onto the floor. He then agreed to talk. This ended the interrogation. The police held the men until their information was confirmed.

I was somewhat shocked by all this and said to the police officer in charge 'This sort of thing savours of the Gestapo.' He seemed amused by my reactions and replied: 'These men have confessed to helping the murderers and now they've told us where they are.' These methods of extracting information, he said, were justified. I expressed some doubts. He added that force was the only language these Arabs understood. Under Turkish rule they had been brought up to respect such methods. 'Where do you think we would get,' he asked me 'if we questioned them like a London bobby? I'll tell you; the police would be laughed at, we should get no results, and our methods would be regarded as a sign of weakness.' 'In these interrogations', he went on, 'I make it a rule never to beat anyone up myself. I let Arab police beat up Arabs, and Jewish police beat up Jews.' It was a golden rule, he added, that women were never questioned or touched.

Conditions were very trying. Many of us went down with sandfly fever. We took many precautions such as having our vegetables washed in disinfectant – which did little to improve their taste. Against the heat we wore pith helmets; it was even forbidden to go about stripped to the waist, though this rule went by the board later in the war. Shirt-sleeves were rolled down at sunset, only long trousers were worn. We took quinine tablets against malaria, smeared a very messy grease on our faces, and slept under mosquito nets. The sandflies won, however, for they were small enough to penetrate the mesh and infect us. It was not a fever that lasted very long, but while it lasted one had a high temperature and felt extremely ill.

As the weather became hotter, so our training seemed more monotonous. Exercises on the plain usually consisted of practising artillery and other formations. In artillery formations we cantered with the whole squadron widely dispersed, so as to give as small a target as possible to either air attack or shelling. After the exercises we often rode into the orange groves where the Arab owners were always ready to let us pick as many as we liked. There was a crisis in the orange industry, owing to the shortage of labour and shipping, and a vast amount of fruit remained unpicked. Oranges in Haifa cost £1 for 1,000, but in the country we could load many more into a three-ton lorry for the same sum.

Our exercises in the mountains confirmed my doubts about the usefulness of horses in a modern war. On the plains the horse was virtually useless as armour could take its place. In the hills a horse could go where a tank or armoured car could not, but the threat of the aeroplane could not be overcome. No amount of dispersion or concealment would hide cavalry from observation or attack by aircraft. The more I thought about this, the more depressed I became, since presumably the same thoughts would have occurred to those who ran the Army. I felt sure that we would never be sent into action, but merely spend the rest of the war maintaining law and order in Palestine.

We still enjoyed spells of leave. One memorable weekend started when a brother officer, Gerard Leigh, and I approached a taxi driver in Jerusalem and asked him to drive us to Cairo – a distance of several hundred miles. He was not in the least perturbed, only asking us to wait a couple of hours while he collected his kit and filled up with petrol. The fare we negotiated was the equivalent of £25 for the return trip. He drove us along a rough road over the Sinai Desert and across the Suez Canal, and thence to Cairo. It was a wonderful place for young men on leave. I already had plenty of friends there and made even more; in addition Cairo offered all the pleasures and vices for which anyone could wish.

Soon after returning from Cairo I was sent as an instructor to the Middle East Cavalry School at Karkur in central Palestine. This was a new unit intended to become the Weedon of the Middle East. Courses were run for officers and NCOs of the Cavalry Division in equitation, horsemastership, map reading and cavalry tactics. Everyone enjoyed the courses, both instructors and students. Some of the students had been well-known jockeys or masters of foxhounds before joining up, but they took their lessons in equitation in good humour. I not only enjoyed the job but benefited from it considerably. Weekend leave was usually spent in Beirut. The town had a French atmosphere and we usually stayed at the comfortable King George V Hotel from where we could swim, go racing, consume excellent food in the company of attractive French girls, and finish the day in one of the many night clubs.

After some months in this job I returned to Tulkarm, where I found that my former troop had been taken over by someone else and I was being given command of another. I asked if I could go back to my old troop but this was refused. I was most disappointed, having commanded it since the beginning of the war; indeed most of the men in it were from my pre-war troop – I knew them well and liked serving with them. I felt very bitter about this and decided to try to find a more active job outside the regiment as soon as I could. I put my name down for parachutists, commandos and a number of other units that were asking for volunteers, hoping that at least it would give me a chance of getting away to the war. In retrospect, I should think that I was a pretty Bolshie officer at this stage, certainly enjoying my leave more than my duty.

During a weekend leave in Haifa I had my first good view of an air raid. The Italians had only recently entered the war against us, and their bombers came over in daylight to bomb the Haifa oil refinery. At the time I was having a drink on the terrace of the Windsor Hotel

Annexe halfway up Mount Carmel. It was an impressive sight as the planes flew over and I could see the bombs leaving the aircraft, follow them as they fell, and observe the bursts. Luckily they missed the refinery but they hit and set on fire three big oil tanks nearby, which burnt merrily for several days. We could see the smoke of the fires from Tulkarm over thirty miles away.

I enjoyed staying at the Windsor Hotel Annexe. Sitting on the terrace one had a breathtaking view. Modern white cubist houses dotted the steep hillside below, contrasted against the blue background of the sea. Beyond the breakwater, built by convicts, was a grey wreck lying on its side; a few white sails in the huge sweeping bay meant it was a fine day for the fisherman. To the north and beyond the outskirts of Haifa, the tanks and ungainly buildings of the oil refinery made a modern contrast with the mouth of the River Kishon, of biblical days, which flowed into the sea nearby. When the heat haze was not too strong, one could just see across the bay the red roofs of the Arab town and the old Crusader fort at Acre.

The hotel was run by an Arab friend, the charming and amusing Roy Boutagy, the owner's son. He was learning the hotel business with a view to taking over from his father, Emil Boutagy, a well-known character who had been a successful agent in the First World War, when he had carried out a series of dangerous operations behind Turkish lines collecting information for the British.

In July I was sent on a field works course near Gaza, where I found myself in a vast camp of Australians. I was beginning to enjoy learning about explosives, demolitions, and the laying of mines when my course was cut short; I had received orders to join the Somaliland Camel Corps. After an alcoholic farewell dinner, I went by train to a camp near Ismalia, embarking next day on a ship where I found eleven other officers from the Cavalry Division who had been sent from their units to join the Somaliland Camel Corps. Among them was Billy McLean of the Greys, who later became a very great friend.

It was unbearably hot as we steamed down the Red Sea with a following wind. All we could do was lie on our bunks naked and pouring with sweat, with an occasional trip to the bar. The temperature in our cabin reached 123 degrees one day, and we were not surprised to hear that two men had died of heat exhaustion. The engines stopped that night while the bodies were dumped overboard.

We had been told that we were making for Berbera, but just as we came in sight of land our convoy was ordered to sail direct to Aden; apparently it had been decided to evacuate Somaliland. On arrival in Aden there were three air raids. The old battleship HMS *Resolution* was a splendid sight as she steamed slowly past us, her decks black from the gunfire of her heavy guns that had been shelling the Italians as they advanced along the Somali coast. As the Italian bombers flew overhead she opened up vigorously but without effect.

During the two days that we stood off Aden we took on board General Legentilhomme, who had been commander of the French troops at Djibuti. He had left to join General de Gaulle. News also reached us on board of the good fight put up by the British brigade in Somaliland, including the Black Watch; together with the Somaliland Camel Corps they had carried out a spirited withdrawal in the face of a reported two Italian divisions. We were not allowed to land at Aden, so we were very glad when, after two days, we steamed off to join a vast convoy from England at the southern entrance to the Red Sea. Apart from two submarine alarms, when our naval escorts dropped depth charges, there were no excitements. We reached Suez rather depressed after our fruitless journey, and even more so when we received orders to rejoin our regiments in Palestine – orders that a number of officers, including Billy McLean and myself, decided to ignore. Instead we took a train to Cairo, where we hoped to find a way of getting a more active appointment.

General Archie Wavell was then commanding the British troops in Egypt. His family and mine were old friends and I had known the general since my Sandhurst days. I decided to go and ask him for his advice, explaining my predicament. He was sympathetic and suggested that I try for a posting to a new unit forming in the Middle East – the Commandos. He gave me a letter to Brigadier John Shearer, the Director of Military Intelligence, recommending me as a suitable officer. The brigadier told me to return to my regiment, but said that I would be summoned to join the Commandos in due course.

My return to my regiment in Palestine was something of an anti-climax after my departure for what I had anticipated would be real action. By now my squadron had moved to Nathanya, a pleasant camp on the coast and cooler than Tulkarm. There was good though dangerous bathing – one of our men had already been drowned.

I was soon on leave again in Haifa when I had another grandstand view of an air raid. This time five Italian Caproni bombers flew very high and dropped all their bombs into the sea where, by a bit of bad luck, one bomb scored a direct hit on a small rowing boat from which an old Arab was fishing. He was the only casualty. After my return from leave in September I saw Italian bombers again; this time they were raiding Tel Aviv. This raid was more effective, for over a hundred people were killed – the highest number, we were told, that had been killed in any raid up to that time of the war.

Early in October 1940 the regiment finally moved from Tulkarm. This turned out to be the last time in its history that the 1st Household Cavalry Regiment moved as a complete horsed cavalry regiment. On the first night of the march no less than twenty men were stung by scorpions. I found one in my fleabag as I was about to turn in, but killed it before it had time to sting me. After a march of four days we reached our destination at Az Zib, which was to be the new regimental camp. Our squadron, however, rode on to a camp near a Jewish settlement close to the border with Syria.

Most of October was spent in carrying out patrols along a wire fence known as McTaggart's Wall. This was a high barbed wire fence that ran along a great many miles of the Syria-Palestine border. It had been built to stop the smuggling of arms and hashish, and was mined in places. Unfortunately the man who had supervised the laying of the mines had died without recording where they were. Every now and then we would hear an explosion as a goat, sheep, or Arab stepped on one of them.

The Arabs were too smart for us. We never caught any of them on our patrols; they were local guerrillas who knew the country and operated at night. The usual Arab trick was to arrange a meeting place on the wire and throw the goods across to an accomplice on the other side. Another habit of theirs was to pull up the iron pickets of the fence and then sell them back to the Palestine Works Department, who had originally issued them. The French soldiers, too, from the other side of the fence also helped themselves to parts of it when they felt inclined. Our relations with the French, whom we occasionally met on patrols, were cordial, but they were heartily disliked by the Arabs, who were continually complaining to us that the hungry Frenchmen had stolen and eaten their sheep or goats.

We used to keep a troop standing by at the customs house at Ras en Naquara, near the coast on the Syrian-Palestine border. There was little to do but I became friendly with the Arab customs officials. One day when I was talking to one of them a car from Syria drew up for inspection. My friend walked over to it, put his head inside the car, and turned to me saying, 'I can smell hashish.' He must have had a very acute sense of smell, for I sniffed and could smell nothing. He turned everybody out of the car – the Syrian driver and passengers protesting volubly – and began a thorough search of the inside, piercing the upholstery with an instrument like a meat skewer. Suddenly he gave a grunt of satisfaction and, turning to me with the skewer in his hand, pointed to a spot of white powder on its tip. This time even I could smell the hashish.

He then slashed at the back of the front seats with a knife, to discover that both front seats had false backs. From the dummy backs he began to unpack small packets of hashish; we counted 125 of them. They must have been of considerable value, for the price of hashish doubled each time it crossed a frontier. Starting in Turkey, where it was grown, it passed through Syria and Palestine to Egypt – usually its final destination.

My friend told me that cars were the usual means of smuggling hashish on that frontier, but from Palestine to Egypt they used camels. 'Not many hiding places on a camel,' I remarked. He laughed. 'The hashish isn't carried *on* the camel, it's carried *in* it.' It was packed in tubes and forced down the camels' throats. After they had been driven over the frontier the camels were killed and the tubes removed. Gold, too, was frequently smuggled, and at Ras en Naquara they had recently discovered a car with sparking plugs that were painted black; they were solid gold.

Apart from our patrols, which were interesting and varied, we also enjoyed some shooting. Not only were there *chicaw* – a large red-legged partridge – but hundreds of blue rock pigeons used to nest in the ruins of the old Crusader castle at Montfort, about a mile from our camp. They made a welcome change in our diet from the usual army rations.

Shortly before I left, some of the buildings in the Jewish settlement caught fire and a party of our troops went over to help. As a result we became friendly, and the Jews invited some of us one day to a meal. I was most interested to visit a kibbutz, where Communism was practised in its truest form. Everything was shared, everyone worked for the good of the kibbutz, even the women were shared and the children became the property of the kibbutz. They gave us a simple meal, including fresh vegetables, and when I left I could not help admiring their energy, enthusiasm, and high ideals.

I was delighted when I eventually received the orders I had been awaiting – to go to Egypt to join the Commandos. I slipped off without any farewell party in case I should find myself back in Palestine. I spent three days in Cairo and then drove down to Geneifa, a vast camp stretching for miles along the Suez Canal. It was then November 1940 and I felt that at last I must be getting somewhere in the war.

3
Commandos

At Geneifa I joined my new unit – No 52 (Middle East) Commando. All the officers arrived first; the men were due ten days later. Before their arrival we had to learn as much as possible from specialist instructors, most of whom had come from England, in order to pass our training on to our men. I was appointed a company commander, which meant promotion to captain.

Intensive training, interesting and wide-ranging, started at once. I was already proficient at compass work and map reading, and had some knowledge of explosives and demolition, but new subjects for me were boat work, weapon training with the new Thompson sub-machine gun, unarmed combat and less orthodox subjects such as camel riding and camel mastership, first aid, and scientific rough-housing.

When the men arrived it was obvious that with a few exceptions – notably the Brigade of Guards and the cavalry regiments – their commanding officers had seized a golden opportunity to get rid of their most undesirable characters. Twelve men came from every unit in the Middle East, some of whom had conduct sheets with up to eight pages of crimes. By the time the last stragglers had arrived under military police escort from Cairo, where they had already been arrested for a variety of crimes, the commando numbered about 600 men.

Some of these were criminal types, but GHQ in Cairo refused to allow us to return them to their units unless they were physically unfit. After a week I took my company on a forced march in full kit, during which we covered thirty-three miles in eleven hours in blazing sun in the desert. Many of the men fell out, and as a result I was able to return some thirty per cent of my undersirables as unfit. Only my orderly knew that I had no skin left on my heels and was almost a casualty myself; but the excercise paid off.

Our commando, being a new type of unit, was used as a guinea-pig for every sort of unorthodox idea. The private soldier was given the rank of 'raider', which was well thought out as it avoided calling men by their branch of service such as 'private', 'trooper', 'guardsman', 'gunner' or 'sapper'. It also fostered an *esprit de corps* which would otherwise have been lacking. For the same reason all identities with former units were dropped, and everyone wore the same uniform and insignia. The majority of men chosen for the commandos were bachelors, on the theory that a bachelor was more likely to take risks than a married man.

Drill and inspections were out, because they were alleged to destroy initiative. We were not allowed to shout orders on parade, but had to give them by hand signal – the object was to ensure silence and keep the men alert. We marched out of step, which was supposed to be less tiring and quieter. Officers were not saluted, to prevent the enemy identifying them. No welfare comforts were allowed, for fear they might make the men soft. On night guards the entire guard stayed awake all night instead of the normal change at regular intervals, though I was never quite clear as to what was the advantage of this method. Even the eating of raw food was encouraged in order to increase mobility; this may indeed have helped those who were taken prisoner and later escaped to the mountains in Crete. In tactics other experiments were carried out such as making an attack without previous reconnaissance in order to achieve surprise. This was a complete failure.

Very early in our training many of the ideas were discarded, particularly since the ill-disciplined men who had been sent to join the commando took every opportunity to abuse them. Parades and marches rapidly became a shambles; even marching out of step proved not only more difficult but more tiring. Gym shoes worn for comfort, silence and speed very soon wore out. It was some months before we were equipped with a rubber-soled commando boot.

Two weeks after training had started we were joined by about seventy Spaniards who had deserted from the French Foreign Legion in Syria, where they were alleged to have shot their pro-Vichy officers. For a time they were attached to my company. They had fought in the Spanish Civil War with the Communists, and were very experienced. They compared well with our troops, especially at fieldcraft and stalking, and also made free use of the 'fanny' – a name given to the special commando knife with which we were issued. It had a blade about nine inches long, with a brass knuckle-duster on the handle, and was later adopted as the official badge of the Middle East Commandos. The Spaniards used them to kill two Egyptians in brawls in Ismalia.

Early in December General Wavell's push started in the Western Desert and Italian prisoners began to appear in the Canal Zone in large numbers. Our morale rose, for we anticipated being used on the North African coast to harry the Italian lines of communication along the coast road. Soon afterwards we were sent on a final leave and informed we were about to be operationally employed. I went on leave to Cairo with another company commander, Richard Boyle of the Black Watch. From there we went down for two days to the oasis at Fayoum, where we shot over a hundred snipe between us.

On returning from leave we were warned that we would be leaving in two days' time for an unknown destination. That same evening, after giving out his orders, the commanding officer was taken ill and retired to hospital – cruel luck after all the hard and difficult work he had done in the formation and training of the commando. He was succeeded by Lieutenant-Colonel George Young, a Sapper, and we embarked at Port Said the day after he took command. We were all convinced that we were going to be used on the North African coast or for a raid on Rhodes or the Dodecanese. To our surprise we sailed south, through the Canal. When we were well out in the Red Sea we were told that our embarkation at Port Said had been a deception plan and that our true destination was Port Sudan, from where we would proceed to operate in Abyssinia. I don't know if the enemy were deceived, but we certainly were.

The journey was not a marked success. Our relations with a battalion of the Highland Light Infantry, also on the ship, were bad – and worsened when they stole all our Christmas comforts, including Christmas puddings and beer. After a stifling journey our arrival at Port Said coincided with an air raid. There was considerable panic in the docks when the dockers, all Sudanese fuzzy-wuzzies, fled in every direction, but little damage was done.

We entrained the same day for Gedaref, the railhead for the troops fighting on what was then known as the Gallabat-Metemma front. Since the Italians were in occupation of Kassala, which was on the direct rail route, we had to make a wide detour via Khartoum.

The journey took three days, mainly through desert and scrubland, with the occasional *jebel* protruding into the sky like some giant rock that had forced itself out of the flat desert. We saw frequent herds of gazelle from the train, and at many stations where we stopped we were surrounded by Dinkas – tall natives carrying spears, with daggers strapped to their upper arms, who stood on one leg as they stared at us.

We crossed the Blue Nile at Sennar, where the railway ran along the top of a huge dam, finally reaching Gedaref at night, to find we were not expected. It was a cold night, we had neither blankets nor greatcoats, and we had to bed down out in the open in only our shirts and shorts. Not many slept.

The next day our troops were given their pay, a fatal error as the majority got drunk and ended up in the black brothel area. The military police were unable to handle the situation alone, so all the officers were turned out to round up the drunks – a most unpleasant job. Two of our men had been knifed by locals. It was hardly surprising.

We drove in a convoy of lorries to our base for future operations. It was a perfect site, situated on the bank of the Atbara river, about three miles behind our own front line and about five miles from the nearest Italians. There was plenty of cover – trees, bushes and elephant grass – and we could camouflage ourselves from detection from the air providing our track discipline was good. The Atbara, one of the tributaries of the Blue Nile, was very narrow and could easily be forded; in some places it could be crossed without even wetting one's feet. We used its water for drinking and washing and, keeping a good lookout for crocodiles, for bathing.

At this stage an irregular front line existed between the Italians and ourselves, running approximately along the frontier between Abyssinia and the Sudan, and between the only villages of any size in the area – Metemma on the Italian side and Gallabat on ours. Gallabat had been captured by the Italians and an attempt to recapture it had failed owing to a poor showing by an English county regiment, who were rapidly sent out of the area of operations for intensive retraining and a change of officers. Gallabat was eventually recaptured by Indian units whose Pathan soldiers proved their fine fighting qualities.

Our first task was to familiarise ourselves with the front. To this end the company commanders were taken on Christmas Day by an officer of the Sudan Defence Force (incidentally a well-known rowing Blue) for a reconnaissance of the Italian front. Since he had previously been the local district officer, he knew the whole area intimately. He pointed out the Italian forward positions and observation posts, and tracks usually taken by their patrols. He clearly resented the fact that the war was taking place in what had been his former district, especially as it had been a game reserve in peacetime and what he regarded as 'his' game were now being rudely disturbed.

We saw a variety of animals, including rhino, leopard, bush and water buck, chimpanzees and herds of baboons, as well as crocodiles. The baboons were rather troublesome, since at night they were continually giving the guards false alarms. By day they had a habit of popping their heads round trees to have a look at you – disconcerting, as their heads looked very similar to those of the native irregulars who were fighting against us. There were also flocks of parakeets and other birds with colourful plumage; also game birds, chiefly guinea fowl, sand grouse and francolin. Once I found some of my men preparing to eat a secretary bird that they had shot. I had brought a shotgun with me and often used to go out shooting for the pot. One day my company sergeant-major and I shot over seventy guinea fowl before breakfast. They fed the whole commando.

We sometimes had Abyssinian officers attached to us, drawn from the Emperor Haile Selassie's bodyguard. Most had been educated at St Cyr and spoke French, but their chief job was to shout with loudspeakers at the Abyssinians fighting for the Italians, calling on them to desert to us. They were unwelcome companions, as their requests were usually answered by a burst of machine-gun fire.

It soon became clear that we were not going to be used in the proper role of commandos, for which we had been trained, but as infantry patrols. Because we were alleged to be, and probably were, fitter than normal infantry, we were to be employed on long-range patrols behind the enemy lines. As yet none of our men had been under fire, and nobody could foretell their reaction. To this end fighting patrols were sent out to probe the enemy positions. It was my company that drew first blood.

We were patrolling along a dried up river bed which formed a part of the frontier between Sudan and Abyssinia. It was then in no man's land. We were moving in a formation we had devised for this type of country during our training. Two scouts were in front, followed by the leading section, then myself accompanied by two runners. Immediately behind me were three platoons, whose actions would depend on the hand signals I made. We were in single file following the game tracks in the elephant grass on the bank of the *khor* (dry river bed).

As we moved along the *khor* I kept hearing a strange bird noise coming from tops of trees as we passed. Looking up, I saw nothing. Suddenly an Abyssinian fell out of a tree about ten yards in front of us; at the same time fire was opened up on us from both sides of the *khor*. We fired at the man, but missed as he disappeared into the elephant grass. Bullets were now whistling overhead fairly fast, the fog of battle had descended, and we were lying down and could see nobody. I called up the Bren gunner behind me and made him spray the grass ahead of us. At once a native soldier sprinted across our front, but was caught by a burst of Bren fire and collapsed moaning on the ground out of sight. Hearing shouts from fairly close to our right front, I threw a grenade and my two runners did the same. I then gave a signal to the leading platoon behind me to make a right hook – a move we had rehearsed against such an eventuality.

The confusion was now increased by the elephant grass on both sides of the *khor* catching fire. I never discovered whether the fire had been started deliberately by the enemy or by our grenades. Through the smoke I spotted an Abyssinian rapidly firing his rifle high in the air without even putting it to his shoulder, and reloading as fast as he could. I took two shots at him with my pistol but missed both times and he bolted. By then the platoon had worked round the flank and the officer in charge of it came over to tell me he had seen the enemy in full flight. He estimated that there had been about fifty native levies and he had seen them led by an Italian officer riding a grey horse. Since the shooting had by now stopped, I decided to call it a day, especially as this was our baptism of fire.

First we carried out a local search and found one dead Abyssinian, evidently killed by one of our grenades. Shortly afterwards we found the man who had received the burst of Bren in his stomach. He was in great agony, making a terrible noise and clearly going to die. He was too bad to move and would not have survived the long march back to base. Furthermore we could not leave him to be burnt by the approaching bush fire or killed off by wild animals. As we were debating what to do with him, Sergeant Harrison, an excellent man from the Scots Guards, suggested that it would be kindest to finish him off, to which I reluctantly agreed. A shot through the head put an end to his suffering, but it was a horrible decision for me to make. In retrospect I feel I did the right thing.

We took identification off the bodies, which indicated that their unit was the Banda Torelli. We returned to base rather pleased with ourselves, for our only casualty was one of our Bren gunners who had been hit in the hand by a shot that had ricocheted off his gun. I was pleased by the way the company had acted under fire for the first time, and relieved at my own performance. I had always feared that I might appear scared in front of my men, but throughout the entire action I was far too involved to have time to be afraid or think of my own safety.

Other companies carried out patrols, but the largest was a raid made by two companies, one of them mine, timed to coincide with an attack made by an Indian infantry battalion. The plan was to march by night down the Atbara river until it reached the Khor Gumsa, about five miles behind the Italian lines. We would lay up there all day and move on again the following night until we met the main road from Metemma to Gondar, the Italian supply base. On reaching the road we were to lay an ambush and shoot up anything that came along.

The first night we marched in single file along the game tracks parallel to the Atbara. It was a fine night, with not too much moonlight, but enough to show up the large trees against the clear sky and brilliant stars. The noises were typical of the African night – a background provided by frogs and crickets, the cough-like barking of the monkeys, the howling of hyenas, the occasional cry or grunt from some other animal. Every now and then we all froze in our tracks as something crashed around in the elephant grass near us – it usually turned out to be a water buck that had come to the river to drink but had dashed off in alarm on scenting humans. The animals caused our leading points to halt several times, but we reached the Khor Gumsa without meeting the enemy.

We lay up in the *khor* next day, sleeping, eating and brewing up tea while patrols were being sent out. We set off the next night, leaving our blankets and food reserves hidden in the *khor*. (The blankets were in shreds when we returned, eaten by white ants.) We again moved in single file, led by an officer using his compass. By marching south-west from the river we expected to hit the main road. We knew from our patrols that the area between the river and the road contained several enemy camps. It seemed doubtful that we would reach our objective undetected.

Luckily their sentries were idle. The Italians and their native levies were singing or talking. As we crept past, crouching and crawling, we could see them sitting huddled round camp fires with blankets round their shoulders. In one camp we actually passed through the middle of some mule lines. In another we heard women's voices, suggesting the rumours that they had brothels in the front line were true.

After some hours' march we hit the road; then things went wrong. Our leading section blundered on to the road sooner than expected, and by ill luck ran into a mule train. Our men were challenged and although one of our officers shouted a reply in Italian, it did not deceive the enemy, who opened fire on us before we could get into a reasonable position. Soon all was confusion, with both sides firing away at each other. I was lying with my company HQ a few yards from the road, being shot at by our own troops from the rear as well as by the enemy from in front. One of my runners beside me was hit in the foot. Some of our shots, however, found their targets for we could hear the groans of the wounded on the road. Spare mules were dashing wildly in all directions and we caught one which we led back to our base, from where it later escaped and was never seen again.

By now the whole area had been alerted, so the colonel gave the order to withdraw. One of my men, Raider Flood, was badly wounded. We put him on the captured mule but he died on the way back. We retraced our footsteps, the same officer leading the way by compass. This time when we passed the enemy camps they were more alert and some fired on us, fortunately without causing casualties. Passing one camp, one of our men, a Household Cavalryman, killed an Italian sentry with a blow from his fanny.

We reached the Khor Gumsa at first light, and it was only then, some hours' march after our action, that we discovered that Sergeant Harrison was missing. Through a muddle the men in front thought he was in the rear of the company, and those in the rear thought he was in front. Going back to look for him was out of the question, and we hoped he might be making his own way back or at worst had been taken prisoner. He was never heard of again, a great loss to the commando.

On our return a post mortem was held on the operation. The colonel was pleased that we had reached our objective, created a diversion and probably made the Italians more jittery behind their front lines. On the debit side it had shown a number of weaknesses, of which the worst was that a few of our men were both ill-disciplined and cowardly. Two were court-martialled for throwing down their arms in front of the enemy and running away. They were sentenced to seven years' hard labour – which no doubt they were happy to receive to avoid fighting the rest of the war. They were bad eggs and I was glad to see them go.

I was very upset at the loss of Sergeant Harrison and Raider Flood. I conducted Flood's funeral service the following day. As their direct commander I had a personal responsibility for what had happened, and in the case of Sergeant Harrison, unless he had been killed at once, I felt his loss could have been avoided.

We spent over two months in the area with a number of other actions, in one of which one of the other company commanders had a very narrow escape. His company were on a night patrol when they walked into the enemy's fixed line of fire. The company commander, lying on the ground, was caught by a burst of machine-gun fire. Six bullets penetrated his bush jacket, scoured through the flesh on both sides of his back but missed his spine; with the result that he had six beautiful wound stripes across his back and twelve neat holes in his bush jacket.

One of his platoon commanders, Max Gordon of the Blues, was less fortunate. One bullet hit him in the neck, another in the hand, and a ricochet off his pistol lodged in his thigh. He most gallantly carried on, helped by the men of his platoon as they extricated themselves and fought their way back a considerable distance to our lines, where he collapsed from loss of blood. It was lucky for him that his men did not comply with the commando order then in force, that all wounded men should be abandoned so as not to handicap the rest of the unit.

I saw Max Gordon as he was carried in, and shared the general opinion that he was certain to die. How he survived surprised us all;

he must have been remarkably tough. He was, I believe, the first member of the Household Cavalry Regiment to be wounded in the war and should have been awarded a decoration for gallantry. That he was not was due to a ruling at the time that no commandos should be awarded gallantry medals as gallantry was supposed to be normal duty. Hence there were no awards to 52 Middle East Commando for any operations on this front.

After about two months there were strong indications that the Italians were about to withdraw, and patrols were sent out to discover if they had left their forward positions. On my last patrol I took a small group to reconnoitre a feature known to have been held by the enemy. We moved in the usual formation – in single file, the leading man armed with a Tommy gun – sticking to game tracks rather than forcing our way through the tall elephant grass. If we came to a rise in the ground such as an anthill, or a suitable tree, we would halt while someone climbed up to see if he could spot any signs of life – smoke, for instance, or vultures circling, or birds in alarm.

We eventually got to the top of the position where we expected to find the Italians. Seeing nothing, we sat down to rest. Hitherto we had been talking in whispers, but when an Italian aeroplane flew over, one of my patrol shouted at me to ask if he could have a shot at it – to which I replied 'No.' The result was startling, for within seconds shots were coming at us from several angles and a red Italian grenade landed and burst at my feet, doing no damage other than making me deaf for several days. I shouted to the patrol to run for it and we all bolted down the hill, pursued by angry bursts of machine-gun fire, which continued for a good half hour after we were out of range. I comforted myself that our ignominious retreat was quite in order: as a reconnaissance patrol we had drawn the enemy's fire and noted their positions. Had we been a fighting patrol we would have to have been more aggressive.

Our last role before the Italians withdrew was not very popular, each company taking over a section of the front line to relieve the infantry. We were in trenches, in which we sat all day under spasmodic shellfire from the Italian artillery. Their shooting was accurate and we had a number of near misses, though no casualties because about fifty per cent of their shells were duds. We resented carrying out this role, which we considered a misuse of commandos.

Eventually smoke was seen rising from several points in the Italian lines and our patrols reported that the enemy were evacuating their forward positions. We were immediately ordered to advance and my company had the task of occupying two features where the Italian brigade HQ had been located. We reached them without opposition and found them completely deserted, except for a few mongrel dogs and vultures. The Italians must have pulled out in a hurry, judging by what they left behind. There was plenty of loot in the way of tinned food, bottles of Chianti, quantities of ammunition, enough medical supplies to equip a field hospital, and a fine souvenir – the flag of the 24th Colonial Brigade, presumably our late opponents. A more important find – by my runner – was a collection of documents that included the operational order for the Italian withdrawal. One of my platoon officers was fluent in Italian, and on examining the order discovered that they intended to withdraw some fifty miles to the Chelga Hills which covered the route to Gondar. The order began by stating that the withdrawal was being made due to 'superior' enemy forces. On this front, in fact, one Italian division was facing one Indian brigade, with our commando in support of it. We hoped that our raids and patrols had helped to foster the belief that we were superior forces.

On the strength of this information a halt was called and after a good looting session we returned to our base, marching through Metemma and Gallabat, which we had not seen before. Both had been reduced to ruins. We also passed the wreckage of a British fighter which must have been brought down before our arrival, for all the time we were on this front we never saw any British aircraft, though the Italians flew over us every day.

Before we finally left our base Colonel Young, Richard Boyle and I borrowed a car and drove down the main road to the scene of our night ambush. It was easy to recognise, though the elephant grass at the side of the road had been burnt. We found many spent cartridge cases and a number of bloodstained field dressings and bandages. We searched the area thoroughly but could find no trace of Sergeant Harrison, nor any grave.

Early in February 1941 we left our base for the last time and marched back to Gedaref, some 120 miles. It was hot and dusty, and we were very ill-humoured, having expected to be taken back in lorries instead of marching. In Gedaref we met No 51 (Middle East) Commando on its way from Egypt to Kassala. Recruited from

Palestine, half were Jews and half Arabs. The only other Middle East Commando, No 50, was, like ourselves, entirely British.

We stayed a week at Gedaref, where many of our men went down with malaria. We had no nets at night and few precautions could be taken. There was a prisoner-of-war camp nearby, filled mostly with Abyssinian irregulars who had been fighting for the Italians against us. They looked quite happy, with numerous relations talking to them through the wire. We were told that when one of these native troops was taken prisoner, such was the bush telegraph that within a week his whole family would be on the move, crossing through both the Italian and our own lines. After walking more than 120 miles to Gedaref they would turn up at the camp asking to see their relatives. Later in the campaign the entire Banda Torelli defected to us and were in action under Billy McLean against the Italians. Billy told me they were excellent troops.

From Gedaref we moved by train to Kassala, which had recently been recaptured from the Italians, and then marched fifteen miles to our new camp at the base of Jebel Kassala. It was a strange-looking mountain, rising steeply from the desert to a height of over 4,000 feet. Its grey rock was almost completely smooth, its sides were vertical, the top itself was rounded. We were told it had never been climbed, which encouraged us to make the attempt ourselves, but having no climbing equipment we never got further than half way to the top.

The country around us had now changed from the bush and scrubland in the Gallabat area to sandy desert, in which Kassala was a large oasis. There was no vegetation except for palm trees near the water holes and wells. The earth itself was more dusty than sandy, and we were cursed with a number of dust storms. Sometimes 'dust devils' – whirlwinds of dust – would pass through our camp, whisking any tent or object that lay in their path high into the air.

We anticipated that we would probably next be employed on the assault on Keren, which would involve the scaling of a series of exceptionally steep mountains. We did a great deal of climbing in our training on the Jebel Kassala, and had just been issued with a new type of boot that was excellent for the job, made of soft leather with very thick gutta-percha soles.

Malaria, however, was still taking a heavy toll and eventually nearly seventy per cent of the unit were sick or on sick leave. The authorities therefore considered that we were no more use as an effective fighting force and ordered us to return to Egypt. It was principally the supply side that was responsible for the high incidence of malaria: anti-malaria pills were simply not available.

When the commando left Egypt no proper quartermaster's staff accompanied the unit. This was because the commando was never intended to be used as a complete unit, but as small raiding parties operating from a permanent base. When we were misemployed on the Gallabat-Metemma front this weakness became all too apparent. We left with mixed feelings, and we all hoped that from Egypt we would be more usefully engaged.

We went by train from Kassala to Wadi Halfa, where we embarked in one of Thomas Cook's tourist boats, driven by a huge paddle at the stern. For company on the boat we had about fifty Italian officer prisoners, for whom we had to provide the guards. It was a pleasant trip down the Nile, with plenty of crocodiles on view sunning themselves on muddy banks, and thousands of duck. The banks of the river varied from sandy hills to high rocky cliffs – reminding me more of a Norwegian fjord.

Our only halt was at Abu Simbel, where we went ashore to visit the famous temple hewn out of the rock. So that everyone could see over it, it was easier to take the prisoners along as well. They seemed to enjoy themselves, particularly when their escorts entered into a furious argument with the elderly Egyptian custodian trying to collect money. Finally we paid for ourselves but refused to pay for the prisoners.

The huge figures carved out of the sandstone cliffs overlooking the Nile made us appear like Lilliputians staring up at Gulliver. Inside there was a tomblike atmosphere, cool but gloomy, about the chambers. Here and there shafts of daylight across the walls lit the carvings and paintings, astonishingly accomplished and in a remarkable state of preservation considering their antiquity.

After passing the half-submerged temple of Philae we docked near Assuan and had a good look at the dam. We then boarded a train which took us to a large camp near Tel el Kebir; from there the whole commando was sent on leave and I flew to Cyprus. Then, on rejoining the commando, which had by this time moved back to its former camp at Geneifa, I went down with scarlet fever and was carted off to hospital. By the time I was discharged the commando had moved to a camp outside Alexandria, where I found a big re-organisation taking place.

Three battalions of commandos had arrived at Alexandria and were living in ships in the harbour. Known as Layforce, they were under the command of Brigadier Bob Laycock of the Blues. Their standards were much higher than ours as their men were all hand-picked volunteers. This time our requests to return undesirable men to their units were approved.

Our working hours in Alexandria were mainly spent in training for amphibious operations such as the capture of Rhodes, though unfortunately none of them materialised. Our leisure hours were dissipated in orgies with our friends from the other battalions. We were living in an atmosphere of 'eat, drink and be merry, for tomorrow we die', but it was all very frustrating, especially meeting friends back from fighting in the Western Desert.

The usual routine in the evenings was to meet in the Union Bar, noted for its prawns, where one could get a very good dinner. We would then move on to the Carlton or Monseigneur's, both of which had bands and a cabaret. As the regulations in Egypt laid down that no alcoholic drinks should be served after 10 p.m. and all places of entertainment should shut at midnight, we automatically went to Mary's House, which was well known to most officers in Alexandria.

In the first place it was a brothel; in the second, if you wanted a drink you had only to ask for a strong coffee and you would get a cup fifty per cent coffee and fifty per cent brandy. It carried on into the small hours of the morning, and as so many customers were fairly high by the time they reached Mary's, incidents were to be expected – such as the night when a drunken Polish officer drew his pistol and shot at the bottles lined up behind the bar. Later Mary's House received a direct hit during an air raid, and afterwards seven officers were gazetted as 'killed in action'. Mary herself was unhurt, and it is said that she wrote a letter to the local military commander congratulating him on the good work and help of his officers after the raid.

The only useful job we did in Alexandria was regular dock guard, which was not as dull as it sounds. Air raids were an almost nightly occurrence and there were other diversions as well. We had one company on guard at a time, with the company commander in charge. On my first night on guard there was an air raid warning and one of the ships that was unloading in the docks failed to extinguish its floodlights. As we heard the bombers approaching and the guns started to open up, we did the only thing possible and shot the lights out. The captain was not pleased. On another evening a German bomber flew in very low, at about 3,000 feet. It was picked up in the searchlights and we could see every detail, including the markings. Everything in the neighbourhood fired at it, from the entire anti-aircraft defences, the Mediterranean Fleet and my own Bren guns, down to an Egyptian policeman whom I saw excitedly firing his rifle. Finally three objects dropped from the aeroplane, opening into parachutes. We thought that the crew were bailing out and expected the aircraft to crash at any moment, but it carried on undeterred and disappeared from view. I have never seen so much fired at such an easy target with so little effect. The next day a ship blew up in the harbour on a mine, almost certainly deposited by one of the parachutes. The harbour was out of action for several days.

The anti-aircraft defences were very strong at this time – some people said stronger than London's. There were both the British and Egyptian army defences and also the Mediterranean Fleet, which included an anti-aircraft cruiser. This added up to a fairly aggressive firework display, though not without its dangers from falling shrapnel and even dud shells. Two fragments of shrapnel fell through the roof of my sleeping quarters in the docks, which had a tiled roof. It was much worse in our camp, for there we were in tents. Apart from the shrapnel, the duds – mainly from naval guns – became so dangerous that we had to go into slit trenches during air raids, more to avoid the hazards of our own making than to escape enemy bombs.

Among our other duties in the docks we had to prevent the pilfering of stores. Local Australian ack-ack gunners were the worst offenders and since their officers seemed to condone it, we gave up handing over any men we caught and merely beat them up. The sailors from the merchant ships were also pretty bad. They would unload attractive stores such as NAAFI supplies during the day, then steal them at night and take them back on board. We caught several and they got quite stiff punishments from their captains when we handed them over. The Egyptian dockers were the other looters, but after we had shot one they became less of a problem.

For some reason the French sailors from the pro-Vichy naval ships that had been interned were allowed complete freedom to wander about Alexandria. Many had pro-Axis sympathies and frequently became involved in brawls, especially with our Spaniards, one of whom died of knife wounds.

During the evacuation from Greece most of the commando was on guard, not only to prevent unauthorised people from entering the docks, but to prevent any from getting out, whether civilians or sevicemen. Most troops disembarked in an orderly manner with their arms, were entrained and taken off to camps; but we had a great deal of trouble with the Australians. They disembarked, luckily without any arms, with the one objective of getting into the town as quickly as possible to have a drink and a woman. They strongly resented our guards for preventing them from leaving the docks. 'Yellow bastards, why weren't you fighting in Greece?' they taunted. 'Why did you run away and leave all your weapons behind?' countered the commandos. They soon came to blows and free fights started. More guards and military police were rushed to the scene to restore order. It was all very unpleasant.

The most impressive disembarkation that I watched was when HMS *Ajax* came in at high speed, made fast, and disembarked a battalion of New Zealanders with their arms in perfect order. She was speeding away again in under an hour, bound back to Greece to carry out further rescue work.

After some weeks in Alexandria life began to pall. In the spring of 1941 I heard that the Household Cavalry Regiment was at last going into action and advancing into Iraq. I wrote to the second in command, asking him if I could come back to the regiment and if so to write me a letter requesting my return. The letter came and I showed it to Colonel George Young, asking for his permission to go. He was understanding and gave it. I left the next day.

The commando only remained as Layforce for a few more weeks. Two battalions were sent to Crete about two weeks after I left, where they fought a gallant rearguard action across the island. Most of them were taken prisoner on the beaches when there were no ships left to take them off. Richard Boyle, who had been my closest friend in the Commandos, and my company sergeant-major, among others, took to the mountains and were taken off later by submarine. Richard Boyle subsequently won an MC with the Black Watch at Tobruk; sadly he was killed during the Rhine crossings in 1945.

Thus the Middle East Commandos came to an end. In the story of Combined Operations, *The Watery Maze* by Brigadier Bernard Fergusson, they were only mentioned in one paragraph, where the author states: 'The locally raised Middle East Commandos had hitherto been having an unhappy and frustrating time. One, operating on the Sudan-Abyssinia border, had only two inconclusive skirmishes to show for many months of effort. The other had been ignominiously expelled from the tiny Italian island of Castelorizzo, off Rhodes, after only a couple of nights ashore.' For years this was all that was written about the Middle East Commandos, but in 1988 a book was published giving the whole story.*

One battalion was disbanded later on and the officers given the choice of returning home or joining units in the Middle East. Most of the Household Cavalry officers joined the 1st Household Cavalry Regiment, where they were very welcome reinforcements. It was at this time that David Stirling and Jock Lewis, who had been in this commando, founded the Special Air Sevice, better known as the SAS.

Another battalion went into action against the pro-Vichy French in Syria, where it incurred heavy casualties while being landed on the wrong bank of the Litani river. Later it was disbanded after a short spell under the command of Lieutenant-Colonel Geoffrey Keyes of the Greys. Keyes was killed leading an abortive raid on what was wrongly thought to be Rommel's headquarters, for which he was awarded a posthumous Victoria Cross.

When I look back on my time in the Commandos I am certain the experience left me a wiser officer. On leaving the Household Cavalry Regiment I had left a unit composed of first-rate NCOs and men with fine *esprit de corps*, traditions centuries old, and a discipline which was unique in the cavalry and to my mind unbeatable. To support us we had an experienced and capable quartermaster's staff, and the men themselves were very adaptable, capable of coping with any change of role or equipment. The commando, on the other hand, lacked all this. It was an *ad hoc* unit with a number of men of low calibre. It was sent into action before it was properly trained and once in action made to perform a role for which it was neither intended nor prepared. It was burdened with too many unorthodox theories, many of which failed in practice.

* Charles Messenger, *The Middle East Commandos*, Kimber, 1988.

4
Iraq

While I had been with the Commandos in Alexandria a momentous change had taken place in the Household Cavalry Regiment (from now on referred to as the HCR). In March 1941 they had changed from horses to 15-cwt trucks, though the organisation of the regiment remained roughly the same. All horses over the age of ten were shot to prevent them from falling into bad hands, as they had in France and Egypt after the First World War. The younger horses were handed over to the few remaining horsed units. My charger Shanter was taken over by our veterinary officer, who kept him as his charger until Shanter went blind from an incurable eye disease and had to be put down.

The same month disturbing events were taking place in Iraq. The pro-British government was forcibly overthrown and the Regent forced to flee the country. The revolt was led by Rashid Ali, who became Prime Minister; he and a number of senior Army officers had very pronounced Axis sympathies and were in contact with the Germans.

In April an Indian brigade was landed at Basra to secure the port and protect the oilfields. By the end of the month hostilities had broken out. The first action of the Iraqi Army was to encircle the British garrison at Habbaniya, a cantonment and airfield at which units of the RAF were stationed under the Anglo-Iraq Treaty of 1930. The garrison, some 2,000 strong, consisted mainly of RAF personnel and the Iraq Levies. The latter had remained loyal, possibly because they were mainly Assyrian troops who detested the Iraqis. Some obsolete aircraft were based there for training purposes. In addition, there were large numbers of civilians in the cantonment, including some British women and children who had been flown from Baghdad, where the British Embassy was now besieged.

In London it was decided that a force should be raised from units in Palestine to go to the relief of Habbaniya, and a column, known as Habforce, was formed under Major-General Clarke, commander of the 1st Cavalry Division. An advanced striking force from this group, which included the HCR, set off from Palestine, moving through Jordan, down the H pipeline towards Habbaniya. I left Alexandria for Haifa a few days later.

On arrival at Haifa I found that the regiment had moved and I did not know where or how to find it. I went at once to the Windsor Annexe Hotel, where I found my friend Roy Boutagy, who usually knew what was going on. He told me that the regiment had left Palestine for Iraq. At the hotel, too, I found the Maharajah of Jaipur, a Life Guards officer, who like me was trying to find the regiment and join it. Unfortunately his efforts were sabotaged by higher authorities, who considered that his war effort would be more effective commanding his own state army than a troop of Household Cavalry.

I took a train the next day down the Jordan Valley, where I transferred to a convoy of requisitioned Jewish buses that were taking supplies to our column. They were desperately slow and kept breaking down, most of us thought deliberately, because the drivers were paid on a timed basis and so tried to take as long as they could. We climbed out of the Jordan Valley, passing through semi-cultivated country until the following day we entered the lava belt, a completely flat and desolate area of broken black volcanic rock. The same night we reached our destination, the pumping station of H4.

The oil flowing in the pipeline from the Iraq oilfields to Haifa could not move by gravity, so pumping stations had to be built to force the oil along. These were built at intervals of about a hundred miles and were numbered H1 to H5, H5 being the nearest to Haifa. These pumping stations were a welcome relief in the desert, for in addition to their pumping machinery they had plenty of water from the wells, ice, air-conditioned rooms for the European staff, electric light and usually a small Beau Geste type of fort, the whole area being surrounded by a wire fence. They played an important part in the campaign that followed.

The H pipeline from Iraq ended at Haifa, while the T pipeline further north had its terminus at Tripoli in Syria. At the Iraq end both pipelines met at K3, where a larger line ran eastwards to the Kirkuk oilfields. These lines ran on the surface of the desert and had a telephone line beside them that provided a useful aid for navigation in an otherwise featureless landscape.

At H4 I found that I had caught up with the rear of our column. I also found the brigade HQ there, and in the mess discovered two officers, both old friends, who like me were trying to catch up with the main column. We heard that it had been attacked by low-flying Messerschmitts but had pressed on and had now reached Habbaniya, where the encircling Iraqis had already been forced to withdraw by the spirited action of the garrison itself. The garrison was so badly off for weapons that some RAF officers had flown unarmed training aircraft and dropped hand grenades out of them. The only piece of artillery was a Turkish 75 mm gun that had been mounted as a trophy from the 1914-18 war. It had somehow been made to fire.

When we lunched in the brigade mess a small, slight officer was conspicuous on account of his uniform. It was a different shade of khaki from ours and his badges of rank and insignia – stars and swords – had an Arab look. On his head he wore a yellow Arab *keffiyeh* round which were two silk ropes, the *aqal*. I looked at the face – blue eyes, a short sandy moustache, and a chin that was scarred and dented – and guessed that this was Colonel Glubb Pasha, the legendary commander of the Arab Legion.

While discussing how to get to Habbaniya, which was clearly our next objective, we were offered a lift by an RAF officer who said he was going to fly there that afternoon. We accepted at once. The plane was a Vickers Valencia troop carrier which looked too antique to fly; its speed was around 80 mph. Before take-off the pilot warned us that since Messerschmitts and Italian fighters were continually patrolling our area, our only chance of avoiding them was to fly at a height of fifty feet and try a crash-landing if they spotted us. This had the disadvantage that we would be in range of any Iraqi who decided to shoot at us from the ground. Also, if we landed our fate would be very uncertain, for the Iraqis had already murdered some RAF officers.

We took off, comforted by the fact that both my companions had a flask of whisky. After a few minutes a burst of machine-gun fire came from the rear. We thought that we were being attacked, but to our relief discovered it was only the rear gunner testing his gun. Next a series of disconcerting messages were passed down the fuselage which we had to repeat to a member of the crew in the rear. First, 'The intercom is useless'; then, 'The batteries are flat'; then, 'The radio doesn't work', and finally, to cheer us up, 'We're lost'. The whisky began to circulate. Darkness had closed in and we were all asked to look out of the windows to see if we could spot a lake. All I could see were the flames from the engines which looked exactly as if they were on fire. On two occasions we saw tracer bullets coming up from the ground, too close to be healthy, and by now the whisky was finished. Finally someone spotted the lake and we landed safely, though our nerves were not in very good order.

In the RAF mess to which we were taken they had no news of the regiment. The next morning, however, I learned it was nearby and found it bivouacked on the shores of Lake Habbaniya near the old Imperial Airways guesthouse, which had been completely looted by the Iraqis. I turned out to be the only Blues officer in a squadron completely composed of Life Guards, but by now the two regiments had been together long enough for this to make no difference except for details of uniform. I met my troop for the first time and was delighted to find a first-class troop corporal of horse in Joe Ratcliffe, whose father had been a corporal-major in the Life Guards in the First World War. I also heard the sad news that on the previous day my soldier servant Morton had been killed. His death was a great personal loss to me for I had come to rely on him for so much. He was a man who never got ruffled and whose cheerful disposition made him very popular in the regiment.

We spent several days at Habbaniya, which gave the men a chance to work on their vehicles after their long march from Palestine. A few patrols were sent out, on one of which a man was killed in an attack by our own aircraft. Thereafter we had to wear a large white patch sewn on the backs of our shirts and paint white circles on the bonnets of our trucks.

When orders eventually came for the advance on Baghdad, the regiment was split into two columns. One was to move directly down the road, crossing the Euphrates near Fallujah, where there had been fierce fighting, and then carry on to Baghdad. The other column had to cross the Euphrates by ferry, sweep across the desert to cut the Baghdad-Mosul railway, and drive south towards Baghdad.

We crossed by ferry at night and next morning set off across the desert. My troop was leading, luckily with a truckload of Arab Legion to guide us. The men of the Arab Legion played a vital role in this campaign, acting as guides, scouts, skirmishers, guerrillas and agents. Their wild appearance, with crossed bandoliers and silver daggers in their belts, their furious driving, bravery in action and gaiety under adverse conditions endeared them to the British troops, by whom they were known as the 'Glubb Girls' because of their long hair and flowing robes. The Arab Legion recruited mainly from the Bedouin tribes from all parts of the Middle East, from Turkey to Southern Arabia, with the result that wherever we were in the desert Glubb could always produce a local man who knew the district, the local sheikhs or headmen and, more important still, the wells.

We hit the railway after a few hours and, as our Arab friends always seemed to carry explosives, they blew up the line. Gerry Fuller, my squadron leader, meanwhile gave me orders to push on down the railway to Taji station, which was reported to be held by the enemy. We drove down the dirt road that ran parallel to the railway, preceded by an ancient Rolls-Royce armoured car, a relic of the Duke of Westminster's regiment from the First World War and now in use with the RAF. It was commanded by a colourful character, Squadron-Leader Cassano. His armoured car was frequently in demand to lead a column ahead of the soft-skinned 15-cwt trucks, a dangerous role he assumed with obvious relish and good humour. I followed him in my 15-cwt and the three remaining trucks of my troop followed me.

In the distance the station looked rather like a Foreign Legion fort. These stations had been built by the Germans in the previous war as part of the Berlin to Baghdad railway, and had been designed to serve also as forts. They had loopholes on the roof and slit windows, and could hold about fifty men.

When we were about half a mile from the station, small puffs of sand began to spurt up from the ground around us. 'I think we're under fire,' Corporal Ratcliffe shouted at me. As he did so, the armoured car stopped and opened up on the station with its Vickers machine-gun. 'Stop,' I yelled at the driver above the din. 'Everybody out into the ditch.' The men needed no second bidding and in seconds were all lying in the ditch at the side of the road. I shouted at the trucks to turn round and get back out of range, which they did without getting hit. I then moved the troop over to the railway embankment on our right and split it into two halves, one on each side of the railway. We advanced forward, the armoured car and the

Iraqis both firing until we were about 200 yards from them, when they stopped. At once we charged the station, in time to see four truckloads of Iraqi soldiers driving away. We sped them on their way with a few parting shots, with no apparent effect, and the fort was ours. We looted it and one of our men climbed on to the roof and pulled down the Iraqi flag – our first trophy.

Next day we resumed the advance, to find that the enemy had left the sandhills and had withdrawn to a well-prepared position in front of Al Kadhimain station, with artillery to support them. When we came within range we were heavily fired on, so the whole squadron dismounted from its trucks, which were sent back, and our troop of supporting 25-pounders opened fire. A brisk exchange of artillery and small-arms fire went on for most of the afternoon, with no forward movement, and as darkness fell we withdrew leaving standing patrols and a section of machine-guns between us and the enemy.

During the night a convoy of Iraqi vehicles drove down the road in close column with their lights blazing. Our machine-gunners fired with such good effect that next morning we found four Iraqi lorries and one motor cycle abandoned, some dead Iraqi soldiers and a quantity of loot including two new Bren guns. These were very welcome, for we were still armed with the upopular Hotchkiss. It seemed illogical to us that the Iraqi army should be armed with Bren guns supplied by the British, while we had none.

The following day our squadron was ordered to carry out a dismounted attack on the Iraqi positions covering Al Kadhimain. The enemy were well ensconced in an area consisting mainly of brickfields, alongside the railway line. Another squadron, which had joined us in the night, was to attack at the same time from another direction.

We moved forward in open formation, for there was no cover, while the enemy put down a very effective artillery barrage in front of us. There was no choice but the very unpleasant one of having to advance through it. As each salvo was fired we threw ourselves on the ground while shells burst around us. It was a relief, as the smoke and dust drifted away, to see the men getting up and moving forward again, although in our squadron one was killed and several wounded.

The barrage followed us accurately until we were a few hundred yards from the brickworks, when intensive machine-gun and rifle fire opened up on us, pinning us down. Had we pressed on, we should have all become needless casualties. Each time any of us raised our heads, or tried to move, a hail of bullets came our way. My troop was particularly unlucky, because we had no cover whatever, whereas the other troops were lying in some undulating ground.

After a while one of my men shouted, 'There's a ditch over there, it should give us some cover.' We crawled over, feeling that our bottoms were very conspicuous, until we reached what transpired to be an irrigation ditch. It gave good cover from the front, though we had to stand in water. From this position I observed a group of Iraqi officers looking towards us with binoculars. I called to the trooper who was in charge of our troop 2-inch mortar, 'See those Iraqis standing beside that house about four hundred yards away?' 'Yes, sir,' he replied. 'Have a shot at them,' I ordered. He carefully sited and aimed his mortar – this was the first time he had fired it in action – then fired. It was an excellent shot, falling exactly where he intended. We saw the Iraqis scatter and some fall. 'Well done!' I shouted. 'Have another go.' He fiddled with the mortar for some minutes, then shouted, 'It's no good, sir, the bloody firing-pin's broken.' From then on our mortar was useless as we had no spare firing-pin.

We spent the rest of the day in this hapless position, sweating in the heat of the sun and waiting for the next shell to fall. One burst on the bank of the ditch about five yards from my troop HQ, showering us with a mixture of sand, mud and filthy water. We were very thankful when we eventually received the order to withdraw, because we could not have driven out the enemy without artillery support, and this we never had. Our brigadier did not endear himself to us when we later heard that he had told our colonel that he did not consider us unable to push on until we had had fifty per cent casualties.

The same night, after we had leaguered, I was sent for by the colonel. 'David,' Colonel Andrew said, 'I've got a rather bloody job for you. I want you to take out a patrol to see if the enemy are in the same positions, and to bring back a prisoner if you can.' He added that my training in the Commandos should stand me in good stead and wished me good luck. I saluted and returned to my troop, where I found six volunteers. We brewed up some tea while I briefed them and at midnight we set off, passing through our standing patrols.

Since local maps were useless and there was little moon, my only help in finding my way was a compass combined with my memory of the ground from the previous day. I led the patrol, carrying my Mauser machine-pistol at the ready. We walked slowly, as silently as possible, halting frequently to look, listen, and take bearings. When I estimated that we were nearing the enemy's positions – I could see the brickworks – the pace slowed down. Suddenly we heard voices; everyone dropped to the ground and remained motionless. We were close enough to distinguish the voices as Arab, and I was deliberating my next move when one of my patrol coughed. Moments later a Verey light went up. We flattened ourselves, but immediately the whole enemy front line started firing. The tracer streaking over our heads showed that thankfully their shots were going high – a common fault at night. I considered that we had achieved our objective, even if inadvertently, of making the enemy divulge their position, and there seemed little hope of taking a prisoner with the opposition so thoroughly aroused. I therefore decided to crawl back until we were out of range, after which we returned to the leaguer safely. I was able to report that the enemy were still in the brickyards.

It had been a nerve-racking night but the next day I was given a much more enjoyable task. Two troops were sent out with six truck-loads of the Arab Legion, accompanied by Colonel Glubb Pasha, and supported by one 25-pounder gun, with orders to capture the railway station of Mashaida, the next station to the north of Taji.

We drove to within rifle range of the station, then came under fire, so we withdrew out of range while the 25-pounder was brought up into action. It did not score a hit on the station until the twelfth shot, whereupon we could see men running away. I fired a Verey light to give the gunners the signal to stop firing, and then, forming a line in our trucks, we charged. It was exhilarating as we drove at full speed over the desert, the Arabs in their trucks firing their rifles into the air and shouting at the tops of their voices. We reached the station in time to take a number of prisoners, most of whom were hurriedly changing out of their uniforms into civilian clothes. We'd come across this before, but they usually gave themselves away by still wearing their army boots, from which they seemed reluctant to be parted.

In the station I found Glubb, who was giving money to one of the prisoners. In some surprise I asked him why. With a smile he turned to me and replied, 'Enlisting a new recruit.' These men, he explained, bore no bitterness against us and, providing we paid and fed them, were just as happy to fight on our side. As we were talking I could see two of his men in the stationmaster's office making unsuccessful and rather dangerous attempts to shoot the lock off the safe. Later someone produced some gelignite, so all was well and the safe successfully blown – though there was no money inside, merely thousands of railway tickets.

While the Arabs were looting the station – they appeared particularly happy at having found a store of blankets – we did even better, for we found a lorry ouside the station piled high with crates of eggs, none of which appeared to be broken in spite of the shelling. There must have been several thousand and the entire regiment lived on them for about a week. The heat at that time was so intense that we could fry them by simply breaking them on the bonnets of our trucks.

Shortly after this episode the 'Cease Fire' blew and the revolt in Iraq was over. We drove back to Habbaniya, where we hoped to link up with the rest of the regiment and enter Baghdad. Instead our column received orders to move to Mosul, where the Iraqis had not yet surrendered. It was rumoured that they were being encouraged to fight on by the German Luftwaffe personnel who were stationed on the airfield with some German aircraft.

We drove up to Mosul without incident, taking two days. On arrival we found the situation tense: the local Iraqi commander was truculent and for a time it looked as if hostilities would break out again. We moved on to the airfield with the barrels of an Iraqi battery of 18-pounders pointing threateningly at us. Shortly after, however, the situation changed for the better when we were joined by a battalion of Gurkhas – it was very reassuring to have them beside us.

There were several wrecked German aircraft on the airfield and inside one of the hangars was a Heinkel bomber. It was intact, with the Iraqi colours painted over the swastika, which was clearly visible below. This was conclusive evidence that the Germans had been collaborating with Rashid Ali. Locals informed us that all the Luftwaffe personnel had made off for Turkey shortly before our arrival.

Our next task at Mosul was to discover the whereabouts of Dr Grobba and capture him. Dr Grobba had been the German Minister in Baghdad when Rashid Ali had seized power, and had supplied him with ample funds with which to organise the revolt. It was thought that Grobba would endeavour to escape to Turkey, possibly with the other leaders of the revolt.

I was ordered to take my troop from Mosul to Rowanduz, about 200 miles away, where I was to set up a roadblock and ambush, as Dr Grobba was expected to pass that way. Taking rations for a week, we set off on what proved to be one of the most agreeable patrols I had done in the war. We drove first to Erbil, alleged to be one the oldest inhabited towns in the world. Built on a large hill in the middle of the plains, it was composed of seven cities all built one on top of the other during different civilisations. It must have been an archaeologist's delight. These was no time for sightseeing, but when I had a cup of coffee with the chief of police, he gave me a lot of useful information. He had hardly heard about our recent hostilities and was very friendly and cooperative.

Leaving Erbil behind us, we drove on through increasingly lovely countryside. The dusty dirt road ran through green valleys, with grassy hills on either side studded with trees and shrubs. Streams of clear water ran down from the hills into the larger rivers in the valleys. We were now in Kurdistan, which made a welcome change from the desert regions of Iraq. The local Kurds differed from the Iraqis by keeping their old customs and manner of dress – turbans and baggy trousers. They were polite and hospitable, told me they hated the Iraqis, and wanted independence to rule themselves. I felt sorry for them as they were also under the rule of Turkey and Persia; they had little chance of gaining independence.

While we were halted at the side of the road a car full of Iraqi officers drove past us at high speed, ignoring our signals to slow down and stop. This seemed suspicious, so we quickly gave chase and after several miles caught up when their car crashed over a six-foot drop at the side of the road. Although the car was completely wrecked, none of the occupants was badly hurt. They seemed hostile and after an acrimonious argument, carried out through our interpreter, I decided to send them back under escort. They were not the men we were after but they were probably trying to escape to Turkey to join the other rebels who had fled there. I never heard what happened to them.

Our drive took us on through the Rowanduz Gorge, a beautiful part of the country. Precipitous red-coloured rocky cliffs towered above the road which wound along the banks of a clear blue river in which we could see numbers of trout. Shortly after emerging from the gorge we came to a junction where one road forked north to Turkey and the other east to Persia. Here we set up our roadblock.

We made good friends with the local Kurds, drinking with them in a nearby coffee shop that was covered with vines. We bathed in the river and I spent hours watching the fish. However, no car came past. After three days we left with regret, to learn on our return that it had been reliably reported that Dr Grobba was in a town called Kameshle, which was just over the border in Syria but also very near the Turkish frontier.

Our column was sent off in pursuit, though with strict orders not to violate the Turkish frontier. We left Mosul in the evening, crossing the Syrian frontier after dark. The head of the column then inadvertently bumped into the French frontier post in the first village over the border. It had been intended to bypass the post because the French in Syria were under the orders of the pro-German Vichy government. Our column commander, Eric Gooch, had to placate the French officer in charge, whose troops had turned out after the trumpets had sounded the alarm. He was reasonable, accepted Eric's explanation that we were searching for Dr Grobba and Iraqi rebels, and let us proceed.

We moved on, cutting the telephone wires from the village as soon as we were out of sight, as we did not want news of our presence to precede us. In the next village the small French post was decidedly hostile, threatening to open fire on us if we didn't go away. We pressed on, but by the time we reached the outskirts of Kameshle we were obviously expected. We halted, while the French, whose artillery we could now see, took up positions to oppose us.

Eric Gooch went on ahead, where he held a conversation with a very smartly turned out officer, complete with sword. This officer politely but firmly informed Eric that he had violated French territory and could not pass. Any attempt to do so, he added, would be resisted by force. He gave an assurance, however, that Dr Grobba was not in Kameshle, as he had passed through there several days previously. We accordingly retraced our steps. As we passed the last village in Syria a dispatch rider appeared bearing a message from the French commander of the post requesting us not to cut his telephone lines the next time we passed.

This expedition had a curious twist to it. On our return to Mosul we discovered that, quite unknown to either the French we had met or ourselves, the British had already launched a major attack on the French in the south of Syria. Had either side known, events might have taken a very different course.

As the campaign in Iraq was now over and the war with the Vichy French had begun, we were ordered to move from Mosul to Habbaniya. From there we advanced on Abu Kemal in Syria, where we linked up with another column.

5
Syria and Persia

The French forces in Syria, having thrown in their lot with the Vichy government in August 1940, allowed German agents to operate in the country. They also allowed German aircraft transit facilities when Rashid Ali appealed to the Germans for help. In May 1941 about 120 German and Italian aircraft landed in Syria. These were among the reasons that the British government decided to attack the French forces and occupy Syria, with the main thrust taking place in the south from Palestine. Our brigade group from Iraq was therefore ordered to strike across the desert – capturing Palmyra on the way – to the Homs area, where we would be able to create a diversion to the enemy's flank and rear.

We stayed at Abu Kemal for a few days, being bombed on each of them by two very old French fighters, on which a great deal of ammunition was expended with no apparent effect. We then moved southwards to the T pipeline, where we joined up with the rest of the regiment at T1, to be confronted with a shambles. The place had been attacked and looted by Fawzi al Qawukchi, an Arab, educated at St Cyr, who had been an officer in the Turkish army in the First World War. After being one of the leaders of the Arabs in the Palestine troubles, he had gone on to serve Rashid Ali as War Minister. Guerrilla bands, well led by Fawzi, had already become a considerable nuisance to us; their chief targets were the rear of our columns and any stragglers. Their treatment of prisoners was not attractive; many were murdered, some by having petrol poured over them and being burnt alive, while others were stripped naked and turned loose in the desert to die. We all but lost our colonel to them. He went down with malaria at T1 and had a narrow escape from capture on his way back to hospital in an ambulance.

The column reached T2, which surrendered after a token resistance, so we pushed on to T3, which refused to surrender. A troop from our column was left to watch T3 while the rest of us moved on.

A few days later the Vichy French came out flying a white flag. When the British troops went forward to parley, the French opened fire on them, killing eight men. The French officer responsible for this disgraceful incident was later captured and court-martialled, but I never heard the result. I hope he was shot.

Between T3 and Palmyra the whole column, including HCR, was subject to heavy air attack. These attacks became routine during the following days, when six to twelve bombers dropped bombs from a height beyond the range of our small-arms fire. Low-flying fighters usually followed with machine-gun attacks. It was both unpleasant and ironic because the aeroplanes, flown by Vichy French pilots, were American Glenn Martin medium bombers, and their bombs were British 200 and 500 lb bombs supplied to the French before their surrender to the Germans.

If attacked on the move we had orders to disperse and keep moving. This was a testing experience for those in the trucks, because the passengers could see the bombs falling and would shout to the driver to take evasive action. The driver meanwhile kept the truck going at full speed over the desert, trying to avoid rocks and other natural hazards, not always successfully. The French fighters were more frightening than the bombers, because they approached very suddenly, usually out of the sun, and could follow and conform to the trucks' movements.

When we halted we all dug slit trenches away from our trucks. As the bombers came over we crouched in the trenches hoping for the best. On one occasion outside Palmyra I was sharing a slit trench with Gerard Leigh, a brother officer, when the bomb we were both watching seemed to come straight at us. I was convinced it would hit us; I think I said 'This is it' and shut my eyes. In fact it burst about twenty yards away, riddling my truck with splinters and ruining my personal kit in the back.

The same day a French fighter came over my troop, flying very low. Four of us fired at it – two riflemen, the Hotchkiss gunner, and myself with a rapid-firing automatic Mauser machine-pistol. From behind us Trooper Reeve, manning a Hotchkiss, also fired at it. It crashed about 500 yards behind us, to the delight of all, and of course we all claimed it as ours. The honours, however, including a Military Medal, went to Reeve. He fully deserved them as he was standing up completely exposed in the open to take on the fighter flying straight at him, whereas we were all firing from our slit trenches.

That afternoon we tried to find the pilot's body, for there was not much left of the aircraft. We found two feet, neatly severed at the ankles, with neither shoes nor socks. These remains were all we could find, so we buried them and erected a cross over their grave. By one of those unlucky chances a piece of the crashing fighter hit and killed Saddler Corporal Fowler, an excellent man who had been in my troop when we had horses.

That night our squadron moved from its rather exposed positions in the open desert outside Palmyra. Casualties that day had been three killed, four wounded and seven vehicles destroyed. We moved into some foothills north-west of Palmyra, where the ground was more broken and gave our vehicles better cover from air attack.

Our forces now encircled Palmyra, but it was heavily defended and a direct attack was unlikely to succeed. We had no heavy weapons and the French had complete air superiority – up to now we had not seen a single British aircraft, which was very bad for morale. We therefore sent out patrols to probe the enemy defences. My troop provided one of the earlier ones, consisting of a ten-man fighting patrol. We left at last light in two trucks, stopping about a mile from Palmyra, which was an oasis of Arab dwellings and French barracks, with some famous ruins outside the town. Dismounting from our trucks in the dark and under cover, we approached the ruins on foot. As we crawled among the Corinthian columns a Cockney voice muttered, 'In peacetime blokes pay cash to come and see these bloody ruins, and here we are doing it *buckshee*.'

We edged right up to the town and entered one of the streets. I noted a vehicle park and some other details of interest. I had meanwhile sent off two men to investigate a dilapidated Turkish fort perched on a hill overlooking the ruins. When we returned to our rendezvous the two failed to appear. We waited for them for some time, too long in fact, for as dawn broke we were still in the ruins and were spotted by the French. Immediately heavy rifle and machine-gun fire opened up on us, and it took us over an hour of alternately running, dropping and crawling before we were out of range. We returned safely to our trucks and then drove back to our lines. I was very crestfallen at having lost two men. Our general, however, who was visiting us at the time, congratulated me on the information we had brought back.

Two days later the missing men turned up minus their boots and rifles. Their story was that they had looked into the fort, where they had seen a dead Arab hanging by the neck. On the way back they had been set on and robbed by the Arabs, who turned them loose after removing their rifles and boots. I knew these two men particularly well and thought it more likely that they never went to the fort at all. Probably they went to sleep and were then robbed by Arabs.

I had felt ill before setting off on this patrol and felt much worse on my return, so Gerry Fuller sent me up to a cave where I would be out of the sun. Someone lent me an old copy of the *Tatler*, in which, by a strange coincidence, I saw a picture of my sister getting married. So erratic was the mail in the Middle East that I had not even heard that she was engaged.

Next day I felt even worse. The medical officer suspected malaria and sent me back to the advanced dressing station. I was made to lie in a slit trench and told I would have to wait until some vehicles could be spared to evacuate the sick and wounded. The French had attacked and destroyed all our ambulances – in spite of the large red crosses painted on them.

We had a marvellous morale-booster the following day. Six Glenn Martins flew over us and began to make their usual bombing runs, when suddenly six Tomahawk fighters with British markings flew out of the sun, each fighter attacking a bomber. Within a couple of minutes three of the bombers were on fire – three aircraft ablaze in the sky was an unforgettable sight. Parachutes then began to blossom. Five of the bombers crashed in flames, the sole survivor flew away belching smoke. All our troops were cheering wildly; this was the first time we had seen our own aircraft, which we later learned came from the Royal Australian Air Force.

One of the parachutes was on fire and descending at increasing speed. Later the airman who had been on it was brought in on a stretcher in a poor way and badly burned. I watched our medical officer cut the burnt skin round his wrists and then remove the skin from each hand in one piece, just as if he were taking off a glove. We were both put in the same lorry for the night, and the Frenchman was moaning most of the time. Though I had been delighted to see him shot down, close proximity to the enemy, as often happens in war, aroused feelings of sympathy rather than hate. At about midnight a Roman Catholic chaplain appeared and said some prayers over him. In the morning he was dead.

I was evacuated from the desert outside Palmyra to a base hospital in Palestine. Our convoy consisted of two trucks of sick and wounded, with an escort of Arab Legion to protect us from Fawzi's bands. I shared the back of a three-tonner with fifteen other sick or wounded men. We bumped along in the July heat and dust, halting three times on the first day while bombers attacked us. Those who could move abandoned the lorry to take what cover they could find, but the more seriously wounded were left. I stayed with them merely because I now felt so ill I didn't care what happened. The bombers scored no hits so we moved on. We spent one night in the desert and next day reached H4, where we were all put in real beds – a great luxury after sleeping rough for so long. The Arab Legion medical officer, who was in charge, was the only one in the force to possess a microscope. He diagnosed I had malignant malaria.

The heat and dust the following day were even worse. Again we travelled in a three-tonner, covering about 200 miles to Mafraq where, the next day, we were transferred to ambulances. I shared mine with a trooper from HCR named Flood-Paddock. As he was six foot seven inches tall the door had to be kept open to let his feet stick out. We drove in a convoy of ambulances across the Jordan Valley to Nazareth, where a monastery had been taken over by the Australians as a casualty clearing station.

The Australian nursing sisters could not have been kinder – I thought them real angels, especially after they gave me unlimited orange juice. I took a more jaundiced view of the male nursing orderlies because they removed my compass, binoculars and Mauser pistol which I never saw again. We were profoundly relieved when eventually the hideous discomfort of our 600-mile journey ended at a base hospital at Sarafand. It had been a ghastly week for the sick and wounded men.

While I was in hospital hostilities with France ended with an armistice being signed. The day after I rejoined the regiment, however, we were on the move again. A new campaign had started, the invasion of Persia, whose Shah was showing distinctly pro-German sympathies. By way of our old haunts of K3 and Habbaniya, we passed Baghdad and finally halted in the desert on the outskirts of the Kirkuk oil-fields, which we could see and smell from our bivouac area.

While exploring Kirkuk I discovered the station rest-house – a notable find, for it had electricity, fans, ice, a bathroom, and a stock of Heidsieck 1928 champagne. Hearing that a volunteer was required as a temporary RTO (railway transport officer) I promptly applied, was accepted and took up residence in the rest-house for the next ten days. I had to supervise the only two trains a day, one arriving and one departing. Nearby was the most excellent sand-grouse shooting. In the evening the birds came over in their thousands to water in one of the tributaries of the Tigris, and I could shoot as many as I wanted. They made good eating, providing you removed the tough skin. Many of my brother officers joined me to shoot, then have a bath followed by a good dinner.

The British government had already sent a strong note to the Persian government, demanding that it expel the large number of German agents who were operating in and from the country. After an unsatisfactory reply, our troops crossed the frontier into Persia. We were told that the Russians were also moving in from the north.

As the HCR was not in the advance guard we had the rather dull role of following behind a long column, usually enveloped in dust. My first impression of Persia was the abject poverty of ther peasants, which was worse than anywhere I had seen in the Middle East. Their appearance was not improved by the law compelling them to wear Western clothes. Arab clothing, however shabby and tattered, always seemed to retain its wearer's dignity. An emaciated peasant wearing a blue pin-stripe double-breasted suit, completely in rags, with a battered green pork-pie hat on his head, created an air of tragi-comedy. The locals could seldom afford meat, and our troops were able to barter a tin of bully for as much as a hundred tomatoes, fifty eggs or twenty cucumbers or honeydew melons.

The Persian countryside through which we drove was a considerable improvement on Iraq. Rolling hills replaced flat sandy desert, there were mountains of over 10,000 feet, and plentiful trees and shrubs. Because it was summer the grass, except near the rivers and streams, was dried up and brown. Small irrigation ditches led to fields where melons and tomatoes grew in profusion. There were attractive gardens in the towns and villages, with bougainvillea making splashes of crimson on the walls, many overhung by vines.

Passing Gilan, where the Persians had put up a token resistance, we pressed on to Kermanshah, where we moved into some hastily evacuated army barracks. Here there was heavy looting and I acquired a very fine new German-designed rifle of Persian manufacture, as well as a prayer mat. In fact the looting became so bad that we had to be paraded in front of the brigadier, who harangued us. The wind was rather taken out of his sails, however, for while he was speaking we could see behind him his brigade major and staff captain creeping furtively out of an arms store with a rifle in each hand. We wondered whether or not they were destined for the brigadier.

From Kermanshah we moved to Senna, where we bivouacked outside the town. From there we carried out a number of patrols, either in futile efforts to make contact with the Russians or to report on the state of the roads. For recreation we shot wild boar, went sightseeing in the town, or visited the local carpet factory. Before leaving we were inspected by Major-General Slim, under whose command we were operating. After ten days in Senna we returned to Kermanshah and from there, passing Qum with its beautiful domed mosque, drove to the outskirts of Tehran. All fighting had now ceased and we were supposed to enter Tehran simultaneously with the Russians at three o'clock the next afternoon. In the event the Russians pulled a fast one on us and occupied the whole town at six in the morning, including the best barracks. We were left to make do with an arms factory, which we shared with the Wiltshire Yeomanry, the 1/5 Royal Gurkhas and the 13th Indian Lancers.

During our stay in Tehran the Russians gave a party to which a number of our officers were invited. It was a somewhat alcoholic affair and after plenty of vodka the Russians had our officers singing the Internationale, while we riposted by getting them to sing God Save the King and the Eton Boating Song. Later we held a joint ceremonial parade with the Russians, at which the salute was taken by General Novikov, commander of the Caucasian Division. It was probably the only time during the war that British and Russian troops had paraded together. The Russian contingent was very smart with green tunics, gold epaulettes and black butcher boots. Of our contingent the Gurkhas were immaculately turned out, while the Household Cavalry troopers, through no fault of their own, looked rather shoddy in pith helmets, open shirts and shorts turned up at the knees. Our brigadier even wore corduroy trousers. The sole British reporter to watch this parade was Richard Dimbleby of the BBC. We all liked him, not the least because he had a bath in his hotel suite and allowed us to use it.

Tehran was a town of contrasts, a fusion of Eastern and Western styles of architecture, clothing and customs. The townsfolk appeared to be better off than the undernourished peasants, though there was no shortage of beggars. The Persian army officers, many of them highly scented, looked slightly comic in their musical comedy uniforms – black butcher boots with high heels and Nazi-style high peaked caps. Some of the buildings were examples of the reigning Shah's grandiose schemes. The railway station, telephone exchange and opera house were typical: there was only one train a day from the station, the town had very few telephones and no opera had ever been performed. We also visited the Royal Palace, where we saw the fabulous Peacock throne studded with precious stones, and the British Legation situated in lovely grounds with a swimming pool. The brigade HQ did itself well by taking over the Summer Legation, which lay some way out of Tehran in the hills where it was much cooler.

Shopping for souvenirs was a profitable occupation, with prices very low and beautifully painted pornographic pictures in great demand. There were also loads of night clubs and girls for company, as well as lavish supplies of vodka and caviar. We probably behaved fairly badly and over-indulged, but we had a very enjoyable time in Tehran. I was involved in one regrettable incident about which I kept very quiet at the time. A party from our squadron, having undoubtedly consumed too much vodka, broke into the German Embassy. We smashed some pictures of Hitler, removed the Nazi flag and took away a bronze bust of the Führer. The Swedes, who were looking after the German interests at the time, naturally complained. There was a terrible fuss and the bronze bust had to be returned from the NCOs' mess, where for obvious reasons it had been put in the urinal. We kept the flag and Gerry Fuller, our squadron leader, who knew the culprits, kept the secret. We heard no more of the incident, but many years later, when I was military attaché in Stockholm, I found myself sitting next to a Swedish diplomat. Somehow we got on to the subject of Tehran in the war, and he told me that he had been in the German Embassy when the nightwatchman told everyone to take refuge on the top floor as they were all going to be murdered by a band of assassins. I did not divulge that I was one of them.

After ten days, which seemed to be the longest time we stayed anywhere, we were on the move again, retracing our steps to Baghdad. During this drive we went over the Pai Tak Pass with a descent of 4,500 feet in four miles of winding road. We took five days to drive the 632 miles to Baghdad and were then ordered back to Palestine. Since leaving Palestine our brigade had travelled 6,300 miles. Our drivers had taken over very old trucks when they handed over their horses, and it was a wonder that they kept them going considering that few had passed a driving test or had any training in maintenance.

In Baghdad I had a recurrence of malaria, so I was left in the RAF hospital in Habbaniya while the regiment moved on to Palestine. After three weeks I scrounged a lift in the rear gunner's seat of a Blenheim and flew direct to Cairo, where I hoped to find out the whereabouts of the regiment. This was not easy. I first went to GHQ Middle East, who told me the regiment was in Persia. When I disillusioned them they suggested that I try HQ of the British troops in Egypt. Here I was told that the regiment was in Habbaniya. I said I had just flown from Habbaniya and the regiment had left there three weeks ago for Palestine. So, in the hopes of meeting someone I knew, I went to the Gezira Club where I met a friend who said 'Go and ask Joe, the barman at Shepheard's, he knows where everyone is.' I did so and Joe informed me that the regiment was in Allenby Barracks, Jerusalem. This proved to be correct. When I arrived there a few days later, most of the regiment was indeed in Jerusalem, although our squadron was in an outpost in the hills above Hebron, where it was very cold with deep snow. There was a very happy atmosphere and we enjoyed Christmas and New Year up there. We started training all over again, and for recreation there was plenty of shooting, with occasional nights out in Jerusalem.

During this period I was sent on what was called a G(R) course, which was a cloak and dagger affair in which we were taught demolitions and sabotage, with a view to training 'stay behind' parties in case the Germans ever occupied Palestine. The course took place at Emwas Monastery, near Latrun. In the grounds were the ruins said to be those of the biblical Emmaus, where Christ held the

Last Supper. We often went over to the big Trappist monastery at Latrun, where monks sold us excellent home-made red wine and cheese. On returning to the regiment I trained a squad of twelve men in what I had learned, and we enjoyed letting off bangs and setting up booby traps.

Early in February 1942 the squadron moved down from the snows to the heat of the Jordan Valley and camped near the Dead Sea, not far from Jericho. In the middle of the month it was announced that a party of 120 of all ranks was to be sent to the Western Desert on a special task – we did not know what. I was lucky to be among those chosen. After a tremendous farewell party at the King David Hotel in Jerusalem we left for Egypt. Our train from Palestine finally stoped at Mersa Matruh, where we took our first steps in the Western Desert.

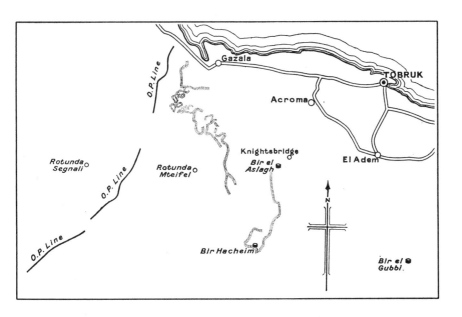

6

Western Desert

From Mersa Matruh we travelled by train and lorry down the Mediterranean coast to Tobruk, on the way passing a number of wrecked tanks from a recent battle. Many still contained dead bodies too mutilated to be removed, so petrol had been poured into the tanks to ignite and cremate them. Our destination was a few hours' drive from Tobruk.

In March 1942 our front, covered by deep minefields with narrow gaps for the traffic, stretched from Gazala in the north to Bir Hacheim in the south. The main bulk of the Eighth Army was behind these minefields, and normally the armoured car screens and the occasional fighting columns, known as 'Jock columns', were on the enemy side of them.

We were now a part of the Eighth Army, with the title 101 Royal Tank Regiment, abbreviated to 101 RTR, named 'Smithforce' after our commander Major Tony Murray-Smith. On arrival in our new area we were met by various officers from the 60th Rifles, from whom we were taking over dummy tanks. They seemed very happy to be handing them over, and once we saw the vehicles we realised why. They were in the most appalling state of repair and virtually on their last legs.

The dummy tank was basically a Morris 15-cwt chassis on which had been welded a tubular metal frame, with the crude addition of three-ply wood, canvas and piping, embellished by some skilful painting. The result to anyone no nearer than 300 yards was an adequate reproduction of the A 15 tank, better known as the Crusader. Enemy aircraft, however, could see that the vehicles left wheel and not track marks in the sand. This difficulty was partly overcome by parking the dummies in the tracks of genuine tanks. When they could be spared, a couple were usually attached to us for making tracks. On the move real tanks raised far more dust than wheeled vehicles, so the dummies achieved the same effect by dragging chains behind them. Chains were also fixed to the bottom of the canvas skirting which covered the wheels and was painted to represent the bogey wheels and tracks. One the chains got torn off – and they often did in thorn bushes – the skirts flapped in the wind.

My new command consisted of eighteen dummy tanks representing a squadron. In addition I had a 15-cwt truck as my personal vehicle, from which I could command my squadron by a series of flag signals – we were not equipped with wireless. The dummy tanks each had a crew of two, one driver and one lookout whose job was both to observe the squadron leader's signals and watch for enemy aircraft. There was some excitement our first morning when three German ME 110s attacked our cookhouse lorry, but casualties were restricted to one saucepan.

Life was very congenial, especially compared with the deserts of Iraq and Syria, for there was a fair amount of greenery with small shrubs and weeds. Much of the debris of war was lying around, again a change from the barren wastes of Arabia. Best of all was the climate, for though the days were sunny and hot, the evenings always brought a cool breeze blowing inland from the sea. The nights were distinctly cold, very often with a heavy dew. It was customary for us to get up wearing thick Hebron sheepskin coats, which we would shed sometime after breakfast; then our battledress jackets would come off, and by midday most people would be stripped to the waist.

Except when there were sandstorms, which were severe and could last for days, the air was remarkably fresh and clear. Even the sandstorms, bad as they were, could be seen aproaching in the distance and there was usually time to take precautions against them. A strange feature resulting from sandstorms was that when we touched our vehicles afterwards we often received quite strong electric shocks.

Most people felt much healthier in the desert than in other theatres of war. The two prevalent complaints were desert sores, when the slightest scratch turned septic, and jaundice. The doctors put the desert sores down to the lack of certain vitamins in our diet. The jaundice was prevalent among officers rather than other ranks, for which nobody seemed to have any explanation at the time.

For food we relied mainly on army rations of bully beef and biscuits, supplemented by such extras as we could buy from the

NAAFI, notably tinned fruit. Water was always scarce and was strictly rationed, according to conditions prevailing at the time. What we had was distilled sea water from Tobruk which made our tea taste horrid and the tinned milk curdle. Apart from drinking and cooking it had to be used for washing our bodies and clothes, for filling radiators, and the cooling system of certain machine-guns. It was not unknown, as a last resort, to fill radiators with urine.

Among the fighting troops in the desert it was a rare occurrence to see any non-combatants. Although some circulated in the rear, the only ones we ever saw making regular appearances in the forward areas were the personnel of the American Quaker ambulances and the Church of Scotland canteen vans. Nor did we see any press correspondents, which was surprising considering the graphic descriptions we read in the newspapers of the fighting in the Western Desert. One story concerning the press related to an Indian Army colonel. He was alleged to be the first Indian to command a battalion and as such was a favourite offering to the newsmen. He became increasingly fed up with being shown off like some prize exhibit and being asked, with regular montony, 'Why are you fighting in this war?' Finally he could stand it no longer and replied: 'I'm fighting for forty shillings a day, but if they pay me twice as much I'll fight twice as hard.' He received no further visits from the press.

Life in the desert at this period was quite social. People were always dropping in to drink our precious whisky and to exchange news, and similarly we used to visit friends in neighbouring units. Tobruk was even more social; there were some extremely pretty girls there, too, serving with the Spears Mission. Sadly there was nowhere to take them out.

Our first spell with 101 RTR lasted two and a half months, during which we carried out our role in cooperation with real tanks, either replacing them when they moved to new positions or, sometimes, making deceptive moves ourselves. On one such move, in April 1942, Smithforce made its name. We received orders to move to a place shown on the map as Rotunda Segnali, which we knew was a strongpoint held by the Italians. Tony Murray-Smith queried the map reference given, but it was confirmed as correct, so we cautiously set forth. Passing through the minefields and then, very much to their surprise, the armoured car patrols of the Royals, we approached within sight of Rotunda Segnali. Here we halted while

Tony Murray-Smith, who had the only wireless contact with the rear, reported back what he could see. He was immediately ordered to move back as we were six and a quarter miles too far to the west. This was exactly one grid square on the map and it was obvious that an error had been made in the coding of the map reference, luckily by divisional HQ as we later discovered.

We had noted, uneasily, that for some time we had been shadowed by a German reconnaissance aircraft, popularly known as the 'shufti-wallah'. This normally meant that he would call up his friends in the Stukas, who would shortly be over to dive-bomb us. While we were turning round we saw some Italian tanks sally forth from Rotunda Segnali, no doubt to investigate what was going on. Soon afterwards we heard the Stukas approaching and when they came into view we expected the worst. However, to our amazement and delight they proceeded to drop their bombs on the Italian tanks. A short while later large numbers of Italian vehicles were seen streaming out of Rotunda Segnali to the rear, and we assumed this to be the Italians in full retreat. If ever Smithforce earned a battle honour it was 'Rotunda Segnali'. The officer who ordered us to move there was awarded the OBE.

During this two and a half month period we had plenty of excitement – reports of impending enemy attacks and numerous air attacks from both German and Italian fighters. The German Stukas were very alarming, for as they dived at you they turned on sirens which made a hideous noise to add to the confusion.

Visits to Tobruk were regarded as something of a treat, so we used to take turns to go there, mainly to draw the pay and do the NAAFI shopping. Air raids were frequent, and an extract from my diary records such a visit: 'March 16th. Drove to Tobruk. Arrived during an air raid. Went to the Field Post Office, another air raid. To the Field Cashier, another air raid. Shopped at the NAAFI, called at the Water Point and AOD. Returned to 101 RTR after taking good action photographs.' The best of these included a view of Tobruk harbour with a ship on fire, anti-aircraft shells bursting in the sky and an aircraft coming down in flames.

Meanwhile all our officers carried out an attachment with the Royals, as by this time we knew that the HCR was to become an armoured car regiment. On my arrival at their HQ I found Major Tony Pepys in charge, very pleased with life as the Royals regimental

HQ had just shot down an Italian Savoia bomber. He was an old friend: I had served under him at the Middle East Cavalry School, where he was the chief instructor. He arranged for me to be attached to one of their squadrons and I spent a week with them.

The chief role of an armoured car unit was reconnaissance. This was normally carried out by the smallest sub-unit, the troop, which contained four armoured cars. A troop would operate in no man's land betweeen our own and the enemy's forward positions – both of which were usually protected by stretches of wired and marked minefields. All enemy activity observed by the troop was immediately reported back by wireless to the squadron leader, whose HQ of two armoured cars was a mile or so to the rear. He in turn could report anything of importance to the colonel, whose regimental HQ was even further to the rear. There was something very satisfying to me about being in contact with the enemy, whether visually or more violently, and an armoured car regiment often drew the fire of the enemy or attracted the unwelcome attention of his fighters. I believe that in desert warfare an armoured car unit had the most exciting and interesting role of all.

At the end of April we were moved back to Cairo to change our dummy tanks for new ones. We had a terrible drive back, with endless breakdowns, but once in Cairo we were all sent on a week's leave, which I took in Alexandria where I had many friends from my commando days – British, French, Greek, Swiss, Copt and Egyptian. There was sailing, horse racing, tennis and, best of all, relaxing in the cool blue water of the Mediterranean and drying off in the soft white sand. On arrival at the Cecil Hotel I immediately indulged in a luxury I had dreamed about in the desert – a long soak in a warm bath sipping a glass of ice-cold champagne. After that I went to the hotel barber, who cut my shaggy hair, shampooed the sand out of it and gave me a face massage that removed all traces of sand from the pores.

After our return from leave we took over our new dummies. This time they represented the American General Grant tank that had now made its appearance in the Eighth Army. These new dummies were so secret that before we left Cairo they were all covered with sacking so that nobody could see what was underneath. Having driven the 500 miles to the battle area in eight days, we finally took off the sacking at night and appeared as tanks the next morning.

As we arrived in our new positions we heard bombing and gunfire; it was obvious that a battle was taking place nearby. It was one of the German probing attacks led by Rommel against the French positions around Bir Hacheim. The Germans were repulsed with the loss of ten tanks.

For the next ten weeks we were very involved in what turned out to be the start of one of Rommel's famous pushes. Our own and enemy columns were constantly milling about, it was often difficult to identify friend from foe, and even more difficult to discover who was winning. We received daily intelligence reports, known as 'sitreps', giving the number of German tanks alleged to have been knocked out, on the strength of which we thought the battle was going our way. We were wrong.

There were many exciting and exhausting days to follow. On one occasion the Germans captured the bulk NAAFI store at El Adem and drank so much beer that it was easily retaken in a counterattack by Indian troops, who drove them out and took a number of very drunk prisoners. The next day General Messervy, commanding the 7th Armoured Division, was captured. He quickly removed his badges of rank before being interrogated by a German intelligence officer. When asked his rank the general replied 'Trooper', to which the German responded 'You must be very stupid for a man of your age still to be a trooper.' The general later escaped.

I myself had one particularly nasty shock. A box of plastic grenades, which we used to make bangs to simulate the fire of our so-called guns, blew up in the back of my truck, blasting the back to bits but fortunately doing no damage to the two of us sitting in front.

Towards the end of the battle we moved to the Bir Hacheim area, being attacked en route by five German fighters who hit one of our dummy tanks and a pick-up. Both went up in flames but by good luck the crews were only slightly wounded. We had a grandstand view of a tank battle and could see all too clearly the effectiveness of each side's fire; from the number of hits it was apparent that the Germans were winning. That night there was a horrible stench of death and next morning I discovered I had been sleeping about three yards away from a half-buried German.

Three days later we were attacked by three Italian fighters who came in about ten feet above the ground. They were all shot down by small-arms fire from a nearby unit. Everyone in the area raced to be the first to loot the wrecks, as the guns and compasses were valuable additions to our own vehicles.

We badly needed machine-guns for anti-aircraft use, so I went into Tobruk to scrounge some. There were large quantities of captured German and Italian weapons at the salvage depot, but the bloody-minded officer in charge refused to let me have any. I was furious; it seemed to me bureaucracy at its worst. Furthermore a few days later Tobruk fell to the Germans and all the weapons went back to the enemy. However, I did make one profitable deal on that last trip to Tobruk. I cashed a cheque with the field cashier and since he was presumably captured along with his accounts, I never had the cheque presented.

The following day we watched yet another tank battle, bigger than the previous one. There was a constant thump of falling bombs and shells and we could see the dust rising in clouds as they hit the ground. Tanks were moving in all directions, aircraft screamed out of the sky with bombs dropping and machine-guns chattering; a flash followed by a plume of black smoke indicated a hit as a tank or a lorry burst into flames. The battle came too close for comfort: when some of our dummy tanks came under fire from enemy tanks, we decided that our role of deception was proving rather too successful. To our relief we were shortly ordered to withdraw, but were less happy to learn it was part of a general wihdrawal by all our troops. We had clearly lost the battle, later to be known as Knightsbridge. The German tanks were better than ours, both out-ranging them and protected by thicker armour. So we joined in the general retreat, finally reaching Cairo where we thankfully handed in our dummy tanks. Smithforce was ordered to rejoin the regiment, which had by then moved to Cyprus.

We reached Cyprus at the end of June, where we stayed for the next two months. It was here that the HCR were issued with their first armoured cars. They were Mark III Marmon Harringtons, with Ford engines, assembled in South Africa. Their chief assets were that they were fast, reliable, seldom broke down and in the desert had proved to be very good runners in the sand. On the debit side they had very thin armour, which could be penetrated by any armour-piercing bullet, and their hitting power was very weak, since they carried only a Boys anti-tank rifle and a Bren gun. Later on in the desert it became the custom to collect enemy weapons and mount them on these cars. The Breda and Solothurn 20 mm guns from crashed aircraft were very popular. An even bigger gun, the Italian 47 mm, was sometimes mounted instead of the 20 mm, but this involved removing the turret.

During our training in Cyprus those who had been in Smithforce regarded themselves as desert experts and indulged in a good deal of line-shooting with those who hadn't been there. We were able, however, to pass on what we had learnt of desert warfare. I was also happy to be back with my old troop in the same squadron, with Gerry Fuller still my squadron leader. On the lighter side there was considerable night life for the younger officers, notably at a night club called the Chanteclair, where mid-European cabaret girls were much in demand. We were outraged when they were all suddenly interned as enemy aliens.

Cyprus was an attractive island but our squadron was stationed in a small whitewashed village on a hot and dusty plain. Exercises that took us to the coast were popular. All the same we felt out of the war, in spite of being told that the main reason we had been sent to Cyprus was to prevent a possible German parachute landing, against which we were continually preparing ourselves and rehearsing alarm schemes. The infantry units expended a great deal of effort digging trenches and enlarging caves, where they were supposed to hide as the German parachutists descended before emerging to shoot them. We little knew that the German paratroops had suffered such heavy losses in Crete that they were not proposing to use this method of attack again. Nor did we anticipate that the carefully-dug hideouts would later be used by Grivas's EOKA.

We were not sorry when, at the end of August, we sailed from Famagusta to Port Said, for we knew we were destined for the Western Desert. We assembled at a huge camp in the Tel el Kebir area where we were issued with our new armoured cars. Nearby was the small village of El Qassasin, in which there was a cemetery containing the graves of Household Cavalrymen killed in their famous moonlight charge in 1882.

Three weeks later we became a fully equipped armoured car regiment. Our morale was very high after the frustrations of the past. In addition to the Marmon Harringtons we also had one Daimler per troop. This was the newest armoured car from England and had all the qualities we wanted – good performance, a hard-hitting 2-pounder gun, and thick enough armour to protect the crew from all but the heavier anti-tank weapons. Its weakness, which we did not find out till later on, was that in soft sand the fluid flywheel was apt to break, rendering the car a write-off.

While we were waiting to move up to the desert several of us were sent to Cairo for a week's course in the 2-pounder and Besa guns. The Besa was a machine-gun mounted in the turret of the Daimler alongside the 2-pounder, and was capable of very rapid sustained fire, being fed by long belts of ammunition.

At the end of September the whole regiment moved up to the Western Desert. Our front line had been considerably withdrawn and shortened since the days of Smithforce. It now stretched from El Alamein in the north to the Qattara Depression in the south; from the main Cairo to Alexandria road we had only a sixty-mile drive to reach our base behind the front line. There we tested and fired all our guns. We also had training in navigation; those who had been in Smithforce were able to instruct in the use of the sun compass and how to read the almost blank maps.

At the end of a week we moved up to the front and took over a sector from the 11th Hussars, then the most famous and experienced armoured car regiment in the Western Desert. This was the first time in the war that the regiment had been in direct contact with the Germans, who held positions opposite us. Between the opposing sides was an intricate system of minefields. The front was stabilised, but intense preparations were taking place in the rear areas as more and more units arrived. Our role was to man a line of observation posts (OPs), from where we could watch for enemy movements. Normally a squadron had three troops up in a line of OPs, with the other two troops resting in reserve.

The first contact made by our squadron was when three German armoured cars appeared about two miles away from my position. My request to go out and engage them with my troop was turned down. Shortly afterwards we were accurately shelled, presumably on the reports of the enemy armoured cars. Later in the morning we were relieved by another troop and returned to reserve. This troop had not been in position long before five British Honey tanks were seen approaching. When they came nearer they were seen to have German markings and were at once engaged. One of our cars scored a direct hit with its 2-pounder, breaking a track on one of the tanks.

By chance Roddie Pratt, the squadron second-in-command, and Corporal-Major Summers were paying a routine visit to the troop in a jeep. As there was supposed to be a troop of gunners on one flank of the troop and a troop of tanks on the other, Summers drove off in his jeep to warn one flank unit about the tanks and Pratt set off on foot to warn the other. While they were on this errand the tanks speedily advanced and Summers was cut off and taken prisoner, together with the two men who had accompanied him in the jeep, one of whom was the driver of one of our armoured cars. When the Germans approached, therefore, this car had no driver, but Pratt, appreciating what was happening, jumped in and drove it off at high speed, with the Honeys in full pursuit. One of them scored a direct hit on the back of the car, wounding all the crew including Pratt, but he managed to carry on and the Honeys withdrew. As the result of Pratt being evacuated to hospital I took over his job as squadron second-in-command.

Next day the HCR were relieved and we returned to our base area. We carried out intensive training for the next ten days, during which we were inspected by General Montgomery, the Army Commander, Lieutenant-General Brian Horrocks, our corps commander, and Major-General John Harding, commanding 7th Armoured Division. On one exercise we acted as enemy to the troops who were to be used later in the attack at El Alamein. A complete replica of the German minefields was laid out and after the attack, in which a number of things went wrong, we carried out a critical post mortem. All the indications were that the big attack was not far off and we anxiously waited to be told what our role would be.

In late October the regiment moved up to the front again and took over from the 11th Hussars. Our squadron was sent to hold the most southerly sector of the entire British line, down in the Qattara Depression, a vast area of soft sand. To reach it we had to drive down a very steep track in the escarpment. The squadron we relieved told us they had been bombed a good deal, losing six vehicles in the previous two days, so we expected trouble.

Next day I took my troop up to relieve a troop of the 11th Hussars and within an hour we were attacked by two ME 109Fs, the newest German fighter. One of my Marmon Harringtons was hit but not damaged. An hour later three 100Fs appeared in line ahead formation and came straight at my Daimler. We fired back at them with all our weapons, including the 2-pounder, but with no visible result. However, it was comforting that their hits on the Daimler did not penetrate the armour and caused no real damage.

Our squadron HQ was also attacked and one man killed. It was impossible for the crews of the transport vehicles to dig slit trenches, as the sand was so soft that the sides continually fell in. But strewn around us were numbers of logs and tree trunks that looked as if they were wood but were in fact stone – we were in the middle of a petrified forest. With these we were able to build sangars (walls) behind which we could take cover.

One night our artillery opened up with a terrific barrage; it was the prelude to the Battle of Alamein. Though we were some distance from the guns, we could hear the noise, see the flashes and watch the lights of the parachute flares. A galaxy of searchlights to our rear made artificial moonlight of the sky. To the north it looked as if some giant Guy Fawkes night had begun.

For a week we remained static, anxiously awaiting news of the battle. In general it was good, though nothing like a breakthrough had yet been reported. At the end of a week our squadron was ordered forward to check whether or not the enemy had pulled out. We moved forward thirty-five miles in very heavy going – the soft sand of the Depression was normally considered impassable for wheeled vehicles. We saw a number of German tanks and vehicles in the distance, but no indication that they were withdrawing. On the way back the transmission of my Daimler broke and the car caught fire. We brought the fire under control before it could spread to the ammunition, which would have been serious, but in any case the car was a write-off. Moreover, the recovery lorry bogged down on the way to tow it out, so the Daimler had to be abandoned after we had stripped everything removable from it. Later we lost a second Daimler in the same way.

Next day we climbed out of the Qattara Depression and rejoined the rest of the regiment. We were told an attack was to be mounted by the 7th Armoured Division that night and if successful the armoured cars would be used to exploit it. After a day's fighting the attack succeeded and 3,000 prisoners were taken, at last giving us the chance to carry out the role for which we had been waiting.

We passed through the minefields late in the evening and advanced for about five miles before leaguering for the night; we also took eleven Italian prisoners, all dead drunk. The next day we came up against the German positions on a plateau from which they showed no signs of withdrawing. Since we had already been machine-gunned by our own fighters and then shelled by our own artillery – we were quite often mistaken for the enemy – we were perhaps more philosophical about coming under fire from German mortars. The German positions were subjected to heavy fire from both our artillery and mortars, continuing throughout the night. We attempted in vain to get some sleep while a regiment of 25-pounders just behind us opened up at frequent intervals.

By dawn the next day the Germans had pulled out and we began to advance with HCR acting as advance guard to 44 Division. We pushed on fast while Italians in their hundreds, and later in their thousands, tried to surrender. As our orders were to press on, we shouted at them from our cars to keep walking east. We came under shellfire again, first from our own artillery and then from the Italians, but we overran the Italian gunners who stopped shooting at us as soon as we started to machine-gun their guns. Another squadron of HCR had the best kill of the day, wiping out a pocket of thirty Germans who fought stubbornly until they were all killed or wounded. A troop of our squadron took twenty Germans prisoner who had air force insignia on their uniforms. These were paratroops, who fought well because they had been told that we shot all paratroops out of hand. Another of our troops of three armoured cars, nine men, took over 600 prisoners.

Just as we were getting into our stride we received very frustrating news: our corps was going into reserve and we were to retrace our steps twenty miles. On the way back we were able to indulge in some profitable looting from abandoned enemy vehicles, and hardly had we reached our destination than we were ordered to advance again to search for lost Italians and to plot on our maps any abandoned lorries or dumps. The squadron spread out and advanced thirty-five miles; we found two parties of lost Italians, each over 1,000 strong.

They were sitting miserably in the middle of nowhere, completely lost, some of them starving, some mad, some dying. They told us their transport had been taken, either by their officers or the Germans, and they had been wandering about the desert for some days with no idea of where they were. They had lost all sense of direction. Our squadron collected over 800 more the next day – the regiment found over 2,000 – and we also found a batch of 150 wounded in a terrible state, having been without water for five days. We had very little to spare ourselves, so the best we could do was to ferry them back as quickly as possible. It was surprising how many men could clamber onto an armoured car and hang on – I had more than twenty on my car, clinging to various parts like monkeys.

A few days later we were told to be out of the battle for good. Though our advance was progressing well, a great many units could not be used because of difficulties of supply. With a sense of bitter disappointment we turned our backs on the battlefield and drove back through Cairo to our old camp near Tel el Kebir.

Here Colonel Andrew Ferguson gave up command of HCR, on promotion, and Eric Gooch took over. He at once went to Cairo to find out the future of the regiment and discovered that we would be staying about ten days in Egypt and then probably moving to Syria. Meanwhile we were all given leave. I went to Cairo where I met Billy McLean. He asked me if I would be interested in joining him in a cloak and dagger operation which involved dropping with him into some region of the Balkans. I told him I was definitely interested.

PART TWO
Albania

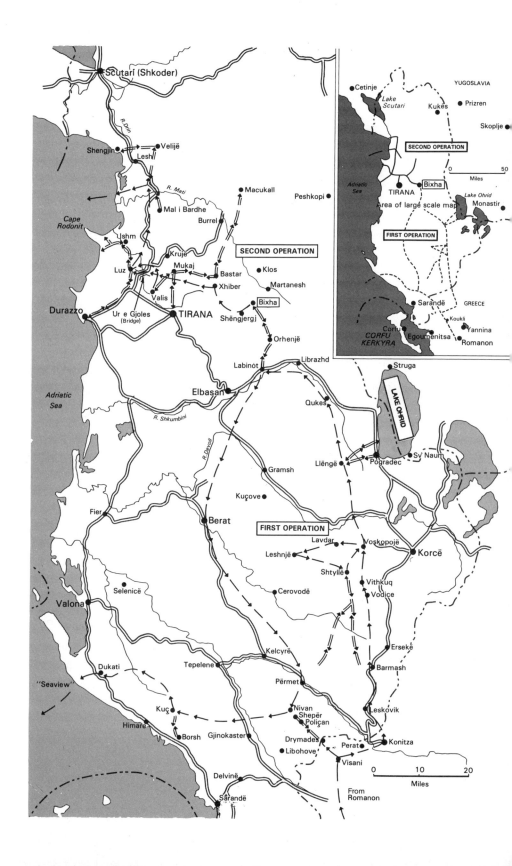

7
MO4 and Parachute to Greece

On New Year's Day 1943 I arrived in Cairo, having left my regiment on the Syrian-Turkish border anticipating a possible German thrust through Turkey. It was another seven years before I rejoined them.

The organisation I had joined was known as MO4. Though I did not know it at the time, this was the cover name for the Middle East branch of SOE – Special Operations Executive. Later, for security reasons, MO4 was changed to Force 133, then Force 366. The HQ of MO4 was housed at Rustem Buildings in a residential area of Cairo. A stale joke relates that it was known to most Egyptian taxi drivers as the 'HQ of the British Secret Service'.

After only a few days in Cairo, where I met Billy McLean and we discussed our plans for a drop into Yugoslavia, I retraced my footsteps to Haifa. There I attended a course at a monastery on the top of Mount Carmel where agents to be infiltrated into the Balkans were trained. Instead of the uncomfortable camp on top of Mount Carmel, I had as my quarters the luxury of the Windsor Annexe Hotel half way up – thanks to my Arab friend Roy Boutagy, whose father owned it. From there I also had a good view one day of Italian bombers attacking the oil refinery.

Apart from the British students there were also Greeks and Yugoslavs. We were taught a variety of subjects, from demolitions, mines and sabotage to lock-picking and safe-blowing, wire tapping telephone lines and the use of secret inks. We went to the Haifa oil refinery and the railway, even learning to drive a locomotive. Our weapon training was entirely with Italian or German weapons, on the assumption that we would capture these from the enemy. We also learnt to identify the insignia on Italian and German uniforms as well as to recognise their tanks, transport and aircraft. We paddled about Haifa harbour sticking limpet mines on an old wreck in the middle of the night.

The course lasted a month and of the forty students about half passed, of which I was one. After this I was sent on a parachute course at Kabrit, one of innumerable camps sited along the Suez Canal. This was where David Stirling had his HQ and where his SAS did their parachute training. SOE agents shared their camp and facilities. We trained for a week, jumping off the back of trucks going about 30 mph to teach us how to fall, doing a certain amount of PT and finally making our jumps.

We did six jumps in all, four from a Hudson and two, at night, from a Dakota. We jumped out of the side of the fuselage of both planes; the Hudson flying at about 120 mph was the more difficult exit. I must confess that I was more scared on my second jump than on my first, and on each jump I was greatly relieved when the static line attached to the aircraft pulled open my parachute. In those days we didn't have a reserve. Our jumps started at 1,000 feet and went down to 500 feet. One of the students had a 'Roman candle' – the rigging lines got mixed and crossed over the top of the parachute, thus spilling out the air so that he came down at such a rate that he sustained fatal injuries.

After completing the course we were awarded our parachute wings and two shillings (10p) a day extra as danger pay. We wore our wings initially on our sleeves but once we had made an operational jump we copied the system used in David Stirling's SAS and transferred them to our chests.

After these two courses I returned to Cairo where Billy McLean told me our plans were changed and we were now going to Albania. McLean had submitted his own plan to Brigadier Keble, then head of MO4, who had given it his approval. Although parties had gone to Greece and Yugoslavia, nobody had gone to Albania and McLean's idea was to go there with the intention of linking up with any guerrilla movements who might be fighting the Italians.

Our only information on Albania came from a woman working in the MO4 office, Mrs Margaret Hasluck. She was a remarkable character who had spent many years living in Elbasan in Albania as an anthropologist, studying their customs and folk lore. The Italians had expelled her as a spy. In fact, at that time, she wasn't, but on moving to Turkey she was recruited by British Intelligence and spent the next two years in Turkey collecting intelligence from, and communicating with, contacts in Albania. She was then transferred to Cairo to set up the Albanian section of MO4. She told us she had received reports of various guerrilla bands in Albania fighting the Italians. She had the names of four leaders of these bands – Abas Kupi, Baba Faja, Myslim Peza and Muharrem Bajraktar. Our intention was to enter Albania to try to find these men.

While in Cairo we had daily briefings from Mrs Hasluck, whom we knew affectionately as 'Fanny'. She also tried, unsuccessfully, to teach us Albanian, which she spoke fluently. We had an opportunity, too, to improve our pistol shooting, as at that time there were two well-known instructors in Cairo. One was Lieutenant Smith, an American formerly in the FBI, whose claim to fame was that he had shot the notorious gangster Dillinger in Chicago. The other, Captain Grant-Taylor, was a crack pistol shot who could literally hit the ace of spades at thirty yards.

We had also, in our short time in Cairo, to get together the team that was going to drop with us. Billy McLean, with the rank of major, was the leader. A regular officer in the Scots Greys, he had commanded Abyssinian guerrillas in Haile Selassie's forces as well as a colonial regiment of Abyssinians who had defected from the Italians. Tall, good-looking, with a somewhat languid and nonchalant manner, he gave the impression of idleness. However, he had already proved himself a fine guerrilla leader, brave and tough, very intelligent, with a strong interest in people and politics. I was to be his second-in-command with the rank of captain. Lieutenant Garry Duffy from the Royal Engineers was the expert on demolitions and Corporal Williamson, from the Black Watch, was to be our radio operator. As none of us could speak Albanian we also had an interpreter – an English-speaking Albanian called Elmaz.

We did a final course in escaping which was taught by Captain Jasper Maskelyne, a peacetime conjuror. He equipped us with various silk maps for sewing into our clothes and a number of magnetic items which would all point north – such as compasses in buttons, pencil clips and even magnetic fly buttons. We also carried gold sovereigns sewn into our trouser turn-ups and our badges of rank were specially made of 24-carat gold.

It was decided that as we did not want to take the risk of dropping into Albania blind, we would drop to the British military mission in Greece nearest to the Albanian frontier. At this time all missions dropping into the Balkans started from Derna in Tripolitania, where a squadron of Halifax bombers was stationed. It was commanded by Squadron Leader Jimmy Blackburn, who was known for the accuracy with which he dropped his supplies and bodies. The Halifaxes had been adapted to drop metal containers about six feet long instead of bombs. These containers each carried three metal canisters about eighteen inches in diameter and about two feet high. In addition the Halifaxes had a large hole in the fuselage out of which the bodies dropped.

We left Cairo by train on 11 April, my twenty-seventh birthday, and arrived at Derna where we were billeted in huts on the airfield. Here we had a slight hitch. As we were drawing our kit on the afternoon of our departure, Elmaz our interpreter refused to come with us. He was insisting on ringing up friends in Cairo, but was forbidden to do so on security grounds. Hence his refusal to come. We decided to go without him rather than wait for a replacement, so Elmaz was handed over to the security officer. We later heard that he spent the rest of the war in a camp in the Sudan.

We took off as it was getting dark, happy to know that Jimmy Blackburn was our pilot. For our jump we wore flying suits over our battledress, padded suits over this and with the parachute harness over all we felt like trussed chickens. As we climbed from the coast of Africa across the Mediterranean, darkness set in but in our uncomfortable positions on the floor it was still possible to read. It was too noisy for conversation. I thumbed through *Horse and Hound* and the *Tatler*; I saw the others were asleep. Our dropping zone (DZ) was to be in the Northern Epirus mountains, about twelve miles north-west of Jannina.

After about two and a half hours we crossed the coast of Greece, where we had been told we might expect flak or enemy fighters. Luckily there were none. After a while the RAF dispatcher told us to get ready. We attached our static lines to a wire running down the length of the fuselage and all gave our own a good yank to ensure it was firmly attached – we had heard of a man who had jumped out without being attached and of course his parachute didn't open.

Once the dispatcher had removed the cover from the hole, there was a bitter wind as we sat dangling our legs over the gap. It was fascinating looking down on the snow-capped mountains and the twinkling lights of the villages. Inside the plane, against the noise of the wind and the engines, conversation was out of the question. Approaching our DZ we saw nine fires forming a 'V', which meant that we were expected. The dispatcher yelled 'Action stations' as a green light went on, and we braced ourselves. When the light changed to red he yelled 'Go', and in quick order we pushed ourselves forward into the hole and dropped. McLean went first, followed by myself, Williamson and Duffy. This was the first time we had made an exit by this method, but we had been warned that people had broken their noses hitting the side of the hole as they dropped out.

All went well and after a few moments a gentle tug told me that my parachute had opened. Briefly I drifted within shouting distance of McLean. As we approached the ground, I could hear first the bells of goats leading flocks of sheep, then voices raised below as the Halifax disappeared between the mountains. The DZ was a dried up river bed and I hit the stony ground hard, hurting a muscle in my leg which lamed me for several days. As I was unbuckling my parachute harness I was grabbed by a bearded man covered with bandoliers who pulled me to my feet and kissed me on both cheeks. He then offered me a drink from a bottle – I took a large swig, thinking it was water. It was ouzo. He led me to McLean who was speaking to a British officer, John Cook, and Duffy and Williamson joined us while the guerrillas – *andartes* – gathered up our parachutes and loaded them onto mules.

The plan now was for McLean to go straight to the HQ of the mission, which was some way off, as he wanted to meet Brigadier Myers, who was holding a meeting there. The rest of us climbed for two hours to a village where we were met by villagers headed by the local priest in his black cassock and stove-pipe hat; he was to be our host for the night. The villagers joined us, took off our boots, fed us and gave us plenty of wine, tucked us up on the floor in blankets and we all quickly fell asleep. Not one of us could speak a word of Greek, nor they English. I did at least discover that 'kala' meant 'good'.

We woke refreshed and set off to rejoin McLean. We found him in the monastery at Romanon where the local British liaison officer (BLO), Major Guy Micklethwaite, had established his HQ. He was an old friend of McLean, having served with him in Abyssinia. I was taken to a room upstairs where I found Brigadier Eddy Myers, wearing the DSO he had won for leading the action in which the Gorgopotamus viaduct was destroyed. He was the senior British officer in Greece and was at Romanon to meet the leaders of two different political parties with a view to persuading them to fight the Germans rather than each other. There were two factions – one, known as EDES, was right wing, loyal to the King, and commanded by General Zervas; the other, EAM, was left wing, under strong Communist influence and commanded by a Major Sarafis. The military wing of EAM was known as ELAS. In general the right-wing guerrillas were known as *andartes* and were bearded, while the left-wing guerrillas referred to themselves as partisans and occasionally shaved. At this stage of the war BLOs were able to cooperate with both parties.

We stayed at Romanon for three days, sorting out our kit, some of which had been stolen – chiefly ammunition, which the *andartes* prized highly. But our most serious loss was our radio, which had been smashed. On Micklethwaite's set we asked for a new radio on the next drop, but so as not to waste time waiting for it we decided to leave Williamson behind to join us later when it arrived.

We set off for Albania with an escort of *andartes*, guides, ten mules and mulemen. We reached the first village, Moshpina, in time for lunch, but there were complications: the *andartes* would not enter it as it was occupied by partisans. McLean and I led our party into the village where we received a warm welcome from the partisans. After our meal we pressed on with a partisan escort to cross the Jannina-Igoumenitsa road at night as it was in use by the Germans. The nearer we got to the road the more nervous our escort became, until eventually they stopped and would not go ahead of us. McLean and I therefore took the lead and crossed the road. On getting to the other side we were challenged. We had no idea what to reply, nor did we know whether we were facing friend or foe. Lying flat on the ground we drew our pistols and remained silent. Luckily some of the bolder elements of the escort came up behind us and answered the repeated challenge. It was from another band that had been sent to meet us.

After two more days' marching we reached the village of Visani on Easter Day. We had an enthusiastic reception, being hailed as 'liberators' and swept into the Easter celebrations. It was a colourful scene with the Greeks all wearing traditional dress. We refrained from telling them that our aim was to get to Albania, for there is little love between Albanians and Greeks. After a night at Vasani we moved on to Drymades, the last village in Greece before the Greek-Albanian frontier.

[82]

We had sent one of the Greek partisans ahead of us and after a day he returned with two Albanian partisans. We gave them messages to take to their leaders. While we waited for a reply we stayed at the house of a man who had owned a restaurant in the United States and had worked there. We were comfortable enough; we slept in beds and one of his daughters was a good seamstress who turned our silk parachutes into pyjamas and shirts. There was plentiful wine and ouzo and the food was adequate, though there were shortages; bread was coarse, made from maize, but we had butter, oil, eggs and cheese, and most meals started with soup. It was here that I ate yoghurt for the first time.

On the third day the Albanian partisans returned with a message that we could proceed into Albania. We crossed the frontier where there was a disused customs house and an unmanned frontier post. In entering the country we had achieved the first part of our mission – quite the easiest part as it later transpired.

8

Albanian Partisans

We moved up the valley in an northerly direction, with high mountains rising on either side, and passed through two villages, in each of which we spent a night, before reaching the village of Nivan on 1 May. Here we waited for the guerrilla leader who we were told was coming to meet us. Bedri Spahiu arrived the next day accompanied by a *çeta* (guerrilla band), all bandoliered and carrying rifles. From the red stars in their caps and their clenched fist salutes it was obvious they were Communists.

Spahiu was a dour character who proved to be uncooperative, if not openly hostile. He advised us to return to Greece as there was what he called 'une réaction fasciste' in the valley. Although we spoke French we did not quite know what to make of this. However, it emerged from our talks that he was a member of the Levizje Nacional Çlirimtare (National Movement of Liberation), LNÇ for short. McLean persuaded him to send on a letter from us to his HQ, wherever that might be. As Spahiu said it would take ten days to get a reply we decided to return to Drymades.

There we were joined by Williamson with his new radio, on which to our great reassurance he got through to Cairo almost at once. We made new plans: McLean would stay at Drymades with Williamson and the radio, Duffy would reconnoitre towards Gjinokaster, a large town to our west, and I would return to Visani and, moving north, attempt to cross into Albania nearer Korça (Koritza) with a view to contacting any guerrilla bands in that area.

On the way I stayed in the town of Konitza which was under the control of the EAM. Here I was approached by several villagers when my escort was not looking, pressing on me notes in which they claimed that the EAM had taken over the town against the wishes of the inhabitants, who were pro-EDES. I could do nothing to help them. I left in the night with two partisans and crossed the frontier again into Albania where, in the next village, I met a *çeta* leader called Sulo Kozelli. He had about twenty men with rifles but they also had two Italian Breda light machine-guns. This time my reception was more friendly and Kozelli showed me a map marked with all the Italian positions in the Leskovik area. He told me they were planning to attack Leskovik and took me with him to have a close look at the town, in which there was a garrison of one Italian battalion. We then moved on to another village where we were to meet another member of the LNÇ. This was Nexhip Vinçani, the leader of all the *çetas* in the Korça district. He was a young man, wore Italian uniform and spoke fluent French. He allowed me to stay with Sulo Kozelli for the attack on the town but insisted that I always had an escort of two partisans with me, 'for your own safety' as he put it. Not until later did I discover there was an ulterior motive for this.

The attack on the town was the first time I had seen the partisans in action. They forced their way in with a good deal of shooting while the Italians withdrew to their barracks; but then the partisans themselves withdrew, losing heart when they were attacked by three Italian fighters. Ambushes on the roads leading to Leskovik, however, were more successful and a number of Italians were killed. Later the Italians burnt down their barracks and evacuated the town.

We moved rapidly after this and after a long march reached the town of Vithkuq. Here to my embarrassment I was treated like a prisoner: I was taken to a house, my pistol was removed and I was locked in a room. My protests were answered with the explanation that it was for my own safety, but apparently they thought I was a Greek spy. I stayed like this for a week until Nexhip Vinçani arrived. I had several talks with him and finally convinced him I was not a spy. He then said that I could come with him on his next action. We moved from Vithkuq to Voskopoj, an old town with many ancient churches which had been ransacked through the ages by a series of invaders – Turks, Greeks, Slavs and Italians.

Here I was given an interpreter who called himself Skender Dine, though I later discovered that his real name was Koço Tashko, a small dark man with shifty eyes who spoke American. He was an obvious townee and extremely unhappy walking in the mountains. He had news of McLean and agreed to pass on a letter to him. Here I met a member of the Central Committee of the LNÇ for the first time – Dr Ymer Dishnica, a fluent French speaker who confirmed that all the suspicions that I was a Greek had been allayed, especially now that McLean had recived a supply drop. He then produced a letter from McLean to myself and said he would send me with a *çeta* to join him.

Accordingly I set off with Skender Dine and a *çeta* of fifteen men. After a long hard march we reached the village of Leshnjë, perched high on the side of one of the Zaloshnjë mountains which had a plateau on top reportedly suitable for a DZ. Here I waited in a house belonging to three tall brothers and was visited by the local commissar, Gjin Marku, with whom I immediately got on well; we shared the same sense of humour. He took me on a four-day tour that included the plateau on top of the mountain which, though too narrow for the dropping of bodies, was suitable for supplies. We also visited a local *çeta* leader called Mestan Ujaniku, who had previously been a bandit – considered an honourable profession. He wore the Tosk white fez and sported a row of medals which Gjin Marku told me he had awarded himself. He had a large moustache and several days' growth of stubble which, as he kissed me on both cheeks, was rather painfully intrusive.

I was much relieved when McLean and his party arrived at Leshnjë. He had been having a frustrating time with the uncooperative Bedri Spahiu. As Cairo had signalled that they were ready to begin supply drops it was agreed that I would move to a shepherd's hut on the plateau and receive sorties, taking Williamson and his radio with me. Meanwhile McLean would leave Leshnjë and try to make contact with members of the Central Council of the LNÇ.

On the DZ plateau I was visited by the local commisar, Ramiz Aranitas, with whom I arranged for a reception party for the supply drops. I also gave him 200 sovereigns with which to pay for the mules and mulemen who would carry the supplies away. The first drop took us by surprise as we had no warning that it was coming. Williamson and I rushed out and lit the prepared fires and I sent Reta, one of our guards, to find Aranitas and his men. Reta returned after ten minutes to say that he had found Aranitas shot dead. Meanwhile Ali, my other guard, had disappeared, as had the 200 sovereigns I had given Aranitas. Ali must have seen me give the sovereigns to Aranitas. I was thankful he did not know there were two bags each containing 1,000 sovereigns buried under my sleeping bag in the shepherd's hut.

I received several supply drops on the plateau, Once a parachute failed to open and the container was smashed. One of the canisters, also smashed, contained a bag of 1,000 sovereigns which were scattered over the DZ. Next morning, as soon as it was light, a search party covered the ground and surprisingly nearly 800 were found and handed in. The explanation of such honesty was that most of them had been bent or buckled and the Albanians refused to accept them, even when we pointed out that they had not lost their weight in gold. Another container was full of boots for the partisans; unfortunately they were all size 6, suitable for children.

While I was at Leshnjë McLean had made contact with the Central Committee members of the LNÇ. It had been arranged with them that we would move to a new and more secure base where there was a good DZ for receiving bodies as well as arms and equipment. It was also suitable as an area where we could train the partisans in the use of mines and heavier weapons.

Accordingly we left Leshnjë with a large party including sixty mules loaded with arms and ammunition. We had a long day's march, first over rocky mountains and then through lovely beech forests, to the village of Shtyllë, which was to become our headquarters. It was at the head of two valleys, one leading by a passable road to Vithkuq and the other to a wide grassy plain which served as an excellent DZ.

At Shtyllë we had the first of many visits from the most senior members of the LNÇ Central Committee – Enver Hoxha, later President of Albania, and Mehmet Shehu, later Prime Minister. Hoxha was a well-built, rather overfleshed man who spoke good French, having been to Paris and Brussels to study law. Although he had never graduated he was known at this time as *Professor* Enver Hoxha. I got on with him fairly well in spite of occasional arguments when he would bluster, lose his temper and spit with rage; but he had a sense of humour. Mehmet was a smaller man who had served in the International Brigade in Spain. Very dour, he spoke good English but made little effort to curb his dislike of the British in spite of all the help we were giving him. He had a reputation for being ruthless and cruel and had boasted of having personally cut the throats of seventy Italian *carabinieri* prisoners. His role appeared to be military rather than political. However, we found out later that Hoxha was the secretary general of the Albanian Communist Party

Central Committee and Shehu was the commisar for the Korça and Valona areas.

We lived in a disused mosque that had been converted to a school on the outskirts of the village of some sixty houses. A stream ran nearby and a beech forest started about a hundred yards away, which afforded a good escape route. We quickly blew up the road to Vithkuq and laid mines on it to discourage Italian visitors from the nearest garrison town of Korça.

The first çeta to arrive for training was led by Petrit Dume and was forty men strong. We trained them in the laying of mines, the use of 81 mm mortars, the 20 mm anti-aircraft gun and the Boys anti-tank rifle. Training continued throughout the last part of June and all July and August. During the same period we received a number of BLOs, Majors Bill Tilman, Gerry Field, George Seymour and Peter Kemp, Squadron Leaders Andy Hands and Tony Neel, and Sergeants Jones and Jenkins. Some stayed with us but McLean sent others to different areas to cooperate with known guerrilla bands.

While at Shtyllë I saw a certain amount of action – the first when I accompanied Nexhip Vinçani and his çetas when they attacked Permet. The action very much followed the style of the attack on Leskovik in that the partisans carried out long-range shooting at the Italians who eventually withdrew into their barracks. Again the partisans were frightened off by the Italian aircraft who bombed and machine-gunned them. Few casualties were inflicted on the Italians in Permet, but again ambushes on the roads leading to the town were successful. However, I was able to check for myself that the partisan claims were as wildly exaggerated as they had been at Leshkovik. For all that, Vinçani was a brave man and I accompanied him on a night attack on an Italian position a few nights later. It was a complete shambles and when I found myself with Vinçani in the no man's land between the Italians and the partisans, and being shot at by both, I said to him that this was not where the commander of the operation should be. He agreed.

One day when I was returning from blowing up a bridge with my small escort, I ran into another çeta which my companions were very reluctant to let me meet. I insisted, however, and it proved to be a Balli Kombëtar çeta led by Safet Butka, a leader of the Balli Kombëtar movement. He was friendly but accused me and the British of helping the Communists and not the Ballists. I replied that if he could prove that he was fighting against the Germans and the Italians, and not collaborating with them as alleged by the Communists, he would certainly get help. This resulted later in my going with one of Safet Butka's *çetas*, much to the fury of the partisans, to carry out an ambush on the Korça-Leshkovik road. The partisans tried to sabotage it and Petrit Dume was sent to compromise us, but I threatened that we would stop all supplies to the partisans if he did so. Reluctantly he took his *çeta* away.

The ambush was a success, resulting in eighteen Germans killed, one 88 mm gun, its troop carrier towing it, and three lorries destroyed without loss to ourselves. This gave the lie to the Communist assertions that Safet Butka was a Fascist working with the Germans. I soon realised that the word 'Fascist' used by the Communists meant anybody who was not a Communist. Safet Butka was later surrounded by attacking Communists and trapped in a house. Rather than surrender to be tortured and executed, he shot himself.

Of the many drops it became my job to receive at Shtyllë, one was extra exciting. We were warned to receive two Halifaxes. The first appeared and we exchanged recognition signals, lit the fires and it began its dropping runs. I heard the second aircraft approaching but at once recognised from the tone of the engines that it was one of the Italian three-engined bombers. I yelled at everyone on the DZ to clear off and take cover. The bomber flew over the DZ and dropped a stick of bombs that blew out most of the fires. Undeterred, the Halifax made another run and dropped a stick of containers. This happened three times, then both aircraft flew away. The second Halifax came and we managed to get new fires going. Afterwards we discovered that the Halifax pilot and crew had no idea that an Italian bomber was taking turns with them over the DZ. Furthermore we did not receive a return visit the next day – which we had thought certain, as the bomb craters would have given the DZ away. The reason, we heard later, was that the Italian bomber crashed on landing at Korça airfield and all the crew had been killed.

Once a sufficient number of *çetas* had been trained, a big parade was held on our DZ. This was the inauguration of the First Partisan Brigade. Some 800 men paraded under Mehmet Shehu. Endless speeches were made – so long that I rather hoped an enemy aeroplane would fly over and disperse us. After a march past, with Enver Hoxha taking the salute, we had a barbecue party of *raki* and sheep roasted whole on spits by our Vlach mulemen. Hoxha was at his most affable.

The next day we asked Mehmet Shehu if he could show us the result of our training by attacking a German platoon position of about twenty soldiers in a post on the Korça-Leskovik road. He flatly refused, even when we taunted him with being frightened to attack twenty Germans with 800 men. This was not cowardice, as we discovered later when we were given a letter by Abas Ermenji, the leader of the Balli Kombëtar. It had been intercepted by the Ballists and was from Hoxha to local partisan leaders, stating that arms and ammunition were not to be wasted on Germans and Italians, but to be conserved to fight the Ballists and Zogists to ensure the Communists had complete control of the country when the Germans and Italians withdrew.

In due course the Italians discovered we were at Shtyllë and launched a full-scale attack on it, using artillery and aircraft. Their shelling was very accurate as they had spotter planes directing the fire. They were held up on the Vithkuq road by Jones and Jenkins laying more mines while we were hiding stores, mainly explosives, in the woods nearby.

We moved into the forest – Peter Kemp was with me – and from a distance heard shots from the direction of Shtyllë. After some hours we went back cautiously to the village. The Italians had departed but poor Shtyllë was smouldering, every house having been burnt down as well as our headquarters. One bonus was that the Italians had not ventured into the forest, so we found our stores intact. We were annoyed that the partisans had made no attempt to hold up the Italians and had retreated to Voskopoj.

McLean now decided that we should move in small groups to a village north of Voskopoj. As I was passing through Voskopoj I met Nexhip Vinçani and groups of partisans. I taxed him on why he had not put up a fight against the Italians; he made poor excuses and we parted on bad terms.

After a long march we reached the village of Panarit where our parties regrouped. Our plan was that McLean and Kemp would go south to contact the Balli Kombëtar with a view to getting them to attack the road, one party including Williamson and his radio would stay at Panarit, and I would move north with Jenkins and Bell, a radio operator who had joined us at Shtyllë, with his radio. I would also have with me an interpreter called Tom, an American-speaking villager we had recruited to replace Skender Dine, who had been sacked by McLean when our NCOs had reported him for trying to convert them to Communism. Tom was a cheerful old rogue who obviously profited from his work with us, but he was a born scrounger and had the advantage of appearing to have a cousin in almost every village through which we passed.

The area into which we moved was known as Mokër, west of Lake Ohrid, in the centre of which the frontiers of Greece, Albania and Yugoslavia all met. We finally reached the monastery of Santa Maria, which stood isolated on the side of a mountain some way from the village of Llengë. The monk in charge was the leader of a çeta and wore a bandolier over his habit and carried a Tommy gun. He also turned out to be a bit of a boozer. He was willing for us to stay in the monastery as long as I paid him a sovereign a week for each room we occupied. When we needed a chicken for our supper he would shoot one out of his window.

The DZ was some way from the monastery and not very suitable as it was too narrow for bodies. It had the advantage, however, of some caves nearby where we could store any supplies that came in. Some drops were rather frightening, as free drops (without parachutes) of coils of Dannert wire sounded like bombs falling and one had to be careful not to be hit by bundles of battledress, blankets or boots. The most memorable drop at Llengë was when a Halifax flew so low that none of the parachutes had time to open. All the containers were smashed or badly damaged, and those containing detonators and explosives exploded on hitting the ground.

I was in the monastery when we heard the news of the Italian surrender. Our monk mysteriously produced four bottles of champagne which he opened to celebrate the event. I set off without delay with some of the çeta and Tom the interpreter to contact the nearest Italians and call on them to surrender, though I had received no instructions on our radio. An Italian battalion and some artillery were stationed at Pogradec, which was the nearest town to us – a day's march away on the southern shore of Lake Ohrid.

On reaching there we sent Tom ahead and he soon returned with a cousin who invited us to his house on the outskirts. From there I wrote a letter to the officer in command, which Tom took, having tactfully removed the red star from his cap. I got a reply saying the colonel would meet me secretly in a private house. Guided there by Tom, I found the colonel and another officer. After a few words the colonel said that as he had received no orders, I could meet him the next day. I agreed; having none myself, I was not sure what my line was to be.

The next day, however, I marched up to the barrack gate and demanded to see the colonel – the sentry must have been a bit surprised to see a British officer in uniform. I was escorted to the officers' mess where I met the colonel who explained to me that his officers were having a discussion as to what to do. I could see a heated debate going on and it seemed that some wanted to join the Germans and some the partisans, but the majority simply wanted to return to Italy. I asked if I could speak on the telephone to General Toriani, the Italian divisional commander, whose HQ was in Korça. I got through to him quite quickly; but as soon as I announced myself in French he said he couldn't talk to me as the room was full of Germans, and hung up.

We finally agreed that the Italians in Pogradec would leave for Korça, having refused to join the partisans, who, I warned them, were now likely to attack them. I managed to persuade them to dump their 75 mm guns in the lake so that neither Germans nor partisans would have them. When the Italians left the town for Korça they were indeed attacked by the partisans and had some losses. Some then deserted to the partisans.

I returned to the monastery, where I found McLean. We had still received no instructions from our office, but we agreed that in order to stop the Germans coming from Elbasan to Pogradec, now taken over by the partisans, the road should be blown. At this time we had partisans, Ballists and Zogists all visiting the monastery and it was decided that I should take a Zogist çeta with me. I took several muleloads of explosives and blew a gap of about thirty yards where the road overlooked the lake. This must have prevented any transport from passing for some time.

We spent about two more weeks at Llengë, during which McLean went as far as the monastery at Shen Naum in Macedonia, where he found partisans fraternising with Bulgarian troops. I went off and destroyed some chrome mines, and also had time to fish in Lake Ohrid with hand grenades, which added to my menu a delicious fish that was a speciality of the lake – pink-fleshed and something like a sea trout.

One day a Ballist *çeta* brought us three German prisoners, all wounded, two of them medical orderlies. The partisans wanted to shoot them but we refused to allow it. As we were about to leave the monastery for another base north of Elbasan, we took them with us and left them on the main road from Elbasan to Struga, and later watched as they were picked up by a German convoy.

During the day I saw German lorries using a wooden bridge which we had to cross on our way north. It crossed the Shkumbini river, which was quite wide. I was with a *çeta* of partisans as we reached the bridge at night, and the *çeta* leader agreed that it would be a good move to destroy it. I sent the *çeta* ahead except for two men and we laid charges set to go off with time pencils. When all was ready I sent the two partisans across the bridge and was about to follow when one of the pencils prematurely detonated the charges, blowing away half the bridge and stranding me on the wrong side. I therefore had to swim across, not knowing when the next charge would go off. I got swept by the current nearer and nearer the bridge and was scrambling out on the far bank as the second charge went off. The main road was about thirty yards from the bridge and as I crossed it a machine-gun opened up from down the road. Luckily I found the goat track where the partisans were waiting. Wet through, I had to climb for two hours, hurried on by the partisans who said the Germans were following us. We got to a village where I tried to dry out and get some sleep but I was awoken by a partisan who said that we had been betrayed and the Germans were entering the village. It was early in the morning and as we set off at full speed up a track at the upper end of the village, we saw the Germans at the lower end. They spotted us and set off in pursuit, following us at a distance for about an hour, now and then shooting at us, though at such extreme range the shots went wide. We snatched a brief halt at a spot where there were masses of wild strawberries which we picked and ate. As the Germans neared we pressed on, only stopping on the high ridge we had to cross. On looking back we saw the Germans had stopped too to pick strawberries, and they then gave up the chase.

Finally we reached the village of Labinot where I found Williamson and a large number of Italian soldiers, mostly Alpini. I had settled down to sleep when Enver Hoxha strode into my room in a fury and demanded to know why I had blown the bridge without asking permission of the Shtab (General Staff of the LNÇ). I replied that I had no intention of asking the Shtab or him for permission to blow up any bridge. I was fighting the Germans which was more than I had noticed his partisans doing. He left me, incensed, and thereafter brought up the subject of this bridge whenever he met any British. I discovered later that the partisans had frequently used the bridge, which was subsequently replaced by a boat ferry.

While at Labinot I received a letter from McLean to say that because of the increasing number of missions in Albania they were going to drop a brigadier and his staff to take over as senior mission. He added that the Shtab had recommended a large plain suitable as a DZ at a place called Bixha, to the west of Martenesh; he wanted me to go there, and if I found it was suitable to set up a base.

With a party including Williamson and his radio, Jenkins, a number of Italians, partisans and mules with their Vlach drivers, we walked for over a day through attractive mountains with beech forests till we came to a large grassy plain that made a perfect DZ. High mountains rose on two sides with lower ones at the ends; the forest came down to the edge of the plain and at one end there was a shepherd's hut that made an ideal HQ. The Italians set to work building more huts, with beech branches and parachutes for cover and camouflage.

I was soon paid a visit by the local çeta leader. This was Baba Faja, about whom Mrs Hasluck had told us. He wore a plus four suit, a priest's stove-pipe hat and bandoliers, and he carried a Tommy gun. He became a regular bore after any supply drop took place as he would appear on the scene the next morning pleading for arms and ammunition. I solved the problem eventually by giving all the arms to Kadri Hoxha, the local commissar, on signature, and referring Baba Faja to him. Baba Faja liked his *raki* and used to burst into song in a deep bass voice.

McLean soon arrived at Bixha, having come from visiting another partisan leader, Myslim Peza. While there he had become involved in a battle between Myslim Peza with his partisans, plus a number of Italians who had defected to us, and a large force of Germans. McLean said Peza's partisans and the Italians had acquitted themselves well but there had been heavy casualties on both sides.

After several fruitless nights of waiting the brigadier and his staff arrived on a night when we had been given no warning. However, all went well. Brigadier 'Trotsky' Davies was a regular soldier considerably older than McLean and myself, who already had two MCs. Among his large staff were Lieutenant-Colonel Arthur Nicholls, Coldstream Guards, as his G1; Majors Alan Palmer and Jim Chesshire, a Sapper; Alan Hare of the Life Guards as staff captain; and a chief clerk, complete with a typewriter and two containers of stationery.

The first morning he alarmed McLean and me by his opening gambit: 'Well, McLean, I noticed there was no stand to this morning.' ('Stand to' is a term referring to that period when soldiers, dressed, armed and at their posts, stand to to repel enemy attacks. There are two such periods a day when attacks are deemed most likely, an hour before dawn until dawn and an hour from sunset.) His second question, 'What time does the sun rise?' had McLean completely stumped. He looked helplessly at me. 'What time do you think, David?' I hazarded a guess, for we seldom rose before about nine o'clock as we usually sat up very late at night. 'Six o'clock,' I told the brigadier. 'Right,' said Trotsky, 'stand to from five to six tomorrow.' Our NCOs looked horrified. Next day we stood to as ordered, then McLean and I went back to bed. The brigadier was not amused.

Nicholls, a punctilious Guards officer, was shocked by the squalor and litter around the camp area, so he organised a big clean-up. Lining up all our camp followers, including Italians and Vlach mulemen, he had them all sweeping through the camp picking up paper, tins, cigarette packets and other rubbish. On getting to the end he congratulated them and told them to fall out. To a man they threw down all the rubbish they had collected and walked away. Nicholls's language was unprintable. One supposed they had no idea why they were picking up all this stuff and did it to humour what they thought was a mad Englishman. (On a later occasion we heard him, through the walls of our hut, admonishing Hare, 'You're getting as untidy as those fellows McLean and Smiley, and they've gone completely native.')

For over a week McLean briefed Trotsky to the best of his ability on the political difficulties that lay ahead of him. Trotsky, who was a kind man, said that as we were the first British officers into Albania, it was only fair that we should be the first out. Accordingly he got approval from our HQ, which had by now moved from Cairo to Bari in the south of Italy, to send us to the coast for evacuation.

We left with mixed feelings. Though keen for a change in our living standards, not to mention some leave, we were sad to part from our friends, though we always intended to return to Albania. I was particularly sad, as we were starting the first part of our return by car, to leave behind my mule Fanny, for she had carried me a good mileage for several months without an accident. I handed her over into what I thought were the safe hands of Alan Hare, who had been a brother officer in the Household Cavalry. Alas I was wrong. After I returned to England I sent a signal to Hare asking after Fanny. The reply came back, 'I have eaten Fanny.'

When McLean and I set off we had misgivings about the brigadier's large HQ. It would have taken over a hundred mules to move it, and we felt that the standards of regular soldiering were not altogether suitable for guerrilla warfare. We travelled light and reached Labinot within the day; there McLean again conferred with members of the Shtab. Next day we reached a health spa where we slept in real beds and bathed in sulphur springs.

Our aim was to reach the coast south of Valona, and to do so we had to pass through areas held by both partisans and Balli Kombëtar, who had already started fighting each other. At one point we met the Ballist leader, Abas Ermenji, and it was he who showed us the intercepted letter from Enver Hoxha to all regional committees telling them to assert themselves against the Ballists so as to ensure the administration of Albania was in the hands of the LNÇ when the Germans withdrew.

We passed through Berat, with a castle overlooking the town, which had just been occupied by the partisans. Here we met old friends, Gjin Marku and Kahreman Ylli, and were put up in a hotel with a sign outside in Albanian which read 'Commissars only'. We moved south the next day and heard that the Germans were advancing on the town, which they later captured. We had a *laissez-passer* from Abas Ermenji and twice passed from partisan to Ballist territory, finally arriving at Shepr, a village where we had spent the night on one of our first days after entering Albania. Now it was the base of Bill Tilman, a distinguished mountaineer who kept fit by climbing the local mountain every morning – to the distress of his minder/escort who had been given orders never to let him off on his own. Tilman complained to us that he could not get the partisans to fight the Germans rather than the Ballists.

From Shepr, where we stayed a few nights and made contact with Bari, we set off towards the coast south of Valona, hoping to join up with Gerry Field who was supposed to have his HQ in the area. I went ahead of McLean to explore the coast and find a suitable spot from where the Royal Navy could pick us up after we had sent them the details. This last part of the journey was very depressing for I passed hundreds of Italian soldiers clearly dying of starvation, and all the villages had been burnt down either by the Germans or in the fighting between partisans and Ballists. At one village the locals showed me a mass grave where they said they had seen the Germans execute sixty Italian officers: their hands tied, they were lined up and shot with a machine-gun and then bayoneted.

I did, however, meet Bedri Spahiu, who was more cooperative this time and gave me a guide who was reputed to know the coast well. I travelled for over a week, going south to within sight of Himare which was still occupied by Germans. Some way north of the town I found an abandoned coastal gun, but as it seemed to be in working order I blew up the breech block to ensure that it was useless. Though it was too cold to enjoy bathing, I entered the sea at several points to test the depth, but found nowhere suitable as all the places I tried were too shallow.

Starvation was rife and the Italians had already eaten all their horses and mules. At one point I joined a meal with some Italian officers in a derelict half-burnt house. We ate a very spicy stew; it was not until afterwards that I was told I had been eating human flesh – I had assumed it was mule. Eventually, after passing two villages in flames, set on fire by the partisans as they were Ballist villages, I found McLean by chance and together we were guided to Field's HQ. There we found a British NCO who told us that Field had moved to a cave on the coast. He added that Field was so disgusted by the activities of the partisans that he refused to have anything more to do with them and surrounded himself with Italians.

With a guide we climbed over the mountains of Dukati, crossed the Valona-Himara road by night and descended sharply down a goat track to the sea. The cliffs were very steep, indicating deep water, and a dog-legged inlet about a hundred yards long led to the open sea.

About a minute's walk above the sea we found Gerry Field in a large low cave with a group of Italian soldiers. Among them was Captain Munzetti who proved invaluable. He had been an intelligence officer in Valona and made several trips to the town to buy food for us and find out the latest news. He was a very brave and intelligent man.

The cave was infested with lice and goat droppings but it was an adequate shelter from the elements that cold November. The drawback was insecurity – there was no escape route except the one goat track down which anyone looking for us was sure to come. There was no water supply and after rain I used to go round the pools collecting water with my sponge. We were also very short of food, for apart from the odd tin Munzetti brought us we were living entirely on one dead mule. In the week that followed we got more and more hungry, the only time in the war I really felt the pangs of hunger. We got increasingly frustrated, too, as the signals from our base kept sending what we considered poor excuses for the non-appearance of the boat to collect us.

Below our cave, which we codenamed 'Seaview', the creek running to the sea was about five yards wide and had steep cliffs on either side. At the end it was possible to reach a rocky point where I sat, night after night, flashing our recognition signal with a torch. Finally I got a reply and eventually a rubber dinghy approached the mouth of the creek with two people on board. On disembarking on the small beach they turned out to be Sandy Glen, a naval officer, and an American OSS officer. Both were to stay in Albania, but on handing over the dinghy to us they informed us it was leaking badly and they did not think McLean and I would make it back to the boat. However, we were determined to try.

Having said our goodbyes we decided that I would row and McLean would bail. Each of us had a briefcase as our only luggage. Mine was full of captured documents, maps, undeveloped films and my Leica camera. We got safely out of the inlet to the open sea, which was a good bit rougher and it became evident that the boat was filling with water faster than McLean could bail. Clearly we were going to sink. This we did about twenty yards from the MTB (motor torpedo boat), so we both swam with one arm, holding our briefcases out of the water with the other. Sailors dragged us out and we were relieved to find we were in the safe hands of a naval officer whom we both knew – David Scott.

[98]

Telling him that those on shore were starving, we persuaded him to take his ship up to the point where a group of Italian soldiers were waiting hopefully. The sailors hurled cases of bully beef to the grateful Italians, then we backed off and set sail for Italy to get to the other side of the Adriatic before dawn. I was feeling very seasick as the mountains of Albania receded in the distance, but I was not sorry to go.

We reached Bari in time for breakfast on a depot ship and must have looked like brigands to our naval hosts. Then a conducting officer from the SOE office arrived and took us to a hospital to be de-loused, which certainly we needed. Here a personal disaster overtook me. While I was soaking in a carbolic bath, some bright spark removed all my clothes and burnt them. I was furious, for I was devoted to my tailor-made corduroy trousers, which furthermore had sovereigns sewn into the turn-ups, and my uniform jacket was riddled with sewn-in maps and other escaping kit. Even my Household Cavalry captain's stars were made of 24-carat gold. In place I was issued with a new battledress.

We were then driven out to General Alexander's HQ, from where he was commanding all the troops in Italy. After questioning us in his caravan, he kindly invited us to stay for lunch – the best I had eaten for months. Then, after three days being de-briefed in Bari, we were sent back to Cairo for further de-briefing and were told to write reports on our activities. We took over a month to do this, during which I spent my happiest time of the war.

Instead of being put up in a gloomy SOE safe flat, we lived in a large house in the residential area of Gezira Island. We named it Tara and the others with whom we shared the house were Billy Moss, of the Coldstream Guards, who had originally found the house, Paddy Leigh Fermor and Xan Fielding of the SOE Greek section, Arnold Breene, who worked in the SOE office, and a glamorous Polish countess, Sophie Tarnowska, who ran the house. We were later joined by Rowland Winn of the 8th Hussars. We led a riotous life, going to many parties and giving many at Tara. We had plenty of money to spend, having saved up all our pay while in Albania, and girls with whom we could spend it.

9
Return to Albania

After a month we flew to England to write more reports, have more interviews, and better still have some leave – we were told we might expect six weeks. While in London McLean stayed at Claridge's and I stayed at the Ritz. Then disaster intervened, for at the end of our first week's leave we were recalled to the SOE office in Baker Street to hear that Trotsky's mission had been betrayed to the Germans and attacked. Trotsky himself had been wounded and taken prisoner and the rest of the mission were scattered and on the run. They were suffering, too, from severe winter conditions. We were ordered to go back to Albania as soon as possible and McLean was to take over Trotsky's command as the senior BLO in Albania.

Before returning we had interviews with Lord Selborne, the Minister of Economic Warfare and head of SOE, and with Anthony Eden, the Foreign Secretary. Eden briefed us on our future role, saying that as we had successfully made contact with the partisans, trained them and given them arms, he now wanted us to go to the north of the country to encourage the tribal chieftains as well as the rival political parties, the Balli Kombëtar and the Zogists, to fight the Germans.

We realised that this was not going to be easy. We had already witnessed the start of the civil war in the south and knew that the right-wing-orientated parties regarded the Communists as their main enemy. It would take some hard talking and bargaining to persuade them to fight the Germans instead.

We flew back to Cairo in February 1944 to find that Paddy Leigh Fermor and Billy Moss had already left for Crete, having told their friends in Cairo that they were going to kidnap the German general. Xan Fielding had brought back enough information from Crete for this to be carried out and indeed the operation was a success but for one thing – they kidnapped the wrong general. While they were at Tara making their plans, the general they were after, who was a real brute and wanted for war crimes, had been replaced by a general who needed a rest from the Russian front and was in no way connected with war crimes or the SS.

In Cairo we met Julian Amery again. He had been there when we first came back from Albania and had helped McLean write the political parts of our report. He was an old friend of McLean and both had the political bug. Furthermore Amery already had Albanian connections, having instigated a resistance movement in northern Albania as long ago as 1940, when he had been working in the embassy in Belgrade. It was decided therefore that he should join our mission: he and McLean would make a strong pair for what looked like being more of a political than a military assignment. We thus became a team of three, with McLean and myself being promoted to lieutenant-colonel and major, while Amery was a captain.

In April we all flew to Bari, where we found Peter Kemp, who had been betrayed to the Germans by the Kossovo partisans and was lucky to have escaped. We also had time to visit Tony Quayle,* who had been running the evacuation point at Seaview but had been brought back suffering from dysentery, jaundice and malaria. He looked pretty ill. He had nothing good to say about the partisans.

The dropping of bodies and supplies to Albania had now been taken over by the American Air Force, whose Dakotas were adequate for the short haul across the Adriatic (the Halifaxes were now used for long-range flights to Poland). So in April we drove down to the American base at Brindisi, accompanied by Peter Kemp as dispatcher. Our first attempt was a failure. We never found our DZ, then we were caught in the searchlights over Tirana and, with ack-ack shells starting to explode around us, the pilot wisely decided to head for home. Kemp had luckily brought a bottle of grappa which helped steady our nerves.

The next night was more successful in that we found the DZ and dropped. The American pilot, however, completely misjudged when to switch on the red light signalling us to jump. Consequently, instead of landing on our plain at Bixha we all jumped too late and came down in the adjoining beech forest above the DZ. McLean went first, followed by me, then Amery, the three of us landing some distance apart. I hit a tree on the way down but was unhurt. Amery

---

* Later Sir Anthony Quayle, the actor-producer.

and I found each other, then started to look for McLean. Eventually we saw a light which turned out to be a torch he had stuck in the snow – he was watching from a safe distance to see whether anyone coming to investigate was friend or foe. It was not until some hours later, as daylight was breaking, that we found our reception party, which consisted of an officer, Jenkins and Jones, and a small Zogist *çeta*. The officer in charge was obviously nervous and urged us to move without further delay. Jenkins told us it was this officer who had stopped them from lighting fires when we were overhead the previous night. In fact we could have dropped perfectly well.

We set off across Bixha plain which was covered with snow blackened by ashes blown across the Adriatic from an eruption of Mount Vesuvius. We saw tracks of wolves and bears on our way to the village of Shëngjergj where, while we were having lunch, a partisan *çeta* under Fred Nosi arrived. He looked angry to see us with our Zogists. The next village we reached was the site of George Seymour's HQ and with him was Alan Hare who told us the details of Trotsky's capture, and also of the terrible conditions suffered by Arthur Nicholls before he died. Nicholls's great courage, apart from winning everyone's admiration, was officially recognised with a posthumous George Cross, while Hare himself was awarded a Military Cross for his gallantry during the attack on Trotsky's HQ.

The next day Abas Kupi appeared with a large *çeta*. The Zogists' leader was an extraordinary man. Illiterate, but blessed with a remarkable memory, he had been a senior officer in King Zog's gendarmerie and when the Italians invaded Albania carried out a determined defence of Durazzo – the only Albanian leader to put up a fight against the Italians. His action enabled King Zog and Queen Geraldine with their newly born son to escape. At one time he had joined the LNÇ and had been a delegate at the meeting at Mukaj where the LNÇ, Ballists and Zogists had agreed to fight the Germans together. Predictably, Enver Hoxha broke his word almost at once, so Kupi left the LNÇ in disgust to take over the leadership of the Zogists, whose party was known as the Legaliti.

McLean and Amery had many discussions with Kupi. He said he would fight as soon as King Zog gave him orders to do so; but he must first be given arms and ammunition. King Zog readily agreed to order Kupi to fight but the Foreign Office, for fear of offending either the Americans – who were anti-monarchy – or the Communists, refused to allow the order to be sent. McLean and Amery, accompanied by Klupi and his *çeta*, set off on a tour of the north to contact the highland chieftains while I remained at the HQ with a radio, an operator, and the reliable Sergeants Jones and Jenkins.

A number of British had gathered at Xhibër whose morale was low and whose health had been impaired by a very hard winter in the mountains. They clearly needed to be sent back to Italy. I was able to arrange the first part of their journey, south to Seaview, which made the HQ much easier to run, more secure, and with less mouths to feed. Those who remained were Alan Hare and John Hibberdine, an excellent young officer from the Cameronians, Corporal Otter the wireless operator, two Italian officers and a number of Italian and Albanian camp followers. Our HQ also included our three interpreters – Halit Kola, Sheqir Trimi and Veli Hassan, though Halit had left with McLean. The other helper – invaluable to me – was my bodyguard, Asslan, who stayed with me to the bitter end. In normal life a *hoj*, or Muslim priest, he prayed regularly and frequently.

Before McLean left we agreed to split our HQ in two. I was to organise an advanced HQ, while the rear HQ stayed at Xhibër. I chose a suitable site in a beech forest near the top of Mount Bastar. It was near enough to a small DZ suitable only for supplies – bodies had to be dropped at one lower down the mountain near Xhibër – and during the three weeks McLean and Amery were away I had a number of supply drops. They were seldom a complete success, with the accuracy of the American pilots not as a rule up to the standard of the RAF Halifaxes. On one occasion the drop was done in one straight run, rather than in several passes, as was normal. We estimated that the string of parachutes must have covered nearly seven miles, as we later heard that some containers had fallen into a German camp. It was just as well that Jack Taylor, an American naval officer seconded to the OSS, joined our group. Not only was he a most useful and congenial member of our HQ, but he sent back signals to the American Air Force in far stronger terms than I should ever have dared, and to some effect.

We had a succession of visitors, including Ihsan Toptani, who had a house near Tirana. He came from a distinguished family and had helped the British missions several times in the past. He was careful not to align himself with any of the political parties, but remained in touch with the leaders of all of them.

After McLean and Amery returned, signals were sent to Bari for onward transmission to Anthony Eden pressing for Zog's order to be passed on. In the meanwhile Hibberdine went off with McLean for a tour of the Dibra area, Hare and Sergeant Pettini, a first-class Italian NCO, moved to the neighbourhood of Tirana to contact possible deserters, and Taylor left with Seymour to be evacuated from Berane, where an airstrip was held by Tito's partisans.

By the time McLean returned an answer arrived from Eden which was completely unhelpful. Instead of letting Zog's message be sent, all Eden's signal said was 'Keep the pot boiling'. McLean and Amery now had the unpleasant task of breaking this news to Kupi, adding that he would get no arms without fighting first. Kupi compromised by saying he would allow a part of his personal çeta, led by his loyal bodyguard Ramiz Dani, to accompany me to blow up a bridge, which I had been longing to do. It was decided that our target would be a bridge at Gjoles which carried the main Tirana-Durazzo road over the Tirana river. I took Veli with me as interpreter, as Ramiz knew no English, and Jenkins to help with the explosives.

With our çeta, twelve men strong, and the mules carrying the explosives, we left the next day. Crossing the Krujë mountain range in a day's march, we finally arrived by night at one of Kupi's farms on the plain. Next day I changed into civilian clothes and, accompanied by Ramiz and his friend Bardhok, carried out a daylight recce of the bridge.

The charges had to be prepared by taking sticks of gelignite out of their boxes and moulding them together. This took the bast part of a day and left Jenkins and me with severe headaches and nausea.

When all was ready we moved off by night and by midnight reached the river-bed near the bridge, under which the Albanians dumped the explosives. Then, making too much noise for my liking, they moved off, leaving Jenkins and myself to fix up the charges. In this we were greatly assisted by the fact that either the Italians or the Germans had built demolition chambers in the concrete piers and had even written under them the exact amount of explosive, in kilograms, that was needed. Concealment, however, was all-important, as German transport was intermittently passing to and fro above us. One lorry actually stopped on the bridge and a soldier got out to urinate over the side, unaware that I was crouching only just out of reach below. We were in very different ways relieved when he got back aboard and the lorry drove on.

After we had set off the time pencils, by crushing the glass phial, we crept back in the dark for a couple of hundred yards to await the explosion. The pencils had a five-minute delay but when several minutes after this still nothing had happened, I foolishly decided to return to the bridge to see what had gone wrong. When I was about half way there I was rocked by a tremendous blast. The bridge had blown. In the moonlight I could see that a span had collapsed into the river.

We quickly made our way back to where the *çeta* and the mulemen were waiting and set off at full speed. Veli the interpreter all but killed me by dropping his Sten gun, which let off bullets in all directions, but we got back unscathed to our base, jubilant at our success – which had the considerable bonus of proving that Kupi was willing to take action against the Germans. This news we signalled at once to Bari, requesting an immediate arms drop for Kupi.

While we awaited the reply Hare left to meet Kupi. He returned with the worst possible news – the First Partisan Brigade had attacked Kupi's forces at Shëngjergj and driven them out. The civil war had reached our area. We had hurriedly to move north to avoid the partisans and Hare agreed to go to negotiate with the LNÇ leaders. Meanwhile we moved first to Matsukull and then on to the glade of Zogolli where Kupi had called a meeting of his northern chiefs. McLean, Amery and I were attending the meeting in torrential rain when a message arrived to say that Captain Victor Smith, a BLO, was arriving with peace proposals from Bari, inviting Kupi and the LNÇ leaders to go there for a meeting. Smith turned up the following morning. Kupi agreed to go at once but Hoxha rejected the proposals out of hand.

The meeting immediately broke up and on our way back to Bastar a messenger arrived with even worse news – the partisans had overrun our HQ there and Hare and Otter and all our supplies had been captured. Smith, who was accompanying us, now elected to inform us that Bari, behind our backs, had come to an arrangement with the LNÇ that all the BLOs with either the Ballists or Zogists were to hand themselves over to the partisans who would 'escort' us to the coast for evacuation. Our immediate reaction was emphatic: in no circumstances would we hand ourselves over to the partisans.

As our advanced HQ was in partisan hands we decided to return to our rear HQ, but found we were cut off by German troops. Our party of McLean, Amery, Corporal Davis, McLean's radio operator, Said Kryeziu, our interpreters, personal servants and some mulemen spent three nights in a beech forest before eventually deciding to split up. All our efforts to leave the forest, however, were thwarted until the news came that our HQ at Bastar had been recaptured by Kupi's men.

Once there McLean sent me off to reconnoitre the coast for a suitable point of evacuation, taking with me Ramiz and Bardhok. Not far from the sea we reached a house owned by a fisherman friend of Ramiz, who warned us that the coast was heavily guarded by the Germans. I said I wanted to go and check their positions, but I had to concede that in battledress I might be rather conspicuous. Ramiz left the house and returned shortly with an Albanian gendarme sergeant's uniform. It was quite a reasonable fit and I wore it for five days while I had a good look at the coast on Cape Rodonit. This was clearly quite unsuitable for our evacuation – there were far too many Germans, not to mention minefields and barbed wire obstacles.

We therefore decided to move further north, taking with us the gendarme sergeant whose uniform I was wearing. We walked along the main road, at one time being joined by a German soldier on a bicycle. Ramiz thought this a bigger joke than I did, but it was nothing to my dismay when, after the cyclist had gone on his way, the sergeant flagged down an approaching German lorry. He spoke to the driver and we all piled into the back, where there were already several German soldiers, all reassuringly unsuspicious. After a while we came to a sudden halt and had to scramble into a ditch as two RAF Beaufighters zoomed overhead, guns firing but, luckily for us, overshooting. One of the Germans alongside me in the ditch shook his fist at the disappearing aircraft, and to show I was one of the boys I did the same. There was no further sign of the Beaufighters, so we climbed back into the lorry and went on for a few miles till the sergeant indicated he wanted to stop. We then got off, very much to my relief.

Again I checked the coast, some of which was suitable for a pick-up, and made detailed notes to signal to Bari. We stopped at a house belonging to Ihsan Toptani where I had the luxury of a hot bath; even pulling a loo plug was a treat, for in Albanian village houses one had to make do with a box-like cabin protruding over the outer wall with a hole in the floor.

I rejoined McLean, Amery, Said Kryeziu and Davis at the village of Mukaj. There McLean and Amery sent off a series of signals pressing for arms and support for Kupi, including a personal one for Anthony Eden, which he never received. This, we later discovered, was because it was deliberately destroyed by one of the officers in the SOE office in Bari.

I should explain here that in the SOE HQ in Bari there were several officers who were either acknowledged Communists, like James Klugman, or unacknowledged ones such as John Eyre, who stood in the next election as a Communist; even the head of the Albanian section, Eliot Watrous, had very left-wing views. In addition, although most of the BLOs attached to the LNÇ saw through the Communist propaganda, a few became staunch supporters and were quite prepared to believe that those officers attached to Ballists or Zogists were Fascists. I was even called one to my face when I got back to Bari.

Still, it all strengthened the hand of those working against us – witness the following signal we received at Mukaj. 'Following message dated August 25 received from Lyon who is with Hoxha. Met Hoxha tonight. Stated McLean, Smiley and Seymour working against partisans with collaborators. Gave ultimatum they must be out of Albania or hand themselves over to partisans for evacuation to Italy within five days of tonight. Otherwise partisan patrols will be sent out to capture them and bring them back for trial by partisan military court.'

This was a bit much even for Bari, and Lyon, having remonstrated with Hoxha, managed to get Hoxha to tone down his demands. A second signal stated: 'Hoxha no longer considers officers with Kupi and other traitors as allied, due their behaviour, but considers them agents of foreign reactionaries who are organising the fight against the partisans.'

Bari sent a signal to Hoxha to the effect that unless he withdrew his threats, all arms supplies would cease at once and all BLOs with the LNÇ would be withdrawn. This had the desired effect, with Hoxha claiming he had been joking. In the meantime we had received news that we been tried by a people's court and condemned to death *in absentia* as enemies of the people. This left us in no doubt of our fate should we fall into partisan hands; moreover, we also heard that patrols had been making inquiries of the villagers as to the whereabouts of the 'British Fascist officers'.

In spite of the civil war having started, Kupi seemed to be concentrating his hostile attentions towards the Germans. He told McLean he wanted to attack Durazzo and I was sent to carry out a reconnaissance of the town and its surroundings, and to give my views whether it was a feasible operation. For this purpose I put on a shabby civilian suit and my white Gheg fez, and was accompanied to Durazzo by Halit Kola and two gendarme officers. It was quite apparent that the Germans were in too great strength for Kupi's *çetas* to take the town, so I returned with Halit Kola to make my report.

We had one particularly nasty moment. We had turned a corner when we were suddenly confronted by three armed Germans who stopped us and asked us for our identity cards. Of course I didn't have one. Halit was passed and waited while the German NCO asked me in German where my card was. I pretended not to understand and kept repeating in Albanian 'I have no document, I am an Albanian.' The NCO seemed reluctant to let me go but Halit called 'Shkojm' ('Let's go') and I slowly walked away. As I did so the German drew his pistol and aimed at my back; then, shaking his head, he lowered it, put it back in his holster and walked off. Halit had unslung his rifle before the German took aim, but he said he was so horrified that he forgot he was carrying it.

We returned to the house from where we had set out and again I was told that it was safer to wear a gendarme's uniform, with which I heartily agreed. This time the jacket had a corporal's stripes on the sleeve. I set off with Halit and a gendarme officer and for the second time we picked up a German truck. I got into the back with Halit and several German soldiers while the gendarme officer got in to the front. We passed through four road blocks but no questions were asked – I assume as I was with German soldiers. Yet again I dismounted with some relief.

McLean and Kupi were awaitng us. After I had discouraged Kupi from attacking Durazzo, he informed us that a Zogist *hoj* had made contact with some German soldiers who wanted to desert. He described them as 'Turkestanis', as this was written on the shoulders of their uniform. We contacted them and on 12 August they murdered their German officers and over seventy of them came to join us. Though they wore German army uniform they carried Russian weapons, including two light machine-guns, and were in fact Tajiks, Uzbegs and Kazaks – all of them with very Mongolian features. They had murdered their Russian officers earlier in the war and deserted to the Germans who had sent them down to the Balkans as garrison troops. They then became increasingly resentful towards the Germans, who, they said, had kept them short of rations and given them no pay for months. They were tough customers, not people you'd want to have taking against you. On the first day they shot their sergeant-major. At least we could pay them in gold and had plenty of sheep or goats for them to eat; but we began to wonder what would happen if these commodities ran out.

A few days later, to test them, we carried out an attack on an artillery camp. We found out that it contained about thirty Germans and thirty Italians, while we had about a hundred of Kupi's men, including his son Petrit, and about thirty Turkestanis. It was a most successful fight – I was giving covering fire with our machine-guns while the rest charged. Amery had a lucky escape when a bullet grazed his chin. Ten Germans were killed and the rest fled; we had two killed. We also took a number of Italian prisoners who didn't want to fight anyway. Before withdrawing we looted the camp and burnt all we could.

During the next weeks we carried out a number of actions in co-operation with both the Zogists and the Turkestanis, who had acquitted themselves well in the attack on the artillery camp. I had my first action in command of the Turkestanis when we went down to the main road, blew a bridge and shot up a German convoy, destroying the first lorry on a mine and forcing the others to stop and back away.

On another occasion I was with a çeta of Zogists on the main road, which we had mined. The first lorry of a German convoy blew up and we killed three Germans who jumped out; but then, as we were firing on the following lorries, we suddenly came under fire from our rear. We thought at first the Germans had outflanked us, but soon realised that the people who were attacking us were the partisans. The çeta retreated in some disorder. Back at our rendezvous I found my mule and muleman had gone. Nobody was in sight.

It had started to rain and when I knocked on the door of an

isolated cottage to get shelter, the owner turned me away saying he was afraid of the partisans. I travelled north, spending a bitterly cold first night in a cornfield. The next day I tried to get shelter in another village, but again the inhabitants were reluctant to put me up for fear of the partisans. They did, however, offer me the services of a twelve-year-old boy who they said would guide me to Abas Kupi. Thanks to him, after another night in the open and having had little food for two days, I eventually fetched up at a village where I found Kupi and his çeta, McLean and Amery.

After some discussion we came to the conclusion we could hardly fight the Germans effectively if we had to contend with the partisans as well. The position seemed hopeless. We had an especially bleak report from a muleman working for Ihsan Toptani. He had been captured by the partisans, who had beaten and tortured him to discover our whereabouts. They told him they had orders to shoot McLean and myself on sight.

We therefore agreed to signal Bari that we wished to be evacuated by sea but would on no account hand ourselves over to the partisans. I was deputed to carry out a reconnaissance of the coast nearest to us, which was between the mouths of the Drin and Mati rivers. I took Halit Kola with me, as before, and we succeeded in finding a beach with a steeply sloping shoreline that I felt would be acceptable to the Royal Navy. The approach to it was fairly secure and there were no German units in the neighbourhood.

I rejoined our group, which consisted of over a hundred of Kupi's men, the seventy-odd Turkestanis, a number of Italians, our Vlach mulemen and our bodyguards, three interpreters, various Albanians, our little British contingent and four Russians who had escaped to us from a German working party of prisoners. We were certainly strong enough to see off any hostile patrols, whether German or partisan.

We moved north to the village of Mal i Bardhe where we spent several days. During that time several notables from Tirana came to see us, including Midhat Frasheri and Ali Kelcyre, who were in the government, and Fiqri Dine, who had been Prime Minister under the Germans. Obviously they knew the Germans were withdrawing and wished to cooperate with us, but after long talks with McLean and Amery they returned to Tirana empty-handed. Another visitor, who did join us, was General Prenk Prevesi, the Commander in Chief of the Albanian Army, booted and spurred, complete with his staff and some sixty soldiers. He stayed with us until just before we left the country.

We spent the next three weeks mainly on the move, avoiding both partisans and Germans, except when we carried out actions against the latter. On one of these Jenkins and I blew another bridge on the main Tirana-Scutari road. We were very tempted by the Zog Bridge, the biggest in Albania, carrying the Tirana-Scutari road over the Mati river; but when we studied it through our binoculars we saw it was guarded by a company of Germans.

As the partisans moved north, pushing back Kupi's men and burning all their villages, we moved north too, stopping next for some days in the village of Velijë, on the lower slopes of the mountain of that name. From there Halit and I, again in civilian clothes, went into the town of Lesh (Alessio) to report on the constant stream of German transport passing through, mostly heading north. We were able to send the RAF some useful targets.

I did a far longer reconnaissance from Velijë to Shengjin, the most northerly port of Albania and not many miles south of the border with Montenegro. I took the interpreter Sheqir with me and we crossed the Drin in a canoe made from a hollowed out tree-trunk. I could not get into the town as there were closely guarded checkpoints and I had no identity card. On our way back I stopped at the house of Bishop Bumçi, the Bishop of Mirdite, and a former Regent of Albania. He gave me an excellent lunch, but ticked me off for blowing Gjoles bridge as he said it interfered with his food supplies.

At Velijë Ihsan Toptani joined us with the news that he was negotiating for a boat in Scutari; but at almost the same time a signal from Bari came agreeing to evacuate us from the coast. When we asked if we could bring out some people who would certainly be killed by the partisans if we left them behind, we were refused point-blank. Those we had named included Abas Kupi, Said Kryeziu, our three loyal interpreters, Sheqir, Halit and Veli, and two Italian officers, Mario and Franco, who had served us loyally for some months. We repeated our request, which was again rejected, so we availed ourselves of a personal signal to Anthony Eden. As on the previous occasion it found its way into the wastepaper basket in the Bari office. This was the work of Communist sympathisers in the office, who even had the nerve, on our return, to say that this had been done to appease Enver Hoxha.

Once it was confirmed that a boat would be sent, we came down from the foothills and crossed the coastal plain at night to position ourselves near the coast in a large house belonging to a friend of Kupi. When we received the signal that the boat was on its way, I set off for the pick up point with the first party, which included Jones and Jenkins. The boat, which arrived on schedule, turned out to be an Italian MAS, similar to the British ML, with an Italian crew under Commander Tony de Cosson, RN. Our party was about ten strong, and the next night a similar boat picked up McLean, Amery and the remainder of those who were allowed out.

In Bari the office personnel were polite but cool. They were distinctly annoyed, however, when we immediately sent another signal to Eden, who replied at once saying that of course Kupi must be evacuated. The Bari office raised difficulties so McLean and Amery flew to Caserta where they saw 'Jumbo' Wilson, our Supreme Commander in Italy, and Harold Macmillan, the Resident Minister of State. They both agreed that Kupi must be rescued without delay and issued orders to that effect. In the event, by the time they returned to Bari this was unnecessary: a British minesweeper had picked up the occupants of a boat it found drifting with engine failure in the middle of the Adriatic and brought them to Bari. To our delight they included Abas Kupi and his two sons, Ramiz Dani, his bodyguard, Said Kryeziu, and Ihsan Toptani who had arranged for the boat. They were all accommodated in a villa near Bari where we could satisfy ourselves that they were safe, for Hoxha, furious at their escape, had demanded their return. We knew some of the Bari office staff would agree to this but we took the necessary steps to thwart them.

We spent a week in Bari writing reports, then McLean and Amery flew back to London. I flew back to Cairo to wind up my affairs there as I was due for a long leave in England. Tara was running down: Paddy Leigh Fermor and Xan Fielding had left, although Billy Moss was still there, having got engaged to Sophie Tarnowska. I was in Cairo for less than a week when a chance meeting changed all my plans.

PART THREE
Thailand

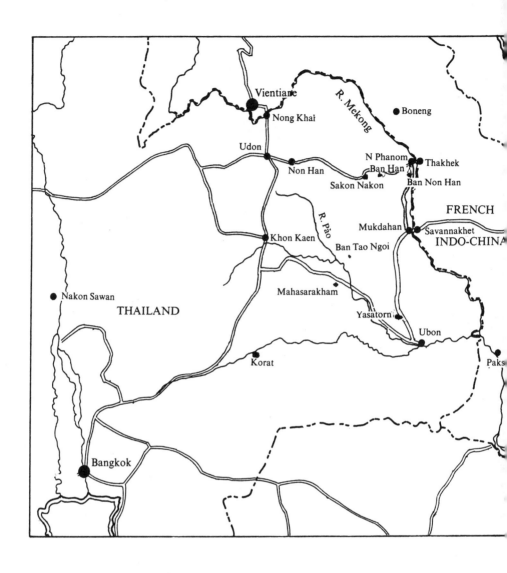

10

Briefing and Training in India and Ceylon

The chance meeting in Cairo that changed my plans was with a very old friend, Prince Subha Svasti, known to his friends as 'Chin'. Before the war I had lived near Virginia Water where King Prajadhipok and a number of the Thai (then Siamese) royal family had lived since the king had abdicated. His wife, Queen Rambai Barni, was Chin's sister. Chin had finished his education by going to the Royal Military Academy at Woolwich and spoke perfect English, while the younger members of the family had mostly been educated at English public schools.

Chin told me that the Thais in England had been put in a very invidious position by Thailand's declaration of war on Britain and her allies in January 1942, which had been done under pressure from the Japanese. Britain had retaliated by declaring war on Thailand; the United States, on the other hand, made no such formal response. Several of the royal family had been serving in the British forces and one had already been killed as a pilot in the RAF.

Chin had been recruited by the SOE, where a Thai section had been formed. He had been given the rank of lieutenant-colonel and was now on his way to the Far East to help organise the dropping into Thailand of a number of his friends and relations. These had volunteered to try to contact their sympathisers and initiate a resistance movement against the Japanese – the alliance with Japan was at best lukewarm. Would I, Chin asked, join the Thai section, drop into Thailand and help with the resistance? I did not need much urging. I was uncertain about my future and had quite enough of the intrigues of Balkan politics. I told Chin I would be delighted to come after I had taken some leave. He signalled the SOE office in London to this effect.

On returning to London I reported to the HQ of SOE in Baker

Street, where I was de-briefed on Albania and transferred to the Far Eastern Section which had the cover name of Force 136. I was sent on two months' leave and on reporting back to Baker Street was briefed on the set-up in Thailand, which was as follows. In March 1943 two groups, one of thirteen and another of eighteen Thai students, had been trained by the OSS in the United States and made officers in the Seri (or free) Thai army. They were selected by Seni Pramoj, at that time the Thai ambassador in Washington. In the same month thirty students were sent from England to India, followed by thirty-two more in August, having joined the British Army. On arrival in India most of these were assigned to Force 136. Twenty-two of them, who had passed the Force training course, were given commissions and codenamed 'Whites'.

In March 1944 the first three Whites, led by Puey Ungpakorn, code-named 'Khem', dropped blind into Nakon Sawan province in north-east Thailand. Nothing was heard from them. In April another team of three was dropped forty miles from the first lot, and again nothing was heard. Both teams had, in fact, been arrested by the local police, who handed them over to the secret police, who kept them in prison in Bangkok but treated them well. In due course Khem established contact from prison with Pridi Panomyong, who was the Regent with pro-Allied sympathies. He in turn arranged for a message to be smuggled out of Thailand to the British consulate in Kunming. As a result of this, in August 1944 the first radio contact was made between Force 136 HQ in Calcutta and Bangkok. In September another team, codenamed 'Brillig', was dropped with a personal message from Mountbatten to Pridi Panomyong.

At the time of my briefing there were certain political complications of which I was unaware. First, a great deal of rivalry existed between Force 136 and the OSS, stemming from American suspicions of British post-war policy towards Thailand. The Americans suspected that the British, by demanding very harsh conditions when the war ended, intended to impose colonial status on the country. The Foreign Office appeared to be hinting at something of the sort when they issued a statement saying that the Thais, 'to atone for Pibul's Quisling behaviour, must work their passage home'. This appalled the Americans and did little to define the British attitude to Thailand. Worse was to follow when Eden, still our Foreign Secretary, called Pridi 'a collaborationist and creature of the Japs' – a statement which could not have been further from the truth. The other factor of which I was unaware was that Chin himself was not popular with the Americans or the students recruited there, nor with some of the politicians in Thailand such as Adul Detcharat – codenamed 'Pulao' by Force 136 – who was Chief of Police and a close friend of Pibul Songkram, the Prime Minister. All these people suspected that Chin, as brother of ex-Queen Rambai Barni, was aiming to restore the absolute monarchy. Strangely enough, Chin got on well with Pridi in spite of the fact that Pridi was directly responsible for the political moves that led to the abdication of King Prajadhipok, Chin's brother-in-law.

While in London I had kept in touch with McLean and Hare. Amery had only spent a very short time at home before flying to Chungking with General Carton de Wiart as an officer on his staff, although this appointment was only a cover for his continuing SOE activities. Both McLean and Hare were still anxious to to go to China and wanted me to go with them, but I preferred Thailand. As a compromise we decided that we would all go out together to India, where we could get a clearer idea of the situation in these Far Eastern countries and make further plans.

In March 1945 McLean, Hare and I set off for the Far East. While on our otherwise uneventful flight to Cairo we were flying over the North African desert at night when suddenly both engines stopped and the aircraft lurched forward into a steep dive. The pilot, who had been sitting with us having a smoke, rushed into the cockpit and the aircraft quickly levelled off; a few seconds later – though it felt more like minutes – the engines started again. 'Sorry, chaps,' the pilot said, rejoining us, 'we were flying on George, the automatic pilot, and ran out of petrol.' It was apparently not among George's skills to switch over to the reserve tanks.

On arrival in Cairo we went straight to Tara, where we could get no reply to our knocks and rings; so we forced the door and found both Sophie and Pixie, the Alsatian, fast asleep. We spent a week renewing acquaintances with old friends, among them, unexpectedly, Peter Kemp. I happened to meet him the very morning he had arrived in Cairo, having last seen him when he had come to dispatch us into Albania. He told me that after we had gone he had been parachuted into Poland, where he had led a very hazardous life, being finally overrun by the Russians, who had put him and his companions in jail for six weeks. He had no idea what his future was to be; but when I suggested that he join me in Thailand it obviously struck him as a good idea. Knowing him so well from our times in Albania, I could not have wanted a better companion. My only reservation was the knowledge that wherever Kemp went there was sure to be trouble.

Another lucky meeting I had was with the Wavells, at dinner at the British Embassy, where they were spending the night on their way to England. Lord Wavell was now Viceroy of India and they invited me to stay at Viceroy's House, the official residence designed by Lutyens on a scale that out-potentated the Indian potentates. I was given a letter of introduction to the Acting-Viceroy.

After a week the three of us set off in a BOAC Ensign in the early hours, only to have one engine fail over the Sinai Desert and be forced to return to Cairo. This was a nuisance but there was some compensation in seeing the expression on McLean's face when we arrived back; he had slept for the entire journey and was still half asleep on getting out at what he thought was Baghdad. We took off at dawn twenty-four hours later, flying to Baghdad directly over the route I had taken when I was with the HCR in 1941. I recognised a number of landmarks, including H4 and the lake at Habbaniya; but further east was new to me.

We felt extremely hot on our arrival in Delhi, as we were still wearing the service dress uniforms in which we had left London. We were clearly not expected at Dolpur House, which was the local HQ of Force 136, but the orderly officer sent us to the Force 136 camp, where we wasted no time in unpacking and putting on cooler clothes.

McLean and Hare decided to move into a hotel in Old Delhi. I rang up Lord Wavell's son, Archie John, an old friend from Sandhurst days, and at his invitation repacked and transferred myself to Viceroy's House, which was a great luxury after the sordid camp. It took several minutes to walk from my bedroom to the drawing room. There were hordes of servants (including 365 gardeners) and I had my first experience of an Indian bearer, who took me by surprise by trying to scrub me in my bath and dry me afterwards. I was even more taken aback when he held out my pants for me to step into and then insisted on putting on my socks for me. I eventually made him understand I was not used to, and did not appreciate, these attentions.

The officers at Force 136 HQ did not seem altogether clear as to what they should do with us, and solved the problem by posting us to Ceylon, where Force 136 had both its operational HQ and some training schools. During the week we remained in Delhi we made copious inquiries about the respective merits of going to China or Thailand. I had a long talk with Colonel Peter Fleming, an old friend, who was then head of 'D' Division which dealt with deception planning; he counselled me not to go to China. Advice from such an expert as Fleming was not to be ignored, so I made up my mind in favour of Thailand. McLean still wanted me to go to China, while Hare was undecided.

We spent a very congenial week in Delhi with plenty to do – sightseeing, shopping, riding, bathing, playing tennis and golf. On most evenings there was some form of entertainment at Viceroy's House – I particularly remember the superb dancing by the famous Indian dancers Ram Gopal and Nina Tamara.

At the end of a week we left, flying in a Dakota fitted up with bunks for hospital cases, which meant we could sleep horizontally for the eight hours it took to reach Bangalore. There we landed for a vile breakfast before flying to Colombo, which was even hotter than Delhi.

It was siesta time when we eventually found Force 136 office, in a house in Mount Lavinia, some miles south of Colombo. It had a beautiful view overlooking the sea and a sandy bay lined with palm trees, with fishing craft on the beach. We were told to come back the next morning. When we did so, we were driven in a truck for nearly two hours until we found ourselves at ME 25. This was the training establishment for BLOs and agents who were going to be dropped into various Japanese-occupied countries of South East Asia.

The camp was situated in a plantation of rubber and coconut trees, where a number of long low huts constructed of coconut fronds served as offices, living and sleeping quarters, and our stores. We were installed in a long dormitory on extremely uncomfortable beds, known as charpoys. These were made of wood, with boards taking the place of springs and a strip of coconut matting on top of the boards a substitute for a mattress. We presumed that this was all to prepare us for the rigours of the jungle, although our previous experience of life as guerrillas had been very much more comfortable than our training instructors led us to expect. Even so, this was the right system of training.

The heat was extreme and we slept on our hard beds wearing only sarongs, sweating profusely. The monsoon season had started and the first night the rain poured down. To our surprise our huts did not leak in spite of their very crude and jerry-built appearance, although next day the camp was a sea of mud. Our spirits were revived, however, by the standard of the food, which was quite good, especially the fruit which included bananas, then quite unobtainable in England, pawpaws and mangoes.

Our fellow students appeared to be drawn from every tribe and race in Asia: Burmese, Malays, Kerens, Kachins, Thais, Annamites, Chinese, Formosans, and even a few expatriate Japanese – there were reputed to be twenty-nine nationalities in all, but of the Europeans only British, French and Dutch were in evidence. Also in the camp was a company of Gurkhas from a secret organisation known as 'E' Force, concerned with the rescue of prisoners and evaders, and it was rumoured that these Gurkhas were going to be parachuted to a prisoner-of-war camp somewhere in Malaya. They operated against us as 'enemy' on a number of exercises and their performance bore out all I had previously heard about them – including that they were the finest fighting troops in the world.

Within two days of our arrival we had an interview with Colonel Musgrave, the commandant of ME 25, who informed us that our chances of going to China were negligible as it had been agreed recently among the Allies that China would become the operational zone of the OSS, our American counterpart. The three of us were given a day to decide whether we wanted another job in Force 136 or, alternatively, to be returned to the United Kingdom. This was no problem to me, for I had already made up my mind that I wanted to go to Thailand, but it was disappointing news for McLean and Hare.

I started training at once, while McLean went to the SOE head office in Kandy, to find our what other jobs they had to offer. Hare had meanwhile contracted malaria and had been sent to hospital in Colombo with a high temperature. McLean returned a few days later, very pleased to have learnt that there was a chance of going to Kashgar, which was apparently not an American sphere of operations. Shortly afterwards Xan Fielding joined from Cairo, hoping to go into French Indo-China and bringing the news that both Billy Moss and Rowland Winn were also on their way out. It seemed that the inhabitants of Tara were gradually collecting for action against the Japanese.

I remained for three weeks at ME 25, during which time we underwent intensive training for living and fighting in the jungle. Some of this guerrilla training was easy for me, especially such subjects as demolition and sabotage, for I knew them already. First aid lectures, on the other hand, had a number of new items to be learnt such as the treatment of tropical diseases and snake bites. In the weapon training we concentrated on the actual arms that we intended to take with us, and we were allowed unlimited ammunition for practice. I kept the two weapons that I finally decided in Albania were the most suitable for a guerrilla: one was a Colt .45 automatic, in my view quite the best and most effective of all types of pistol; the other was the American .30 carbine. The Colt had the hitting power that smaller pistols did not possess; it was also very reliable and not prone to jams. Its only disadvantage was that it was a bit heavy. I found the best way to carry it was in a holster slung from a waist belt and strapped to the right thigh – it was the nearest point to the right hand for a quick draw.

The American .30 carbine that I invariably carried had been a gift when in England after my first mission to Albania. I had only seen one before, in General Alexander's HQ in Italy. After I had given a lecture to a group of British, American and French officers known as 'Jedburghs', the American commandant handed me the .30 carbine with the words 'Try this out when you go back to Albania, and let me know the results.' It was highly satisfactory: it was very light to carry and easy to handle, it held fifteen bullets which it fired semi-automatically, and it had a very accurate killing range up to 300 yards and a less accurate one up to 500. It later became the standard weapon of the American parachutists.

We were trained to shoot with this weapon in an entirely new way. Whereas the usual method in firing a rifle is to take a steady aim with one eye closed, the new system was to use the weapon like a shotgun, in other words to keep both eyes open and shoot instinctively without taking deliberate aim. The very good reason for this was that in the jungle things happened so quickly and at such close quarters that a person who fired his shot first usually came off best. The method had already been proved in Burma against the Japanese, who had a habit of sitting up in trees. I found that with practice one soon became quite accurate and could be remarkably quick into action.

We carried out several exercises in the jungle, at first going out for a single day but then progressing to schemes of four or five days. We found these most useful in familiarising ourselves with our new conditions of warfare, for the various aspects of jungle lore and survival were very different from the Balkan mountains. On some of the exercises we were expected to procure our own food, learning from local guides the various fruits and berries that could and could not be eaten. We shot for the pot, and any animals or birds that we shot we had to gut, clean, skin or pluck, and then cook ourselves. I ate some excellent wild boar on one scheme and some deer and jungle fowl I shot myself on another, but I jibbed at eating a monkey that a French officer shot – it looked uncomfortably human.

On the last week of the course I was given my preliminary briefing by the chief instructor. I was to be dropped into Thailand, he told me, during the next moon period. That would be in about three weeks' time. He added that I would get a fuller briefing from the Thai Country Section in Calcutta, which controlled the operations in the field. Meanwhile I was to choose from the Thais on the course two men to go with me as combined interpreters and bodyguards.

I selected two men whose training reports had been good, and whom I knew personally from working with them on exercises. They were fit, tough, spoke passable English, and were above all cheerful – this was a most important requirement under guerrilla conditions. They had been corporals in the Bangkok CID when they had been brought out of Thailand some months previously, Their real names were Sudhi Sudisakdi and Santa Sintavi, but they were allotted the more easily remembered codenames of 'Chat' and 'Pun'. I still had the codename 'Grin', and the fourth member of the team who eventually joined us was 'Gunner', who was the same Sergeant Collins who had dropped to us in Albania.

I already knew Gunner to be a first-class wireless operator and a courageous man. He had served most of his time in Albania as wireless operator to Major Tony Simcox, and had suffered from both German and partisan attentions. After a number of narrow escapes they were finally captured by the partisans and were marched as their prisoners through the greater length of Albania, being subjected to a number of indignities and humiliations along the way. When I heard that Gunner was in London I had immediately signalled a special request to have him as my operator. He was flown out, too late to do any training in Ceylon, but in time to join me in Calcutta.

I had a number of amusing nights out in Colombo with McLean and Fielding, and later with Hare when he came out of hospital. Hare found a job on the staff of the HQ of Force 136 in Kandy, and I did not see him after I left Ceylon until we met in Bangkok after the war had ended. Then one evening, just as I was setting off for a night out in Colombo, I was summoned to the commandant's office and told that I was to leave for Calcutta at three o'clock the next morning, together with Chat and Pun. McLean and Hare nobly got up to see me off, a gesture which I much appreciated. It was sad that we would not all be together in Thailand.

A comfortable flight in a Liberator bomber fitted with seats for passengers took ten hours non-stop to Delhi. There by good luck I found one of the Viceroy's ADCs waiting at the airport to meet the Governor of Burma (or what there was of it to govern, since at that time the Japanese were occupying most of it). I got a lift with him and found myself sitting next to an amusing Burmese who had been introduced to me as U Tin Tut. In the car he turned to me and said with a smile and evident relish, 'You may think my name is odd but one of my political colleagues is called U Tin Po.'

The next day we flew to Calcutta, where we were taken to the Force 136 office, headquarters of the Thai Country Section. The first person I met there was the G1, Major Ben Hervey-Bathurst of the Grenadier Guards, who, after being wounded in Europe, was now doing a staff job. We had been at preparatory school together at Hawtreys many years before, and it was now his job to brief and administer me while I was in Calcutta. He would also be my rear link after I landed in Thailand. He took me in to meet the head of the section, Lieutenant-Colonel Peter Pointon, who was not a regular soldier but had served for many years in the Bombay-Burma Trading Company and had a considerable knowledge of the Far East. Finally I met the section intelligence officer, Lieutenant-Commander Hopkinson, RNVR, known as 'Hoppy', who had worked before the war for the Swedish Match Company in Bangkok.

All these officers were friendly, capable, and quietly efficient. The office itself, in a requisitioned private house, was a rather untidy collection of rooms and partitions, but it had a decidedly happy atmosphere, not to mention a complement of very good-looking secretaries. With my memories of Bari still very fresh, I felt it essential that the officers with whom I should be in wireless contact from Thailand should be the ones in whom I had confidence, and better still personal friends. On this score throughout my time in Thailand I never had any doubts; for the duration of my mission I received the greatest cooperation and help.

Chin was not in Calcutta and nobody seemed to know quite where he was; he was more difficult to trace since he had changed his name to Chin Arun. But I found that he had left a letter for me to the effect that he had spoken to 'CHM' (Colin Mackenzie, the head of Force 136), naming me as his first choice of a British officer to join him. I also met a number of my Thai friends, who all wore British uniform with the words 'Free Thais' inscribed on their shoulder titles. So many of them had been educated at Eton, Harrow, and other well-known English public schools that they were known as 'The Old School Thais'. My most frequent companion was now Karawik, whom I had known at Virginia Water, and whose cover name was 'Rasmee', though he was known to all his friends as 'Sunshine' from his round and ever-smiling face. We played tennis every day in order to keep fit, and I often had meals with him and his companions. Meanwhile I gradually got used to the change of Siam to Thailand and to referring to the inhabitants as Thais and not Siamese. I stopped short of extending the change to cats or twins.

My briefing gave me the first indication of the extraordinary political set-up in Thailand. Technically, my briefing officer told me, Thailand was at war with the Allies, against whom she declared war when she was occupied by the Japanese. 'Didn't she fight against the Japanese when they invaded Thailand?' I asked. 'And why did she have to declare war on us?' She only offered 'token resistance' against the Japanese, I was told, and declared war on us 'under strong Japanese pressure'. She was, however, a most unwilling ally of the Japanese. 'How do you know that?' I said. One had only to look, he replied, at the size of the underground movement. It included not only a number of high-level politicians, service chiefs and government officials, but was led by the Regent himself. He went on: 'You'll hear a great deal of the Regent from now on. His real name and title is Luang Pradit Pridi Panomyong but he is known to all of us as "Ruth", which is his codename.'

At the end of April 1944 the first British officer from Force 136 to visit Siam was Brigadier Jacques, codenamed 'Hector'. He and Chin had been landed off the coast of Siam by Catalina flying boat and had then transferred to a fishing boat that took them to Bangkok. Hector had been a prominent lawyer in Bangkok before the war and had many friends and contacts there; he also spoke the language fluently. In Bangkok they had meetings with Ruth and some of Ruth's friends, then returned the way they had come.

After Hector had reported to Mountbatten he returned to Bangkok by the same means, taking with him a radio and radio operator. He came out once more, when I met him, then stayed until the end of the war. As a soldier he insisted on wearing uniform, which caused Ruth a security problem. However, Ruth found him a safe house either in his own palace or the University of Moral and Political Science, where he was in daily communication with Force 136 HQ. As he was in close contact with Ruth, who had frequent meetings with the Japanese, he was able to pass on much vital information which would be on Mountbatten's desk in Kandy within twenty-four hours. Hector remained the senior BLO throughout his time in Thailand.

The first Thais to be dropped into their country had been dropped blind, a very different proposition from dropping to a reception committee as I was about to do. They showed great courage, for it was by no means certain how they would be received. Some had been captured and imprisoned, but others were more fortunate and had contacted friends, a few of whom had influential positions in the country; and in this way they got in touch with Ruth. The resistance movement gradually expanded all over the country. Not only were good radio communications established with Calcutta, but a two-way traffic in bodies began, with a number of Thais being brought out by sea or air, or a combination of both. A high percentage of those who came out volunteered to go back, and having done a course, often at ME 25, in underground warfare, intelligence duties, sabotage, and wireless training, were returned by various methods – most commonly by parachute – to become active agents. It was thus that Chat and Pun had elected to leave their work as detectives in Bangkok and found themselves at ME 25, where we had all linked up. We were to be dropped to join the guerrilla organisation, the 'Free Thais'.

My briefing was very thorough. Unlike Albania, which was a completely unknown country in which McLean and I were the first two BLOs, much more was known about Thailand, and we already had Thai agents operating there with whom we were in wireless contact. The first section of my briefing order defined the area in which I was to operate. This area was known as 'Candle', the codename of my mission, and it was very large. Roughly it was the north-eastern area of Thailand, covering about one third of the country, but to be more exact it was defined as follows: 'That part of north-east Thailand bounded on the west by the railway running north from Korat to Udon and the road on to Nong Khai, on the north and east by the Mekong River (where it forms the frontier between Thailand and French Indo-China) and on the south by the railway from Korat to Ubon.' The brief further stated that to the west of Candle area was 'Coupling' area, in which Major Hudson would be operating, and to the north and east, in French Indo-China, French Force 136 officers were active. In the south there was reported to be an American OSS mission.

The brief listed eighteen tasks in all, the main ones being the organisation and training of the guerrillas and the reception of arms for them; the selection of DZs and the construction of landing strips; the sending of intelligence reports on Japanese dispositions and moves, and details of roads, railways, and bridges; the locating of prisoner of war (POW) camps, if possible making contact with the POWs and helping them to escape; helping any other evaders such as bailed out airmen or civilian refugees; and the last, but an important one, which I quote: '18. At all times to remain clandestine and on no account to take any action against the Japanese.'

There were very good reasons for this order, because policy of SOE in South East Asia at this time was dictated by one big event – the projected D Day, when Mountbatten, the Supreme Commander, was to launch an attack on the Japanese which would include a seaborne invasion, and which it was hoped would drive them out of South East Asia. All efforts of SOE agents were therefore concentrated on preparing the ground for this event, so that by the time D Day came the areas in which they operated would rise against the Japanese simultaneously. It was already known that Thailand was ready, and her military services organised, to turn on the Japanese; her alliance with the Japanese would be revoked, her allegiance transferred to the Allies, and she would thereupon attack the Japanese by all possible means. It was for this object that we all worked, but because of the dropping of the atomic bombs on Japan this D Day never took place. In the event, during my time in Thailand I never fired a shot in anger before the end of the war. When the war ended quite a different situation existed and I saw my first action.

After four days in Calcutta I drove in a jeep with Hervey-Bathurst to the airfield at Jessore, about ninety miles north east of Calcutta; this was the operational base for all sorties in South East Asia for Force 136 agents and supplies. There were two squadrons of Liberator bombers and one of Dakotas employed on these duties, and they also dropped pamphlets as a cover for their more clandestine roles.

There was also a training school at Jessore, where courses were run for parchutists, under a commandant who was reputed to be 'jump-happy' from the vast number of drops he had made. Another course at Jessore was the 'pick-up' course, and it was this that I had come to do. The object was to train people in organising landing strips behind the enemy lines, to be used by our own aircraft for landing and picking up people who were required to enter or leave the country. Most of the short-range work was done, mainly in Burma, by Lysanders and American L 5s, both of which required only a very short run for take-off. Dakotas operated for the longer ranges.

I was in Jessore on 8 May 1945 which had been officially designated as VE (Victory in Europe) Day. Celebrations were the order and everyone in the rear areas had a holiday. Even the RAF suspended their fighter and bomber sorties for the occasion, though some of the pilots to whom I spoke were not too pleased; nor, presumably, were the soldiers who were still fighting the Japanese. The day itself created little impression in India, where the majority of the inhabitants were rather more concerned about the war on their own doorstep. Nor were the British troops madly enthusiastic, when their efforts in Burma had received such scant attention in the British press. They had been fighting a very tough campaign under extreme hardship, only to have the newspapers at home make little or no mention of their activities in comparison with the fighting in Europe. It was not surprising that they referred to themselves as 'The Forgotten Army'.

Nevertheless VE Day was celebrated in fine style by the company of Gurkhas on the parachute course. The officers were invited to their sergeants' mess where they kindly produced their entire month's ration of whisky, which we shared and which was quickly consumed. Large numbers of Gurkhas passed out and we finished the evening carrying them to bed and tucking them up under their mosquito nets. They were blissfully happy, singing lustily, extremely funny, and no trouble whatsoever.

Four days after I had been on the course I was asked if I would like to go in a Liberator on a supply-dropping operation over the area in Thailand where I was to be dropped myself. I naturally accepted. The flight was due to last twelve hours non-stop, the Liberators having been fitted with special long-range petrol tanks. After we had been airborne for about an hour, however, fire broke out in the fuselage. It burnt strongly while the dispatcher, the rear gunner and I fought it for over fifteen minutes, using up all the fire extinguishers and finally managing to beat out the flames. We carried on after this, but after another hour one of the engines developed a bad fuel leak and was stopped. I was very relieved when the pilot wisely decided to return to base, although I had considerable misgivings about our chances of getting back. I felt sure another engine would pack up and it was common knowledge that the four-engined Liberators could not maintain height on two engines. To make matters worse, our parachutes had been burnt in the fire, so there would have been no question of bailing out.

As it was, we got back without further incident. We then discovered the cause of the fire. A special device was carried to destroy the secret radar in the aircraft in the event of a crash or forced landing in enemy territory. This incendiary device had somehow prematurely ignited, though nobody knew how or why. After this trip I finished my 'pick-up' course and returned to Calcutta for a week of briefing and final preparations.

During the day I read the files on Thailand and studied the signals sent from the field in the Candle area. I saw a lot more of the Whites and also had a number of discussions with Major 'Soapy' Hudson, who was going to be my neighbour in Coupling area. Hudson, who had won a DSO with the Maquis, got on well with the Thais, being a personal friend of Chin. I was very glad that he was to be my neighbour; he was quiet and reserved and gave the impression of being very sincere and dedicated to helping the Thais.

My evenings became more social when Julian Amery appeared from China on his way home to stand in the forthcoming General Election. I had a number of meals with him at places ranging from Government House, where he was staying, to small Chinese restaurants. One evening I drank a very rare Chinese liqueur reputed to be over a hundred years old, and alleged to be the more delicious because there was a pickled lizard in the bottle.

There was another Liberator due to drop supplies to the Candle area on 20 May, and I was offered a ride. In spite of my last experience I accepted, though I was glad to see when we took off that the pilot had a chestful of decorations. After flying for three hours we crossed Foul Island, off the coast of Burma, then altered course to follow the 18th degree of Latitude eastwards. The Irrawaddy, Salween, and Mekong rivers all made landmarks among the vast expanse of hilly forests and jungle, and after six and a half hours' flying we were over Sakon Nakhon.

We dropped leaflets over Sakon Nakhon as part of the cover plan, and a few minutes later were over the DZ where we could see a number of people on the ground. After the supplies had been dropped successfully and I had taken a number of photographs of the drop, we flew in a wide circle over what was to be the Candle area. We also flew in extremely low, literally a few feet off the ground, to look at a landing strip that guerrillas were constructing. As darkness fell we headed west and climbed steadily until night gave us cover from the unwelcome attentions of any stray Japanese fighters.

We landed safely at Jessore after a thirteen-and-a-half-hour flight, an extremely long hop in those days, considerably further than crossing the Atlantic, and for three-quarters of the time we had been flying over Japanese territory. It was not only a very good experience for me but it made me appreciate the efforts of the RAF Liberator crews on whom we had to rely for our supplies. Apart from possible enemy action, they had to contend with some of the worst weather in the world. There had been heavy losses solely due to weather among aircraft flying over the Hump to China. Psychologically it was bad for the crews, as the majority would have much preferred to be dropping bombs on the Japanese rather than dropping supplies to agents who might or might not be doing a good job.

During my final week in Calcutta I met Brigadier Victor Jacques for the first time – he had only just arrived from Bangkok. A tall thin man, with a scholarly appearance, he looked more like a professor than a soldier; he had, however, a Military Cross and bar from the First World War. He was very helpful and gave me a lot of useful tips as well as bringing me up to date on the political situation, which was developing favourably for us. On the last day I had my final briefing from Colonel Pointon and gave a farewell cocktail party for a number of my friends, after which I finished up in a night club called The 300 with Julian Amery and two FANYs from the cipher section.

We left Calcutta in two jeeps, one of which contained Hervey-Bathurst, who as conducting officer was coming to see us off, Gunner and myself (with a bad hangover); the other contained Chat and Pun. We should have left Jessore that night but the sortie was postponed because of bad weather, and then postponed again the following night. There was a cinema in the camp, at that moment showing Hemingway's *For Whom the Bell Tolls*. I had seen the film before, but I took Chat and Pun to see it, thinking it was good stuff to show potential guerrillas. On the third night we finally took off from Jessore.

11

Reception, Activities and Evacuation

On 29 May we took off in a Liberator with a very friendly all-Canadian crew. The first stage of the flight was in daylight, much of it over the Sunderbunds. These were seemingly endless swamps at the estuary of the Ganges, with no signs of human life – only occasional flocks of white birds. Then we crossed a distinct dividing line in the water below us where the blue sea met the mud-coloured Delta. We landed at the island of Akyab, which had recently been recaptured from the Japanese, to refuel and rest before it was time to start on our final lap. That night, after a good meal, we lay down on the concrete runway under the wing of the Liberator. The hardness of the ground and the prospect of the next day's hazards did not make for much sleep.

We left at two in the morning so as to fly over Japanese-held territory in the dark and arrive at our DZ at first light. After crossing the shining sinuous outlines of the Irrawaddy, Sittaung and Salween rivers, we saw the smoke, fires and flashes of a battle below us, but we were too high to make out any details.

We had to climb to 15,000 feet to cross some mountains, which in those days of unpressurised aircraft entailed using oxygen masks. It was bitterly cold in spite of the amount of clothing we wore, and Chat and Pun looked miserable. After so many flying misadventures, I confined myself to speculating what would happen if we came down in the jungle below, not knowing where we were or what we might encounter. We steered an erratic course, taking avoiding action from the large cumulus clouds, the despair of Liberator pilots. If you flew into these clouds the most extraordinary things were likely to happen to the aircraft, all of them unpleasant. A pilot told me that he was flying his Liberator over Burma when he flew into a cumulus cloud. Suddenly there was a terrific crash. He had a momentary blackout and the plane got completely out of control. When he came to a few seconds later, he was flying upside down and 2,000 feet higher up.

After getting our bearings from a bend in the Mekong river we started to descend towards the lake adjoining Sakon Nakhon and, flying very low, dropped thousands of leaflets and propaganda-inscribed matchboxes on the town. We got no reaction from the Japanese garrison, who were probably still asleep. At dawn we sighted our DZ, which was situated about twenty miles south of Sakon Nakhon, at the village of Ban Non Han. On the ground we could see three signal fires burning and the DZ appeared to be swarming with men. We made a wide circle, and as we did so the dispatcher made us climb onto the wooden chute that was rigged up in the fuselage and had its exit lowered under the rear gunner's compartment.

As soon as the light flashed red for 'Action Stations' we were all seated on the chute, with myself in front, followed by Chat and Pun, and Gunner last. We gripped the sides of the chute firmly until the lights changed to green and the dispatcher yelled 'Go'. I gave myself a shove on the sides and started to slide down. Nearing the exit I saw the ground for the first time and can only recollect the rear gunner giving me the thumbs up sign before there was a tug as the static line pulled out my green camouflaged parachute. I preferred this type of exit from an aircraft to hurling oneself out of a door or a hole in the floor.

It was a much lower drop than the one I had done the last time in Albania; during the descent of 500 feet the only thing I noted with any clarity was the fact that nobody had followed me out of the plane, which was fast disappearing from view. This was a bit disconcerting, and not at all according to plan, but before I had time to think what had gone wrong I landed with a splash in a paddy field. Though wet and muddy it was the softest landing I had ever made, and no harm came to the two bottles of whisky that I carried in the leg pockets of the flying suit I was wearing over my jungle-green battledress.

I was immediately surrounded by a party of Thais. 'I'm Pluto,' said one, in English, 'welcome to Thailand.' 'I'm Kong,' said the other, 'we are very happy to see you.' There was no sign of the aeroplane and I was beginning to get anxious when we heard the sound of its approaching engines and it came back into sight. As it flew across the DZ three bodies dropped out, their parachutes opened, and they all landed within a hundred yards of where I was standing. After two more runs, dropping containers with our stores and weapons for the guerrillas, the Liberator came in for an extra low final run, roaring over our heads as we waved to show we were all right. It then waggled its wings in farewell, climbed steeply, and headed west. We watched it getting slowly smaller until we lost sight of it on its long journey home.

When I asked Gunner why nobody had followed me out of the plane, he told me that Chat had got stage fright. Having never done a jump before, he had hung on to the side of the chute instead of sliding down it after me. The dispatcher told the pilot on the inter-com, and the pilot began to circle back. Pun meanwhile was swear-ing at Chat. On the return journey the combined efforts of Pun and Gunner, with the dispatcher using gentle persuasion, had finally got Chat out. He was visibly embarrassed and came in for a good bit of leg-pulling from Pun and Gunner.

The first objective had been accomplished, for we had all landed safely at the right place in the north-east corner of Thailand; and although we were well over 1,500 miles from our base in Calcutta and over 1,000 miles behind the front lines, we were among friends.

Our reception committee consisted of about a hundred men, most of whom were armed with rifles and wore khaki shirts and shorts. These were the guerrillas, while those who wore a sarong and were unarmed were the local villagers. They had brought twenty bullock carts, each drawn by two fine-looking animals, and as soon as the parachutes and supplies had been collected and loaded, Pluto invited us to get into the back of a cart which had a long low roof made of wicker. 'The camp is about two miles away,' he said. 'Don't show yourselves.' The local villagers had aparently never seen a white man before; the sight of one would cause gossip, and then the Japs would know we had landed.

After a bumpy ride of about forty-five minutes over muddy cart tracks we reached the camp, where the guard turned out. I got out of the back of the bullock cart and the guard gave a praiseworthy 'present'; having returned their salute I was invited to inspect them. Pluto led us through the camp, which contained a number of bamboo huts in a sugar plantation which was Pluto's property. The brand new house where we were going to live had been specially built for us out of bamboo and, like all houses in that part of the world, was perched on stilts about five feet off the ground. It had four rooms, a bath house attached to the back, and a well-constructed deep trench latrine abour forty yards away.

We were immediately given an excellent meal, the basis of which consisted of sticky rice, which we were supposed to roll into a ball in our fingers and then dip into a chili or soy sauce, and pork and buffalo meat. At first Gunner and I were hopeless at making our rice stick as it should, and most of it stayed on our fingers; but gradually we got the knack and I was beginning to enjoy myself when I ate a minute green chili, which was so hot that my streaming eyes and hiccups gave much amusement to Pluto and Kong who were eating with us.

After the meal I had my first long talk with Pluto. He told me his real name was Nai Tieng Sirikhandra. He was the people's representative, or deputy, for the province and town of Sakon Nakhon.' 'What's a people's representative?' I asked. 'The same as your Member of Parliament,' he replied. I liked him at once: he not only gave the impression of being genuinely glad to have us with him, but seemed frank and sincere. He spoke good English and was evidently intelligent. He added that he was one of the founders of the resistance movement, for he and Nai Chamrong Daurong, the people's representative for Maha Sarakham, had been the first two members of the Thai House of Assembly to vote against the Thai declaration of war against the Allies. They had consequently come under suspicion from the Japanese.

Pluto was a close friend of Ruth and, partly to keep him away from the Japanese, Ruth had sent him back to his own province to organise a resistance movement there. Pluto was now the head of all the guerrillas in the area. He spoke in strong terms of his dislike of the Japanese, referring to them as invaders, and bitterly condemned the present Prime Minister, Marshal Pibul Songkram, whom he regarded an an out-and-out collaborator.

Pluto was in his thirties (though I always found it hard to assess the ages of the Thais, for they usually looked to me much younger than they were). He was of medium build but tallish for a Thai, with a complexion a shade darker than most of his compatriots. Born of a well-to-do family in Sakon Nakhon and brought up there, he had a wide circle of friends and contacts and knew the area thoroughly. He had an engaging smile, like so many of his countrymen, and an excellent sense of humour, though his moods could quickly change from gaiety to seriousness. His abilities as a leader of men and as a guerrilla organiser were to prove the mainstay of our mission, and he was soon to become my closest friend there.

Kong, whose real name was Kris Tosayanonda, had parachuted into Thailand nine months previously. He had been operator for Ruth in Bangkok before moving to Pluto's area, where he had been working ever since. Trained as a wireless operator, he had dropped in with a wireless set, with which he had maintained contact with Calcutta; his signals had been responsible for our successful arrival. He was a good-looking young man, of sturdier build than Pluto, and spoke good English, for he had at one time studied medicine at Edinburgh University. He had received the full Force 136 training. Like us he wore jungle-green battledress, with the badges of rank of a captain in the British Army. Many of the Thais who dropped into their country were given a British commission, the senior being Chin Svasti who held the rank of lieutenant-colonel.

The plantation in which our camp was situated was in a clearing, with the jungle surrounding us on all sides. Oil lamps were lit as night fell, and sparkling fireflies and other insects buzzed around them, many of them burning their wings and falling to the ground. We slept well the first night in spite of the unusual background noises. These sounds of the jungle became a regular nightly feature and we got quite used to them. There was one very high-pitched chirrup made by crickets which seldom stopped, and the frogs, too, kept up an incessant chorus. Another very persistent noise was the 'kaw-kaw' made by the lizards, while geckos were constantly making themselves heard on the ceiling or walls of the house, to which they clung by tiny suckers on their feet. They entertained us in the evening by stalking flies and mosquitoes, then catching them with their long tongues.

The following morning Gunner made contact with Calcutta, and from then on his daily 11 a.m. schedule never failed. Considering that his wireless was the same type of small suitcase set that had been used in the Balkans (the B 2), that the distance was nearly 1,600 miles, and that it was the monsoon period with endless rain and electric storms, it was remarkable that he made contact at all, let alone every day. It was a tribute to both his skill as an operator and his perseverance.

At our first meeting Pluto told me that there was an American officer in the area. I decided to contact him as soon as possible, so leaving Gunner, Chat, Pun, and Kong to deal with a supply-dropping sortie that was shortly expected, Pluto and I drove out of the camp in a truck belonging to the Public Works Department. Our heavily armed bodyguard piled into the back. After an hour's drive, in the course of which we passed several road blocks manned by Pluto's guerrillas, we reached Sakon Nakhon where the Japanese had a garrison. Our party seemed quite unconcerned by this and drove through, following the straight red laterite road to Udon and passing several Japanese army lorries on the way. When we reached the town of Ban Han, we turned off to the south, then took a rough track, passing more guerrilla camps, till we came to a camp consisting of a number of huts in a clearing in the jungle. As the car stopped a man emerged from one of the huts wearing the uniform of a major in the US Army. Pluto introduced us: 'This is Major Holliday.' The American greeted us warmly and invited us into his hut for some coffee. It was well furnished and stacked on the shelves were American food tins and other signs of the supply drops he had been receiving from American aircraft.

His American instant coffee was excellent, and over it we talked for about two hours. Of medium build, in his forties, he looked somehow out of place in uniform. I asked him how long he'd been in the Army. 'Only since we came into the war,' he replied. 'What were you doing before that?' He told us he had been a missionary in Thailand, but after the war started he was recruited by the OSS, presumably because he knew the Thais and could speak their language, and sent back there. Later on I asked him what was the purpose of his mission, for he was in the area in which I had been ordered to organise and train guerrillas. I wanted to make sure we worked in harmony and did not tread on each other's toes. 'I'm here purely to collect intelligence,' he told me, adding that he was in no way connected with the guerrilla movement – 'though naturally I have to rely on our good friend Pluto's men for my security.' 'Do you intend to travel much?' I asked, 'No,' he replied; he would stay as long as the Japs allowed it, and his agents would send him the information that he required. I saw that he had a wireless set manned by a Thai operator, who he told me had been trained in the United States. To complete his entourage he even had a monkey and a parrot. I liked Holliday very much. He was kind, hospitable and cooperative.

I spent the night in his house and the next morning found 800 guerrillas outside, summoned by Pluto and lined up for my inspection. They looked a keen bunch of young men, but only about a hundred had rifles; the rest had dummies made of wood. I assumed the parade was a hint from Pluto.

After arranging with Holliday to keep in touch, we drove back the way we had come, stopping at Pluto's house at Sakon Nakhon, which was next to the Japanese barracks. His very attractive wife, the first Thai woman I had spoken to since my arrival, cooked us a most agreeable dinner before we drove on to the camp. She had the dark dreamy eyes and long lashes with which so many of her compatriots were blessed. She spoke a few words of English, but Pluto acted as interpreter to pass on her offers to help our mission in such domestic matters as mending our clothes or lending us bedding. It was at this meal that I learnt my first words of the Thai language – 'kop jai' meaning 'thank you', and one sounding like 'gin kao' meaning 'food', or translated literally 'eat rice', for to the Thais rice is the staple diet.

It was the monsoon period, which lasted another two months. That meant that it rained every day, frequently, though for short periods; but it came down in sheets, worse than anything I had experienced before. The tracks were always muddy and full of puddles, streams were in spate, the trees and our houses dripped continually. As a consolation, everything was lush and green, with the lovely fresh smell that follows rain on the ground.

After Pluto had given me details of his camps, I decided to visit as many as possible, preferably all of them. I was worried about the security aspect and told him so; he and his guerrillas did not seem to take the Japanese very seriously. After all that I had previously heard of them, the last thing I wanted was to fall into their hands. Their methods of treating ordinary prisoners were notorious enough, and what they would do if they caught someone like myself was something I didn't care to contemplate. However, Pluto was reassuring. He said that the Japanese only had a company at Sakon Nakhon and they were communications troops who would be unlikely to disturb us. Even if they did, his guerrillas would see them off. I made it clear to him that our policy was against this. If the Japanese came, I told him, we had to withdraw because no action was to be taken against them except as a last resort. He seemed disappointed at my reaction.

The first camp I wanted to visit was at Maha Sarakham, as it was alongside the large landing strip under construction that I had seen on my first flight over the Candle area. We codenamed it Heston – we found the long Thai names confusing and usually replaced them with short codenames which were both more convenient and secure. I took Gunner on this trip because I wanted to keep in touch with Calcutta and possibly take a supply drop at Heston.

Pluto normally used to visit us in a Ford two-seater car, but this time he came in a Ford utility van and we all drove for two hours to Ban Tao Ngoi, where we stopped at the village school. It housed 120 teenage students whose studies were not exactly orthodox – their main classes were in Brens, Piats, Stens, rifles, carbines and explosives. We stayed the night there and were woken at five in the morning by a class doing PT outside my window. Later I made a short speech to them, translated by Pluto. As we left they gave three cheers, 'Khio! Khio! Khio!'

At Ban Tao Ngoi we changed our means of transport and for the first of many times I rode a Thai pony. They were bred for riding rather than pack-carrying and only stallions were used; it was considered undignified and bad form to ride mares. The ponies were extremely nimble, moving with a strange action, tripling – trotting very fast with their forelegs and cantering with their hind legs. They kept up this pace for hours while an experienced rider could sit very comfortably in the saddle. Gunner was a regular soldier who had served with the Royal Horse Artillery before the war, so he and I were more than happy. Chat and Pun, however, both townsmen from Bangkok, looked most uncomfortable and finished the journey very sore.

We rode all day through the flat, characterless forest – following the jungle tracks through mile after mile of grey and ochre woodland, relieved occasionally by the bright yellow-green of the paddy fields and banana plantations round a village. It was a dreary landscape by daylight, yet haunting under a full moon. Had we met a Japanese patrol it would have been possible to leave the tracks and make our way through the undergrowth on foot, but the ponies would have had to be abandoned. We always carried a *dah* as part of our equipment – a special type of flat-bladed knife, about a foot long, that was very useful for hacking through the undergrowth. The bamboo in particular was very difficult to cut unless one had learned to handle the *dah* properly.

The deciduous trees that grew in these rain forests were quite the largest that I had ever seen; the Thais called them *mai teng* or *mai rong*. They were not a species of the teak for which Thailand was famous, for that grew in the west of the country near the border with Burma. The undergrowth was mainly bamboo, fern and the stumps and fallen trunks of old trees, over which creepers of all types grew in profusion. The forest was dense and dark. Most of the time we never saw the sun, but here and there a long shaft of light would penetrate the canopy of trees above us and illuminate the undergrowth almost like a spotlight. The interplay of light and shadow could be extraordinarily beautiful.

There were countless wild orchids growing on the trees, and also a curious navigational guide that Pluto pointed out to me – a fungus that grew only on the south-west side of tree trunks. Of animal life I saw little. Pluto told me that there were leopard, panther, tiger, bear and various types of deer; and although I did occasionally hear other animal noises, all I ever saw were flocks of monkeys, occasional exotic birds including peacocks, and the most enormous butterflies – brilliant colours, the most striking being a very vivid blue.

We met several villagers on the way, and I was surprised at the manner in which they removed their hats and bowed very low until we passed. The women, on the other hand, prostrated themselves on the ground and did not look up at us at all. The older women's teeth and mouths were horribly discoloured by the purple stain from chewing betel nuts, but the young girls were very lovely, with bare breasts and long black hair. We also met several hunting parties later on, armed with bows and arrows, or crossbows. Pluto told me they could hit a running boar at fifty yards; and since their arrows were poisoned, a pig that was hit anywhere eventually died. All the hunters had to do was follow its tracks.

We reached Heston late at night and next morning I went out to look at the work on the landing ground, which was about three-quarters finished. There had been a strip there earlier, but a Dakota needed a runway 1,000 yards long and 50 yards wide, and the old surface was not good enough. The new runway was being made on a base of rock a foot deep, on top of which there was a four-inch surface of earth and sand. This was a formidable project – not least because the rock had to be brought from a hill five miles away – and over 3,000 villagers with 1,000 bullock carts and 2,000 bullocks were working almost non-stop. I was very impressed by the condition of the bullocks pulling the carts, and also of the water buffaloes pulling the ploughs in the paddy fields; the animals in Thailand were on the whole treated much better than those I had seen in India. The only exception to this rule was that the Thais' Buddhist principles did not allow them to put badly injured animals out of their misery.

A Liberator was expected that evening and while we were waiting for it I played Thai football with the guerrillas. This was a good game, in which any number of people stood in a circle and endeavoured to keep the ball, made of wicker, off the ground. You were allowed to kick the ball, or hit it with any part of the body, usually the hands, elbows, knees or head, but you were not allowed to catch it or hold it with your hands. You lost a point if you were the one to let it hit the ground, and I have seen good players keep the ball going for as long as three minutes. After all that, the Liberator never came.

The next day I was visited by the people's representative for the province of Maha Sarakham, in which we found ourselves. His real name was Nai Chamrong Daurong, codenamed 'Cato'. A close friend of Pluto and Ruth, he was the organiser of the resistance movement in his constituency and led 3,200 guerrillas. He was a very cheerful and jolly companion, spoke comic broken English, and though his political views were, like Pluto's, radical, I could never feel that he took them as seriously as Pluto. He was rich: when I first met him he owned twelve cars, two of which he placed at my disposal – lovely Studebakers but unfortunately with very bad tyres. He also shared with me a liking for good food and drink, and the two of us would often sit together in the evening round large earthenware pots, out of which we sucked rice wine through long bamboo tubes, getting slowly tight together. The building of the airstrip at Heston was his responsibility, and he took a great interest in it, especially as he saw its post-war possibilities. He was a brave man, going to Bangkok several times on our behalf at the risk of his life. Later he sheltered Gunner when Gunner was on the run and the Japanese were getting close on his heels.

I waited five days at Heston for the Liberator that never came, but then had to send off Gunner to get the wireless batteries charged. The hand charger was broken, and the petrol generator was already damaged and rusted when it was dropped with us on our arrival. We were hoping for a new one on the Liberator. Meanwhile our evenings were enlivened with music, either from an instrument called the *kan*, or by a full-sized band. The *kan* was made from a series of bamboos of different lengths joined together, with holes in the tubes. It was a kind of wind instrument on which the player blew in much the same manner as on a flute, using his fingers on the holes to make the different notes. The resulting music was not unpleasing, rather like a cross between the bagpipes and a harmonium.

When the band played, it consisted of the *kan*, two drums, one flute, one Thai violin, two normal violins, and a strange instrument best described as a cross between a harp and a xylophone. Very often the guerrillas and the local girls would dance the *ramwong* to the music; it was very graceful to watch, for though they danced in couples they never held or touched each other, the principal movements being made by the hands, while they shuffled their feet. I enjoyed Thai music, for it had distinct tunes and rhythm – unlike Indian music, which I could not appreciate.

After five days I gave up hope of the Liberator and decided to join Gunner, who was at Ban Tao Ngoi, which we had renamed Kempton. When I got there he told me that the Liberator we had been expecting had been reported missing, and we were asked to make inquiries about it. I asked Pluto to contact the governors of all the provinces in the Candle area, but it was never traced. It cast a gloom over us, for these Liberators and their crews meant something personal to us and we felt a responsibility for their loss, since they were coming to us. This particular one was probably lost over Burma or the Bay of Bengal.

On the way back from Kempton I had a bad fall; my pony slipped on some wet rocks while crossing a riverbed and we both fell about five feet onto the rocks below. The pony did not seem to be hurt, but I was cut on the elbow and back, and one little finger stuck out at right angles to the back of my hand and looked most odd. I was lucky to have Kong with me; he pushed and pulled until the finger went more or less back to the right position. But it was well and truly broken, and has been crooked ever since.

I spent a week visiting more camps, after which we decided to move. This was dictated partly by reasons of security and partly by convenience, because our new base would be fairly central for the other camps that were now in existence. The place we chose was Ban Non Han, five miles from Kempton, and we named it Ascot. There were already 1,000 guerrillas in the camp, which was sited near the bottom of the hills, with a good DZ nearby and a stream. Pluto had ordered our house to be built in a clearing at the top of a hill, from which we had a wonderful view, including the town and lake of Sakon Nakhon. It was put up very quickly, a very fine house on stilts about five feet off the ground. The floors and furniture were made of teak, the rest of the house of bamboo, and the whole building was made without the use of a single nail – everything was joined together by twine made from a jungle creeper. It had one very large room in which Gunner, Chat, Pun and I both lived and slept, a bathroom which consisted of an enclosure at the back in which a huge urn of water was standing, a kitchen, and a long verandah facing the view. We had real beds, for which Pluto's wife provided the sheets. The guerrilla life was not proving so tough as our instructors at ME 25 had led us to believe.

On the first morning there I found fifteen young girls and women sitting on the verandah with baskets of fruit which included mangoes, pineapples, bananas and jackfruit. The vendors interested me more than the fruit, and I must also have been making some sort of an impression on them, as they were giggling at me so much that I had to ask Pluto what the joke was. He said that they had never seen a European before, and thought my fair skin and hair very funny. They were more intrigued, however, by my blue eyes, for they thought only devils had blue eyes. These women became a daily feature, and after supply drops were always on the scrounge for bits of parachute, which we used as currency – half a parachute would buy a pig. We used to get them to sew up the strips of parachute for use on our DZs as signals to the aircraft, and they would also wash and sew our clothes. The two best-looking were eventually engaged as our resident cooks.

While at Ascot we started a regular courier service to the various governors, all of whom were very useful sources of information. The governor of Nakhon Phanom, which was on the Mekong, wrote to say that he was in touch with three groups of guerrillas across the river in French Indo-China. This news was passed on to Calcutta, as were details of the Japanese units in the Candle area.

We had a number of callers, two of the most frequent being Pluto's wife and their five-year-old son. He was a bright little boy, who picked up English very quickly. He never called me Nai Pan To (Major) Grin, which was my customary name, but 'Maksida' which was some little joke of his own, for maksida was a type of fruit. He was a great favourite of us all and we looked forward to his visits.

Our visitors were varied, some of them having come long distances. One was a doctor from Bangkok, who brought a letter from Ruth and having drunk us out of whisky informed me that he thought the life of a guerrilla so comfortable that he would leave Bangkok and join us; but he never did. Another very optimistic arrival was an official from the Ministry of Education, who asked me to keep a list of all the arms I distributed – which I did anyway, having found it so useful in Albania – as it was going to be his job after the war to collect them again.

I spent a week at Ascot before my next move, during which time we had two supply drops. I issued the arms to the guerrillas, the majority of whom were schoolmasters and students. They were very keen to learn and easy to train. In the evenings we would have concerts round the camp fires, and sometimes dancing, for Pluto had by now recruited a number of girl guerrillas. The men, as was customary, often wore flowers stuck behind their ears, but I stopped this on parade as I did not think it very military, however decorative.

Chat and Pun were my constant watchdogs. Although they were not much use as interpreters because they could not understand the local dialect, they made excellent bodyguards. They also saw to my comfort, making tea or coffee at just the right moment, and always had bright smiles. They regarded the locals as foreigners. Our coolies, who carried the stores whenever we moved, were Laos of a type known as the 'tattooed Laos' and were tattooed blue from the waist to below the knee. Others, more brave, were tattooed blue from head to foot, for it was a sign of valour and a woman would seldom marry a man who was not tattooed. I was rather pleased to be able to show off the tattooed figure of an officer of the Royal Horse Guards that I had on my right arm.

We fed very well at this time, with our two girl cooks showing plenty of initiative. The basis of all our meals was sticky rice, but with it we had a variety of other food, which included water buffalo, bamboo shoots, mushrooms, coconuts and all sorts of fruit. Eggs were rare, usually duck or goose. We drank water with our meals, and rice wine or spirit after supper. Of our own supplies that were parachuted to us we had tea, coffee, whisky and rum. The items we missed most were bread, butter, milk, and cheese, for these were unobtainable.

I was very happy in this HQ: we had all we wanted, intelligence started to flow in to us, and I could reach most of our camps in two or three days' march. We now had twelve camps, with approximately 1,000 men in each, but we were very short of arms. With enough supplies of these, our force of some 12,000 would make a good showing when the order to fight was given. As I went about visiting the camps I felt rather like the squire in his parish, but this pleasant life was too good to last. We kept getting signals from Calcutta saying that they had heard from Bangkok (presumably from Ruth via Hector) that the Japanese were aware of our activities and were sending up a company of Kempai Tai (security police) to Sakon Nakhon to track us down. This proved to be true.

Later more Japanese moved to Nong Khai, Udon, Sakon Nakhon, Nakhon Phanom, and Mukdahan, but the local governors kept me fully informed of their movements. We were not unduly alarmed, but our HQ clearly was and eventually all supply drops to us were stopped as a security measure. Pluto was convinced that there was a political motive behind this, for Pulao, the chief of police in Bangkok, was a bitter enemy of his. Pluto was certain that he was spreading alarm deliberately to cut off the supply of arms to the area, afraid that Pluto was getting too strong and well armed for post-war politics.

A special joint mission of Japanese and Thais was eventually sent up with the task of investigating our activities, with special reference to DZs, landing strips and camps. They sent out patrols of about fifty Japanese, guided by a Thai officer, to the suspected areas; but we were still not worried, for the Thai officers on the mission kept us fully informed of the Japanese intentions well in advance, and the Thai officer leading the Japanese knew of our whereabouts and so would lead the Japs on a wild-goose chase elsewhere. On two occasions we received requests from the Thai officers with the Japanese to vacate our camps because the Japanese knew of them and were determined to go there, and they could not refuse to lead them without incurring their suspicion. Pluto immediately ordered the camps to be burnt down, and so the Japanese found only ruins, though they did find one landing strip and for the rest of the war kept a guard on it. We felt very frustrated that we were not allowed to attack these guards, for they were an easy target for the guerrillas. One Japanese spy, however, was caught near one of our camps and shot after having been interrogated. Otherwise we were given away only twice, on both occasions by Chinese, who informed on us for cash. Luckily we got warning in time.

On 23 June I was at Ascot when word came that one of our agents had made contact with a large prisoner of war camp in Ubon. Ubon was also a base for a battalion of Japanese troops as well as a Thai army garrison. I decided to go there and moved to Heston, intending to stop there for the first night. While we were there we received news that a number of Japanese trucks were approaching our camp. We put our emergency alarm procedure into operation: Gunner had all the wireless kit loaded on to coolies and I packed our code books and other secret documents into a special SOE briefcase.

This brief case had five pounds of thermite concealed in a false bottom, and could be used either as a booby trap, set to blow up anyone trying to open it, or for quick destruction of itself and its contents. It was operated electrically with batteries, and while I was putting all our documents into the case it exploded prematurely – probably owing to a short circuit. I was squatting over it at the time and the blazing thermite showered all over me. As I had my sleeves rolled up and was wearing shorts, I was burnt severely and but for the help of Gunner and Kong would probably have died. I had shut my eyes at the moment of the explosion, and my face was so burnt, with the skin black and hard, that I could not open them again. I was burnt on my arms, knees and hands; all the nails were burnt off both hands, and the flesh was burnt to the bone on four fingers of the left hand. Gunner led me and we hid nearby for a while, but the Japanese never appeared and we returned to Heston, where I swallowed two morphia pills and Kong rubbed coconut oil on the burns.

I shook like a jelly all the first night while Chat, Pun and Gunner took turns to sit up fanning me. I was in agony in spite of the morphia, which did not seem to take effect. Calcutta was informed and they said they would send a Dakota to Heston to pick me up, for by now the landing ground had been completed. I was very pleased to hear this, for we had no medical supplies for burns after using up one small tube of aquaflavine in the first aid kit. Cato suggested the local remedy, which was the juice of squashed prickly pear cactus rubbed into the burns. It did relieve the pain a little and certainly did no harm.

Gunner had already radioed Calcutta for medical instructions and they replied 'Keep the burns covered but bathe frequently in salt and water.' We had access to salt and strips of parachute served as bandages. However, the next problem was caused by maggots entering my wounds. Only irritating at first when they ate the burned flesh, they became more painful when they ate the live, so I had a relay of boys picking them out with tweezers. Gunner reported this to the medical officer in Calcutta and was ordered to have the boys stopped immediately, as the maggots were doing me good by preventing gangrene from setting in, which might have been fatal.

Then my spirits dropped, for we heard that the Dakota would not be coming. I was still in considerable pain and unable to sleep, so Cato brought me an opium pipe to smoke. This made me feel sick, but also a bit drowsy; and because it lessened the pain I smoked it quite a lot. I had none of the dreams that opium is supposed to produce, probably because I did not normally smoke and could not inhale.

After three days the burns, which had raised blisters ranging in size from golf balls to tennis balls, became raw as the blisters burst and the skin came off. My eyes were open now, but I couldn't use my hands at all. My face, too, was still bad – I couldn't open my mouth and could only take liquids through a bamboo tube. I realised that I was only a handicap to everyone and had my fingers been functioning I would have shot myself; but Gunner found me trying to get my automatic out of its holster and removed it from me. By their nursing care Gunner, Kong, Chat and Pun undoubtedly saved my life, for without their attention I would have died of shock.

We still had hopes that, although the Dakota was cancelled, a Liberator would drop medical supplies. In the meantime Kong had contacted Ruth's operator in Bangkok (quite illegally, for all communications between missions in the field were supposed to be passed through Calcutta), and a sympathetic message came from Ruth saying that he would try to help and would send a doctor.

Then, at the end of the week, we received a signal to say that a Liberator would drop medical supplies. As the reception committee was waiting, a Japanese fighter suddenly appeared over the strip and everyone rushed for cover. On the second circuit the fighter came down and landed on the strip, and two officers in the uniform of the Thai Air Force got out. When our men went out to them, the pilot said they had been sent by Ruth to collect me and take me to another clandestine air strip further to the west, from where I could go on to Calcutta.

I said goodbye to my friends and was taken out to the aircraft. It was a Japanese Nagoya fighter-bomber with only two seats – for the pilot in front, and the observer behind. I climbed into the observer's seat, which I had to share with the second officer, and found it very uncomfortable and painful in such cramped conditions. We took off, the first aircraft to do so from our new strip, and flew over two hundred miles to the west, landing at Non Han about fifty miles west of Khon Kaen. It was a strange experience for a British officer to be flying around in a Japanese fighter. I hoped we wouldn't meet any RAF.

At Non Han we were met by a doctor who had been sent by Ruth from Bangkok, the governor of Khon Kaen, and Noon – one of the Force 136 trained operators. I was very well looked after, but had a bad time when the doctor tried to rip off the strips of parachute we had used as bandages and which had stuck to the raw flesh. I stayed two days at a house by the airstrip where twelve camouflaged Corsair fighters were dispersed, awaiting the long-expected D Day for action. Their presence was completely unknown to the Japanese. On the third day I was flown in a Corsair for about a hundred miles due west to a place called Naarn, where there was another clandestine airstrip. I was met by Major Paul Ashwell, a Force 136 BLO, the governor and chief of police of Loey, who were the local resistance leaders, and Noo, another Force 136-trained White. They could not have been kinder or more helpful. I hadn't slept at all since my accident seven days before, but this problem was solved when the chief of police made me drink a complete bottle of very strong rice spirit. I passed clean out and was carried to bed. The treatment was worth it in spite of the hangover the next day.

There were five Thai officers and fifteen cadets at this camp waiting to be evacuated for training in Ceylon, and they were a very cheerful and friendly bunch. I had a five-day wait until a Dakota arrived, complete with a stretcher for me, though I was able by then to walk quite well. We flew in three hours to Rangoon which had recently been recaptured from the Japanese, and after refuelling flew on for a further four hours to Alipore, near Calcutta. I was met by an ambulance and a large party of friends who seemed surprised to see me on my feet.

The ambulance took me to No 21 Combined Military Hospital in Calcutta, where I was thankful to receive treatment at last for my extensive burns, some of which were classified as third degree. The doctors forecast at least a month in hospital, but luckily they were wrong.

12
Return to Thailand

I entered hospital thirteen days after being burnt. The staff were kind, the treatment was good and the ward air-conditioned. But there was a problem in the frequent visits I received from Force 136 officers such as Ben Hervey-Bathurst and Rowland Winn (Winn had been earmarked, at my request, for Candle area). Force 136 activities were still top secret, so conversation in a large ward with no privacy was virtually impossible. The difficulties were resolved when Richard Casey, the governor of Bengal, whose wife was a friend of my mother, very kindly asked me to stay at Government House.

The Caseys, both Australians, were wonderfully hospitable. I stayed a week in the luxurious Curzon suite in the house which is reputedly a replica of Kedleston House in Derbyshire. One afternoon Gandhi came to tea. He seemed to have a good sense of humour but looked a little incongruous in the drawing room wearing his *dhoti*.

An official car took me to the hospital daily for my saline bath. By the end of the week my burns had healed so well that I had bandages only on my hands and arms. Soon I had recovered enough to visit the office, briefing them about the Candle area and exchanging signals with Gunner and Pluto. I was very touched by all the messages I received; and a bundle of letters that had been brought in from Thailand included some from Pluto, Cato, Gunner, Chat and Pun. I discovered, however, that a security ban on flying over Candle area had prevented the aircraft landing at Heston. This puzzled me, for I knew that Holliday was still getting supply drops. Orders for the ban had come from higher up than Calcutta, and I wondered if Pluto's theories were correct and his political enemies in Bangkok were responsible.

Calcutta was uncomfortably hot at this time of the year. Lady Wavell, having heard of my predicament, asked me to stay and convalesce with her family up at Simla, where the household moved in the hot weather. The last part of the journey was in a small rail car that climbed up a winding track amid lovely scenery in the mountains. The single track twisted and turned its way upwards, in and out of tunnels, with the hillside becoming steadily greener and the views more impressive. In Simla itself it was delightfully cool, the clean white houses with their red tiled roofs in marked contrast to the villages of mud and straw that we had passed on the plains. No cars were allowed, there was a peace and detachment about the place that was wonderfully soothing, with the birds in full song and nothing more disturbing than the occasional barking of a dog or the braying of a donkey. It was an exhilarating change from Calcutta. Suddenly the war seemed far away.

I was met at the station by one of the Viceroy's ADCs and taken to Viceregal Lodge in a rickshaw propelled by four men – two pulling and two pushing – dressed in smart red and blue uniforms. The house was immense, in Scottish baronial style, set in a commanding situation with a lovely garden and views that stretched in the far distance to the snow-capped Himalayas. I spent a month there. Thanks to the kindness of the Wavell family and their staff, it was a very happy convalescence. Life was gay and social. There was one night club with a band completely made up of Italian prisoners of war, who seemed to enjoy their new role. Kemp came to stay, and we planned that he should join me in Candle area.

The bandages were gradually removed from both my arms and then one hand, and to get fit I played tennis regularly with various members of the staff and the tennis pro, an old Sikh with a long grey beard whom we irreverently nicknamed 'J.C.'. In spite of his baggy trousers and voluminous clothes, he beat us all. Tragically, he was one of the thousands killed in the inter-racial massacres after partition.

After three weeks I failed a medical board but passed a week later. I still had a bandage on my left hand and wore a cotton glove on the other to keep off the sun, but I was keen now to rejoin my friends, especially when I heard that Japanese were getting more active and there were distinct possibilities that we might soon be allowed to take more aggressive action against them. I made my grateful farewells in Simla and returned to Calcutta. There I found Kemp and Winn engaged on their final preparations for dropping together into Candle area. I was looking forward very much to having them attached to my command; in operations of this nature it was a great asset if one's comrades were personal friends. I had heard of a number of missions where the officers did not hit it off, and, where there was no return ticket, this led to most unhappy situations.

While we were in Calcutta the atomic bombs were dropped on Japan, causing mounting speculation as to whether or not the Japanese would fight on. It was essential that we reach Thailand as soon as possible, for the prisoners of war would be our first concern. It was vital to ensure that the Japanese, as a last-minute gesture of barbarity, did not attempt to massacre them. We had also to be prepared to help and succour these unfortunate men, some of whom had been over three and a half years in captivity under appalling conditions.

Kemp, Winn, Sergeant Lawson, who was Winn's operator, and a Thai interpreter, Toy, left for Jessore to join their Liberator and were expected to parachute within a few days. I was to follow shortly afterwards, but then a sudden offer came my way: Brigadier Jacques was wanted in Bangkok immediately, a special Dakota was to take him, and I was told that if I liked I could go with him. I needed no second invitation. Within a few hours I was sitting in a Dakota containing only the brigadier, a Thai wireless operator and myself as passengers on the way to Rangoon. On landing there we were told that there was engine trouble and we would have to wait for two days, which gave us the chance to do some sightseeing. The most impressive feature was the large temple that stood on a small hill dominating the city and visible from almost any direction. Rangoon itself seemed largely unscathed, except for the bombing of the dock areas. Most of the main residential areas were on the outskirts, and we stayed in a house taken over by Force 136 in a row of neat white houses with red roofs that had their own gardens.

We flew on again in the Dakota and landed on the same strip from which I had been evacuated. We were met by Hudson, who had arranged for the brigadier to be flown on to Bangkok. Then Hudson and I flew on together to Non Han; from there we contacted the governor of Khon Kaen by telephone to ask him where Pluto was. Later in the day a car arrived with a Thai Army major, who had orders to take me to Pluto. We set off for Khon Kaen, but by chance met Pluto on the way and had a happy reunion. He told me that Kemp and Winn had dropped successfully the day before, so we decided to join them as soon as possible. We drove to Phannikhom, where we found Gunner, Chat and Pun all looking well and in good spirits.

We stayed the night at Phannikhom and the next day Kong arrived in a truck with Kemp, Winn, Spider (Lawson's codename) and Toy. It was Kemp's birthday, an excuse for Pluto to arrange a big party at which Kemp and Winn had their first experience of the *ramwong*, the local Thai dance, which by now I had a vague idea how to perform. The evening was exceedingly festive. We all went to bed the worse for wear.

Pluto and I had already discussed Kemp's and Winn's future areas of operation. With the situation changing so rapidly, it was not easy to decide where they would be most profitably employed. Candle area covered a vast expanse of territory. We knew that the Japanese now had garrisons at Ubon, Nong Khai, Udon, Sakon Nakhon and Mukdahan, with smaller detachments on the various roads between these places. The Thai Army, on whom we knew we could rely, also had its own garrisons in the area. Korat, situated at a point where Candle and Coupling areas joined, held the biggest Thai garrison, both army and air force; but some time ago I had agreed that Korat should be the responsibility of Hudson, for our mutual convenience. We knew that an armistice had been signed, but not if the Japanese had accepted the terms of surrender. When they did, the first priority would be the PoW camps and the second the disarming of the Japanese. The only known PoW camp in the Candle area was at Ubon, which also contained the largest Japanese and Thai garrisons. I decided to make this place my responsibility. I allotted the north-east area of Candle to Kemp, with his HQ at Nakhon Phanom, and the north-west area to Winn, with his HQ at Nong Khai. Both these towns were on the Mekong, with fair-sized towns on the opposite banks – Vientiane opposite Nong Khai and Thakhek opposite Nakhon Phanom. I wanted to keep Kemp and Winn to contact any French Force 136 officers in French Indo-China, as it was rumoured that there were a number of civilian internees on their side of the river.

My orders to Kemp and Winn were very vague, as were my own from Calcutta, for nobody knew what the Japanese reactions would be, or whether they would obey orders to cease fire. Nor did we know how they would react to solitary British officers like us: they might treat us correctly, or shoot us out of hand. On one point our instructions were firm. We were to remain underground until the receipt of the codeword 'Goldfish', when we could make our presence known to the Japanese, calling on them to surrender and ordering them to treat all PoWs with utmost care and attention, until we could take over the camps and arrange their repatriation.

Luckily Pluto had already summoned the governors of Sakon Nakhon, Nakhon Phanom and Nong Khai to a meeting, and I was able to introduce them to Kemp and Winn, who later left with their respective governors. Winn had Spider and his wireless set, but Kemp was still without a wireless, though Calcutta had promised to send him the next one available. However, I could keep in touch with Kemp by courier, because the distance by main road from Nakhon Phanom to Ubon was only about 170 miles – a short day's journey by car, providing the ferry was functioning across a river that ran into the Mekong.

The same day that Kemp and Winn left I drove to Sakon Nakhon down one of those straight and dusty laterite roads that we had throughout the Candle area. Driving could become very boring after a time, with scarcely any change in the scenery for hundreds of miles, though this time the monotony was broken by several lorryloads of Japanese soldiers. I made no attempt to conceal myself; but if they saw me their blank and impassive faces showed no signs of it.

My plan was to get to Ubon as soon as possible and after a good dinner with Pluto and his wife we pushed on to Mukdahan. The *amphur*, an official corresponding to a sheriff, was waiting for us on the road outside Mukdahan with the information that there were two Japanese battalions in the town. Furthermore the colonel in charge had approached him to say that he would like to surrender to the British officer whom he had been chasing for the past six months. Much as I should have liked to meet my ex-adversaries, I had to refuse. The codeword 'Goldfish' had not yet been received.

After staying the night with the *amphur* we continued south, passing long columns of Japanese marching dejectedly towards Ubon. We went into some Thai barracks at Yasatorn where I met Major Chris Blathwayt, who was one of Hudson's Force 136 officers from the Coupling area. He had been sent over with offers of help, for Hudson had no PoW camp in his area. We discussed plans for contacting the PoW camp at Ubon, and then drove to the Thai barracks

[153]

at Ubon, where it had been arranged for us to stay and make our HQ.

My first object was to get a letter into the PoW camp. This I did through Colonel Prom Pot, the helpful Thai garrison commander. I addressed my letter to 'The Senior British Officer'. In it I asked for details which would enable me to give immediate help when I was allowed to make open contact with the camp.

I received a reply written on a scrap of paper, which was all the PoWs had as the Japanese forbade the use of writing materials. It was written in tabulated form in answer to my queries.

Camp Strength	British 1,458
	Dutch 1,472
	Australian 101
	U.S.A. 4
	Total 3,035
Requirements	Clothing etc. 4,000 blankets;
	3,000 prs of shorts;
	3,000 shirts
	4,000 prs of boots;
	10,000 razor blades;
	3,000 razor blade holders;
	6 open razors.
Medical	50,000 Atabrine tablets;
	500 GMS (1lb) Yatren;
	100 ampules of Ephedrine (asthma);
Food	500 tins of milk;
	cigarettes and tobacco.
Health of Camp	Good in general;
	Approximately 20 stretcher cases;
	Approximately 300 sitting cases.

At the end of the letter he added: 'Japanese still here. All hoping to welcome you very soon.' It was signed in the official Army manner:

I am your obedient servant,

E.A. SMYTH
Major, R.A.M.C.
S.M.O., P.o.W. Camp, Ubon

I had asked Colonel Prom Pot if he could arrange for me to meet a British PoW officer the next day. He replied that he would try but it would be tricky, for the PoWs were still under Japanese guard. As I was still 'underground' he had to make sure that the Japanese escort did not see me. His plan succeeded, however, for the next day he sent for three PoWs on some pretext and they were brought under escort to the officers' mess of his barracks. I was living in a room on the top floor of the officers' mess, and from my window I saw the three PoWs being escorted by Japanese. They were shown into a room downstairs and deliberately kept waiting by the colonel. During the wait it was arranged for each one to go to the lavatory, a Thai officer firmly telling the Japanese soldiers he would escort them. The Japanese remained behind and the Thai officer brought each prisoner in turn up to my room.

They were Major E. A. Smyth, RAMC, Captain L. D. Stone, RAMC and Regimental Sergeant-Major A. M. McTavish of the Argyll and Sutherland Highlanders. It was a great moment for all of us – I was the first British officer from the outside world that they had seen for three and a half years, while they were the first PoWs with whom I had made direct contact. In the short time available we exchanged news and I promised all possible help in getting the supplies that they needed as soon as I could. But I had to tell them I was still restricted because I had not yet received 'Goldfish'. Smyth told me that there were thirty medical officers in Ubon, but all the other officers were in separate camps. As soon as they had gone, I got Gunner, who was with me, to send a detailed signal to Calcutta concerning the PoW camp and its requirements. Then, the same day, we heard that the Japanese had accepted the terms of surrender. We waited in vain for 'Goldfish', increasingly frustrated. The sooner we could openly declare ourselves to the Japanese the better.

Calcutta had signalled that a Dakota was arriving at Ban Han with a jeep for me on board. This was the first transport to land at Ban Han, so I asked Pluto to drive me there. On the way we passed numbers of Japanese. I made no attempt to hide as we drove by, and quite a few of them rather surprisingly saluted – perhaps more in honour of Pluto's smart car rather than in any deference to me. The only time I tried to conceal myself was when we approached the ferry, where we saw six Japanese lorries full of soldiers queuing up to cross. Pluto stopped the car about 200 yards from the ferry and made me get down on the floor in the back. He covered me with a blanket, on top of which he put some baskets of fruit and a very smelly basket of fish. He then drove to the front of the queue, where the ferryman, who was incidentally one of our guerrillas, embarked us in front of the Japanese. The ferry was very small and only carried one car at a time. To my dismay about twenty Japanese joined us, sitting on the running boards and mudguards of our car while I cowered under the blanket inside, fortunately undetected; but I was very relieved when we drove off the ferry and I could surface.

I dined with Kemp at Nakhon Phanom, exchanged news, and drove on to Ban Han. Kong, who had been left there with his wireless to receive aircraft, told me that a signal had come saying the aircraft had been cancelled. There was therefore nothing for it but to drive another monotonous 200 miles back to Ubon in a bad temper. On the way Pluto crashed into a water buffalo and killed it, with the result that we were drawn into an argument about compensation with the villagers who owned the animal. Later I dropped Pluto, who was going to reorganise the dispositions of his guerrillas. A large number had been concentrated in the jungle near the PoW camp to give help if necessary.

The following day a party of British officers arrived at Ubon, under command of Lieutenant-Colonel Philip Toosey, RA. They had all been PoWs and belonged to the same units as the POWs in Ubon, where up to now there had only been medical officers. Now the troops there were going to be commanded by their own unit officers again. Meanwhile for me the situation was getting ridiculous. Colonel Toosey and all his officers were armed and had complete freedom of movement, while I was still compelled to remain underground until I received the codeword It was two more days before the signal at last arrived. From that moment I could consider the war officially ended and regard myself as a normal officer again.

The morning after we received 'Goldfish' Hudson arrived fron Korat. He brought with him Major Alec Griswold, a very agreeable American from the OSS, and we drove together to the PoW camp. At Toosey's request our first action was to attend a parade in which all the PoWs, except those who were sick, were lined up on the camp parade ground. Their dress was makeshift. They had an assortment of hats, the commonest of which were of straw, home-made; they had no shirts, but wore either a tattered pair of shorts or a 'ball-bag', which was a piece of cloth tied with a string to cover their private parts; and their feet were either bare or in home-made clogs. Some of them had sold clothes to raise money to buy food.

As we came on parade Toosey called the men to attention. The Japanese flag was hauled down from the flagpole and a Union Jack, which had been kept concealed by one of the prisoners in the camp throughout the war, was hoisted in its place. As they sang the National Anthem, standing proud and erect, I had great difficulty in holding back my tears. This was the official liberation of the camp. The guards had withdrawn to their quarters.

The morale of the PoWs was very high after the years of hardship they had suffered. Toosey addressed the parade and the men were dismissed. They crowded round us, shaking us by the hand and asking innumerable questions about the war and the outside world. They had seen no newspapers, heard no news and had no letters from home. There was so much they wanted to know that I returned to the camp in the evening and went on the stage at the camp theatre, when questions were fired at me for about two hours on end.

The camp was situated on the Ubon-Mukdahan road at kilometre 9 north of Ubon. It was surrounded by two high bamboo fences, usually patrolled by guards. In the camp were a number of long huts built of bamboo, with atap roofs and bamboo matting sides. Two long rows of sleeping platforms ran the length of the inside of each hut, with a narrow passage down the middle. The men slept shoulder to shoulder on the platforms, about six or seven men to four yards, with no form of bedding but plenty of bed bugs. Each hut had up to 150 men in it and was about 50 yards long. There had been some very clever improvisation by the PoWs, often with the use of bamboo, and I was very impressed by the bamboo pumps with which they could draw water out of the ground. The camp hospital was full, the majority being dysentery cases, though I was told that malaria was the commonest disease.

On the very first day two Liberators dropped supplies on the Thai barracks, consisting of blankets, clothes, toilet sets and cigarettes for the newly freed prisoners. The following day two more Liberators came, dropping medical supplies and two medical officers and two sergeants. They formed an administrative team from RAPWI (Relief of Allied Prisoners of War and Internees), an organisation for the repatriation of PoWs. They were an enormous help, not only to the

PoWs but to me, for they took a lot of work off my shoulders at a moment when I was very hard pressed.

I was trying to cope with three different tasks, all urgent, with few resources at my disposal: first, the repatriation of the PoWs; secondly, the disarming of all the Japanese in the area; and thirdly, the evacuation of French civilian refugees from French Indo-China. I might one day be working in the PoW camp, the next driving off to see Kemp or Winn and dealing with their problems in neighbouring French Indo-China, the next taking over arms and equipment from a Japanese unit.

On the first day, after the parade, I sent for Major Cheda, the former camp commandant, who took me to his office to discuss various problems. The first thing he did on entering the office was to offer me a State Express cigarette out of a packet which had obviously come from the Red Cross supplies. I refused. I had already discovered that the Japanese had used all the Red Cross supplies, whether medical or welfare, for themselves. When I asked what had happened to the mail for the PoWs, Cheda blandly offered to hand it all over to me. He took me to a room full of letters – the POWs had received nothing for months, yet their mail had been in the camp all the time, withheld by the Japanese. It was a despicable performance.

The camp guards, apart from the officers, were Koreans and many PoWs told me that they were more brutal than the Japanese. They had subjected the prisoners to forms of punishment that may have appeared normal to them but were barbaric by Western standards – frequent beatings with bamboos and floggings; having to stand to attention for hours on end naked in the sun; holding a heavy object above the head until you dropped unconscious; being tied up to poles or trees for long periods in cramped and unnatural positions. All these were common occurrences. There were also many worse crimes alleged, such as where men had been executed or disappeared under mysterious circumstances. One case was reported to me of a British soldier being murdered by being buried alive in a deep trench latrine. All these crimes had to be investigated, and later many of the culprits were tried before a war crimes court.

The worst offenders were known to the PoWs by nicknames such as 'Efficiency', 'Squint Eyes' and 'Joe Penner', and these were amongst the first to be arrested as war criminals and sent to Bangkok under escort. It said much for the discipline and self-restraint of the

PoWs that they did not take the law into their own hands and carry out summary justice. To be fair, however, the guards were not all bad; indeed a few went out of their way to help the POWs – two in particular were commended to me, one known as 'Russian Joe' and the other as 'Take It Easy'.

Under Colonel Toosey and his second-in-command, Major Reggie Lees of the Gordons, with the excellent Sergeant-Major McTavish in support, the camp was soon running very smoothly, and the PoWs were usefully employed or entertained until the day of their departure. I had moved my HQ from the Thai barracks to Ubon airfield, nearer the camp and more suitable for receiving supply drops. From then on supplies dropped at the airfield were received by the PoWs themselves, who collected them and drove them back to the camp.

I was allotted a good house at the edge of the airfield, and to my own staff of Gunner, Kong, Chat and Pun I added three more from the PoWs. These were Sergeant Neave of the Gordons, who helped Gunner with all the extra cipher work and did a lot of clerical work for me; Corporal Phillips, RASC, who became my driver mechanic and helped keep the various Japanese staff cars on the road by his skills of improvisation; and Sergeant Thomas, RAOC, a fluent Japanese-speaker who became my interpreter. He had been the camp interpreter and had suffered many humiliations at the hands of the Japanese, not only because his mother was a Japanese, but because interpreters were always used by spokesmen making complaints and were frequently beaten as a result.

These three men volunteered to stay behind with me after the rest of the PoWs had been evacuated – a most unselfish offer, which I accepted as they were invaluable. I think they enjoyed their new roles, not only as a change from PoW life, but because we lived a very unmilitary and happy-go-lucky existence, with plenty to do. They remained with me until my final return to Bangkok two months later.

Some entertainments were organised by outsiders for the PoWs, others they arranged themselves. Though still living in the camp, they were free to go out when they wished. I was very surprised to see so many of them fraternising with their Korean guards, and thought the British soldier must have a very forgiving nature. In the camp there were concerts and sports meetings, the governor of

Ubon organised some pony racing, followed by tea for everyone, and on the final day the whole camp was given a dinner by the Thai Army.

A number of parties were also given for the officers by the governor, the Thai Army officers, and other officials; and in return the officers invited them to entertainments in the camp. The party I enjoyed most was given by Pluto to celebrate the news that he and Cato had been made ministers in the new government headed by Ruth, and it was also to celebrate my recent promotion to lieutenant-colonel. We were delighted to hear that Marshal Pibul was now under arrest and awaiting trial as a war criminal. As the chief Thai collaborator he had condoned the Japanese atrocities on their prisoners.

The behaviour of the British troops from the camp was of a high standard, but that of some of the Australians very bad. After the Thai chief of police had been plagued with incidents – drunkenness, housebreaking and rape being the most frequent – Captain Tom Phillips of the Norfolk Regiment was appointed town major and came to live in my house. I was very relieved that the Australians were among the first to be repatriated. In fact the four Americans, all survivors of the USS *Houston*, were the first to go, followed by the Australians and 250 British three weeks later; the remainder of the British left a week later.

One big problem concerned sex. Many of the men were apparently worried that after three and a half years of celibacy they might have become impotent, and they hoped to disprove this before they returned home. (I suspect that the eagerness to test themselves out-weighed any genuine anxieties about their capabilities.) I consulted my friend the chief of police and we organised a system of brothels, several for the troops and one for the officers christened the 'Chinese Hotel'. It all worked well until the question of payment arose. Some of the Dutch officers had paid with the official requisition form, which they had filled in requisitioning a girl. The girls then came to me, asking me to redeem the forms! In the end I held a conference with the chief of police and a girl representing her colleagues, and we reached a very felicitous solution. I agreed to pay three panels of parachute to each girl for each performance. This probably saved a lot of money, for I had already sent 850 parachutes back to Bangkok by train and they never arrived. Presumably someone had made a good profit, for the black market value of a parachute was 2,000 ticals (about £24), and as a parachute had 28 panels this was almost a £1 per panel. I thought the parachutes were being better used to pay the girls than being sold on the Bangkok black market. For the record, I was told the results were quite satisfactory as far as the PoWs were concerned.

On 25 September 1945, twenty-six days after I had first entered the camp, all the British PoWs left for Bangkok by train. As they drove out of the camp all the camp guards, now disarmed, lined up at the gate and bowed at each lorry as it left. The PoWs were delighted and cheered them; I discovered later that the guards' gesture was completely spontaneous. Major Cheda had already been sent to Bangkok to await trial as a war criminal, accompanied by some of the Korean guards and Lieutenant Hoseda, who faced a murder charge.

I was very sorry to see so many newly made friends leave, but happy to think that they would soon be reunited with their families, thanks to the air ferry service operating from Bangkok to the United Kingdom. Meanwhile 1,500 Dutch still remained, and I maintained close contact with their commandant. The problems of repatriation were more difficult for these men, for apart from twenty-four Dutch officers the majority were Asian inhabitants of the Dutch East Indies with Dutch nationality. At that moment their country was in the throes of a civil war, and before they left I was ordered to re-equip them with Japanese weapons as it seemed likely they could get involved in still more fighting.

One of my first contacts in Ubon was a Chinese girl named Jin. Just before I had been burnt I was on my way south to Ubon, as Pluto had told me that one of his men had made contact with the PoWs in the camp. The contact was in fact Jin, for she had the contract for supplying the camp guards with ice and other supplies, and entered the camp every day. One day she passed a note to a PoW and later took out an answer, eventually becoming a regular courier carrying notes from the PoWs to Pluto's man. Quite what we could have done for them is open to question. I asked some of the prisoners if they would have escaped if I had guaranteed to get them out of the country, but they said 'No'. The Japanese had threatened to shoot ten prisoners for every one that escaped, and they would not have risked this.

Jin was very vivacious, intelligent and an astute businesswoman.

She spoke fair English and she was a wonderful intelligence agent, knowing exactly what was going on in both Thai and Japanese circles; she would even tell me which British officer slept with which girls in the Chinese Hotel. (The building was owned by her uncle, who, I suspected, took his cut out of the three parachute panels.)

I used to go to Jin's shop whenever I could spare the time, to have coffee with her and hear all the gossip. She was also invaluable out shopping, being a great one for getting a bargain, and she used to help the officers from the camp, and myself, over buying jewellery — rubies especially were common and cheap in Thailand. She was not an exceptional beauty, but she had a sister called Prapussorn who was lovely, as well as being an excellent seamstress. She made me several shirts and pyjamas from parachutes.

One of the more unpleasant jobs I had to undertake at Ubon was to condemn and destroy the Japanese army horses. They had already marched over 1,500 miles from China and were in a terrible condition, both from starvation and ill-treatment. I had Tom Phillips to help me, who had been a racehorse trainer in Norfolk before the war, and out of 1,200 horses we inspected, we condemned 700 to be shot; they were dying at the rate of about ten a day from starvation and had only their droppings to eat. Some of the saddle sores were so big and deep that I could put my fist in them; I had never in my life seen such ill-treated horses.

Tom Phillips and I shot a great many, and I was often sick afterwards. The first day a deputation of Thais formed up and asked me not to kill the horses because it was against their Buddhist principles. I replied that it was a duty I very much regretted. I noticed plenty of Thais around afterwards removing their horses' tails, before they were buried in huge pits dug by Japanese working parties.

Word reached me after the first day that the Japanese were saying that I had shot the horses for motives of revenge, because we had won the war. I therefore had them all paraded and through Sergeant Thomas told them that I was not shooting the horses because we had won the war, but to put them out of their misery after the ill-treatment to which they had been subjected.

I did not understand the Japanese mentality, for when leading their horses up to be shot, many of the men were in tears, and after they were shot they would take off their caps and bow at the graves, and even put flowers on them. A signal came from Bangkok suggesting that I was killing these animals unnecessarily, and that a veterinary officer would be coming to Ubon to inspect those that remained. A few days later a very fine-looking Indian colonel arrived and the Japanese paraded the remaining 500 that we had not shot for his inspection. He promptly condemned a further 400 to death.

Tom Phillips had left when I still had to shoot these 400 horses, and so I gave some of the Japanese vets back their pistols and told them to help me. After I discovered that they were taking up to three shots per horse, and found that some of the horses were being buried still alive, I stopped them and had to deal with the rest myself. Out of the 700 horses that I shot personally with an American .30 carbine with a folding butt which I used like a pistol, I had to give only one horse a second bullet. This was a horse that I shot in the correct place – at the centre of the X drawn from the ears to the eyes – but it trotted off apparently uninjured. When it was caught and brought back again, it was found to have a neat bullet hole in exactly the right place. It did not appear to be either frightened or in pain, or upset in any way. I fired the next shot downwards into its skull from above its ears and it dropped dead – I can only think it had a freak skull. I was very thankful when this distressing job was over.

13
Incidents in Thailand and French Indo-China

The disarming of the Japanese took up a lot of time, though there were few difficulties, owing to the rigid Japanese obedience to orders. At the end of the hostilities there were some 112,500 Japanese troops in Thailand, of whom 9,200 were in the Candle area, mostly from 22 Division of the Imperial Japanese Army. Those in Candle area were ordered to concentrate at Ubon, under the command of Lieutenant-General Hirata, the divisional commander.

My first contact with the Japanese, apart from Major Cheda, was with Colonel Hosumi, commander of the Ubon garrison. I went to see him, accompanied by Colonel Toosey. His head was bandaged, seeming to confirm a report that I had heard from a friend in the Thai police, who said that he had been attacked by one of his own soldiers in a drunken brawl in a brothel. He was somewhat truculent at first, and at one stage I drew my pistol and placed it on the table in front of me. His response to this threat was to produce a bottle of Japanese whisky and some salted prawns.

From then on things went smoothly and arrangements were made for the Japanese chief of staff to report to my house daily, where a short conference was held at which I issued orders. A British general, Major-General Geoffrey Evans, had arrived in Bangkok to command all the British troops in Thailand, who were only a small token force. He was accompanied by a large staff of officers, many of them members of various missions such as RAPWI.

General Evans gave his orders to the Japanese Lieutenant-General Hamada, who committed hara-kiri after ordering the surrender of all the Japanese troops. The Japanese were to be concentrated in eleven areas in Thailand, of which Ubon was one. They accordingly assembled in one large camp they had built for themselves on the road north of the town. They were also ordered to hand over all their arms, in the presence of a British officer, to the Thai Army, who would take them on their charge and store them in the Thai barracks awaiting orders as to their disposal.

To help me in dealing with this matter at Ubon, an officer was sent up from Bangkok belonging to 207 Military Mission, which was responsible for supervising the disarming of the Japanese. This was a very amusing but eccentric officer, Major John Hedley. He was an Old Etonian, a good deal older than myself, very tall, and weather-beaten from many years of service with the Bombay-Burma Trading Company before the war. He had distinguished himself with the Chindits.

He wore an Australian Terai hat with a chinstrap, carried a rifle slung over his shoulder on all occasions, and proceeded at a very fast walk wherever he went, refusing with disdain any offers of a lift in a car. My staff, with little respect for rank, referred to him as 'The Mad Major'. He was a very great help, except in his dealing with the Thais, with whom he had little patience and whom he used to curse heartily. I was continually getting complaints from Colonel Prom Pot or the chief of police that Hedley had insulted their officers. My profuse apologies usually resolved the matter.

After the formal disarming the Japanese were allowed to keep only a very limited number of weapons, chiefly for the use of their guards on, for instance, fuel dumps. Theft by the Thais was a recurrent problem, but at Ubon it ceased after a Japanese sentry shot and killed a Thai who was stealing petrol. The governor expressed himself delighted.

I had no compunction about equipping myself, my staff and my friends at Japanese expense – looting has always been a victor's privilege, though not officially allowed by British Army Regulations. I had heard that General Hirata had a huge Straight Eight Cadillac saloon and this was produced forthwith for my personal use. The impressive-looking machine had a slight snag, in that its self-starter did not function and there was no starting handle. The only means of starting it was by pushing, and this required at least eight men. Until I got a new self-starter, the problem was overcome by having squads of eight Japanese soldiers stationed at the various places in Ubon I normally visited during the day or night; so whenever I required a start, a 'pushing party' was on hand. Another good car I spotted was a Chevrolet 1942 drophead coupé, whose hood went up and down

[165]

automatically at the press of a button. I gave it to Kemp. He wrecked it shortly afterwards, nearly killing himself in the process.

I equipped many of my friends, and myself, with excellent binoculars. To others I gave pistols. But swords were the most popular gifts; I collected fifty from the Thai barracks and gave them to the officers in the camp. They were not valuable family or ceremonial swords, and we strongly suspected the Japanese of destroying or hiding these. Even so, American soldiers in Calcutta were reputed to be paying £50 for an ordinary one.

Thanks to the help that I was receiving from Hedley, I was able to leave Ubon at intervals to visit the rest of my area. On one occasion I drove to Mukdahan to make arrangements with the Japanese colonel there for a number of boats to be handed over that their troops had been using as ferries across the Mekong. The interview was hilarious. The colonel started by telling me he was glad the war was over as his piles were getting very bad, and we were continually interrupted by a lizard of the gecko family which ran around the walls and ceiling emitting rude noises (best described by the British troops who christened it the 'fuck you' lizard). The noise, or rude remarks, infuriated the Japanese colonel. He summoned half a dozen orderlies who rushed around the room with fly-swats trying to swat the gecko. They were too short to reach him, however, and he stayed on the ceiling cursing us to the end of our interview. We made arrangements for the ships to be handed over, but before the date agreed they had been hijacked by the Annamite Communists and taken back across the river to Savannakhet.

On 22 October all the Japanese in the area were concentrated and ready to be counted – our HQ in Bangkok had ordered a physical count to be made by a British officer. Hedley and I went to the camp, where we had arranged for the men to be drawn up in blocks of a hundred, in lines ten men long and ten men deep. The Japanese officers took such a long time in shouting out their orders and reporting to me that we evolved a system whereby I stood in front of each unit taking the salute while Hedley, at his usual high speed, strode down all the lines counting them. We counted 8,000 in under an hour. After the parade we went to the hospital lines to count the sick, and even the worst cases were standing to attention supported by their comrades. I thought this was carrying discipline a bit too far and ordered them back to their beds, which seemed to surprise them.

[166]

The camp guards were dealt with early on, but there were other Japanese who were wanted for trial as war criminals. A number of prisoners had been badly beaten by Japanese soldiers when working on a landing strip near Ubon that the PoWs had, contrary to the Geneva Convention, been forced to build. The Dutch especially had suffered, so I ordered a parade of the 300 Japanese who belonged to the unit concerned. The Dutch officers walked slowly down the lines pointing out the offenders. As they were identified I ordered them to be marched off the parade, escorted by two Thai policemen, and lodged in the local jail. The Japanese officer in charge of these men walked behind me shouting abuse at each man as he was arrested. When all the men had been picked out, I turned to him and said 'Major Sensui, you are the last, hand over your sword.' His face fell, and he protested that he had been ordered to beat the prisoners. In spite of all his pleas he was marched off, much to the delight of the Dutch, for he had been quite the worst offender.

The most embarrassing of my prisoners were the Japanese comfort girls. One day fifteen of them turned up at my house and asked to speak to me. They were not particularly attractive, and I discovered they were Koreans not Japanese. They spun me a long story to the effect that they were being held by the Japanese against their will, and wanted to be taken over by me. I took the matter up with the Japanese, who said that they had paid the girls 10,000 ticals (or bahts) for services that they did not consider had been rendered, and they were therefore reluctant to let them go. I accordingly wrote out a large official paper in which I declared the debt null and void and ordered the girls to be released. From then on they were housed in the town, though I had to put a Thai police guard on them for their own safety. They seemed very grateful and offered me their services. Sometimes they came over to my house in the evenings and would sing when I was entertaining officers from the camp to dinner. I still have a souvenir of them, for before all the Korean guards left Ubon an official photograph was taken. I sat in the centre of a large group, flanked by Thai policeman and Buddhist priests, with several rows of Korean guards standing behind, and seated at my feet a row of comfort girls.

While there was plenty to do at Ubon, I could not neglect the rest of the Candle area, for Kemp and Winn had problems on the other side of the river. French Force 136 officers were operating there against heavy odds, for the Japanese had armed the Annamites in their initial fight against the French. Although the area was in the province of Laos, the majority of the population in the towns were Annamites. The Laos were loyal to the French, but the Annamites had the declared intention of driving the French out of Indo-China; it was for this reason that they had openly collaborated with the Japanese. China, their source of Communist influence, was also arming them. More extraordinary still, they were at the same time being supplied with arms by the American OSS, who were operating from Chungking and dropping officers to them from there.

Kemp was already in touch with two French parachutists who had been dropped near Thakhek after the Japanese surrender. One was Lieutenant François Klotz, the other his female wireless operator – Edith Fournier. They both belonged to the organisation called 'E' Force, concerned with the repatriation of prisoners, whose HQ worked closely with Force 136. I met both at Nakhon Phanom after receiving a signal from Kemp asking me to go and see him. Klotz was a young man, who spoke slow but excellent English. Edith Fournier was about the same age, capable and tough in her jungle-green battledress. She spoke only a little English, but my French was adequate.

As soon as I arrived I held a conference with Kemp and Klotz. I asked about the situation across the river, for Thakhek, in French Indo-China, was separated from Nakhon Phanom, in Thailand, by the Mekong river, there three-quarters of a mile wide. 'The Japs still have a company in Thakhek,' replied Kemp, and Klotz added, 'There are a number of French civilians there too.' 'Where are the civilians?' I asked, 'and who are they?' Klotz told me that they were all held prisoner by the Annamites, who claimed them as hostages against the French. Most of them were women and children. When I asked what the Japs were doing about it, Kemp replied that all these French were held as civilian internees by the Japs up to the time of the surrender, upon which they withdrew their guards and the wretched internees were promptly re-arrested by the Annamites, who had put their own guards on them. 'The Japs don't appear interested in them any more.' 'What happened when you were last in Thakhek?' I asked Klotz. 'The Annamites gave us a pretty hostile reception,' he replied; they certainly could not have remained in the town without trouble starting. 'I asked François to make his HQ with me here,' Kemp added. 'It wasn't safe for him to remain in Thakhek.'

[168]

From what they told me, it was clearly necessary for me to cross the river and investigate, and so the next day Kemp, Klotz, and I, together with the governor of Nakhon Phanom, embarked in the governor's launch and crossed the wide, fast-flowing river – in flood after the monsoons. A local official met us and took us to the convent where the civilians were interned under Annamite guards. There we found eighteen French women, five men, one of whom was a priest, fourteen French children, and five French nuns in charge of forty Eurasian orphans. I asked the guards who was in charge, and we were taken to a group who called themselves the 'Delegates'. We argued with them for over two hours, threatening and cajoling until they finally reluctantly agreed that the whole party could be evacuated by us across the river to Nakhon Phanom.

These Annamites were distinctly menacing and had already threatened the French, who appeared to be vastly relieved at the results of our talks and had started to pack their belongings. As they were doing so, a Japanese patrol appeared, very rough and truculent, some of them, I suspect, drunk. Pushing Kemp, Klotz, and myself in front of them, they motioned us to move off. When we stopped to remonstrate, we were prodded in the backs with bayonets. Though we still had pistols in our holsters, we were in no position to argue with a larger number of Japanese with their rifles at the ready. We were thus ignominiously marched down several streets in front of the gloating Annamites till we came to a house by the river. There we were pushed upstairs into a room where a Japanese officer was seated at a desk, which appeared to be the only furniture in the room.

He was a good-looking man, and behaved very correctly, introducing himself as Captain Nakajima. He said at once that he could not let us evacuate the French unless he had orders from his superiors. It was obvious that he had been tipped off by the Annamites, otherwise he could not have known of our intentions. I replied with considerable heat, starting with a strong protest at our treatment by the patrol, for which he apologised; but he was adamant about releasing the French. I did, however, persuade him to replace the Annamite guards with Japanese, and told him that under the terms of the armistice he was responsible for the safety of internees. I added that I would go to Ubon and return with superior orders for him. After this interview we left, this time without an escort.

The French were filled with dismay at this turn of events and some of the women became hysterical. To give them some confidence, I left Kemp with them for the night. Before leaving I checked that the Japanese had replaced the Annamite guards, and while doing so I found a Japanese soldier trying to steal the watch off a nun. I went up to him and swung him roughly round, whereupon he drew his bayonet and made a lunge at me. Luckily he was drunk and I was able to seize his arm and shout for the guard commander. A Japanese corporal came running up, grabbed the guard and started to slap his face, while I went off to report the incident to the Japanese captain. He returned with me, and the drunk soldier was brought up to him, whereupon his well-bloodied face was slapped again.

I returned to Nakhon Phanom with Klotz after witnessing this interesting piece of Japanese discipline, and drove as fast as possible towards Ubon; but about five miles short of Ubon the track rod broke and the car ran off the road into a ditch. The Thai sitting beside me was knocked out, cutting his head quite badly on the windscreen. We were unhurt and, being near the PoW camp, quickly found help.

I went at once to Colonel Hosumi and told him that I wanted immediate orders sent to Thakhek stating that the French civilians were to be evacuated at once. At his suggestion he not only wrote out the order straight away but sent a Japanese officer to accompany me to ensure that it was carried out. This officer was the notorious Lieutenant Hoseda who, so my interpreter Sergeant Thomas told me, had murdered a British PoW. He was arrested and charged with this crime later.

I drove the 170 miles back to Nakhon Phanom and crossed the river at Thakhek. We passed through a sullen-looking and scowling crowd of Annamites; they wore grey topees, some had a uniform shirt, and all carried rifles. I then found Captain Nakajima and gave him his orders, which Hoseda confirmed, telling him to have the streets cleared of all Annamites by the next day, when we would evacuate all the French. To this he agreed. I was relieved to find Kemp in the convent, not having had any incidents. I left Klotz in the convent for the night and returned to Kemp's HQ where I found Winn. We had been invited to a party given by the governor, where we enjoyed ourselves with plenty of good food, drink and attractive girls. I was presented to the local officials, one of whom was introduced as the 'Director of Humanity'. He turned out to be the schoolmaster.

Next day, taking Winn for support, we crossed the Mekong to Thakhek and found the streets deserted. The governor of Nakhon Phanom had been very efficient and his boat was at the jetty. The French and their charges, together with an immense amount of baggage, filed on board without incident and the boat chugged across the river. The governor had arranged to billet them in the local hospital and they were pathetically grateful. But for our intervention there was little doubt that the Communists would have murdered them in due course. For many years after the war I received news at Christmas from Soeur Marie Céleste, the Superior of the convent at Thakhek, who was in charge of all the orphans.

That evening Kemp arrived with three French civilians, one a young girl who had been shot in the stomach by a Japanese soldier. Kemp said that there were reports of more civilians at the tin mines near Boneng, about twenty miles away. We decided to go there the next day, this time with an escort. I went to Captain Nakajima, who, since he had been told by Hoseda to take orders from me, had been most cooperative. He provided me with a platoon, including a machine-gun, under a lieutenant, and we drove off from Thakhek in a convoy for the fifty-mile journey to Boneng.

The road to Boneng was made of the same red laterite as the roads in Thailand. For most of the journey it ran through forests of giant trees and creepers, with occasional clearings where paddy fields indicated that we were approaching a village. These clearings were a reminder that we were following a deep valley, flanked on both sides by craggy mountains, their tops wreathed in cloud, that rose steeply out of the forest on each side. There was a certain austere beauty in the colours and the shifting light, but to me the whole area felt sinister and oppressive.

For about the first half an hour we met no vehicles; then we saw several lorries filled with armed Annamites who were heading towards Thakhek. They were flying the red flag on each lorry, and from the clenched fist salutes that they gave us it was not very difficult to determine their political affiliations. Then, on arrival at the outskirts of Boneng, we came upon an excited group of Annamites. I stopped the car and got out. 'What's going on?' I asked them in French. 'French bandits are attacking our village,' one of them replied. Certainly a battle of some sort was in progress. The cracks of rifle shots and the occasional stutter of a machine-gun sounded quite close, so I ordered the Japanese soldiers out of their lorries and told their officer to deploy them for action.

With the Japanese as escorts, Kemp, Klotz and I strode down the main road leading to the centre of the village, from where the firing seemed to be coming, ready for action but totally ignorant as to who was fighting whom and whose side we should take. For my own part, it seemed to me that the best for all concerned would be for the fighting to stop.

On reaching the centre of the village I saw a lot of Annamites – well over a hundred – shooting at the village school house. I went over to their leader and asked him what his men where shooting at. He replied that a French robber band was in the school and shooting at everyone on sight. This did not ring very true as the house seemed to be completely surrounded by Annamites who were keeping up a steady fire on the building. I ordered him to cease fire at once and told him that I would go and speak to the French in the school. He seemed reluctant to obey. He walked over to a group of his companions and for some minutes they engaged in a animated discussion about the merits of my demand. While they were doing this my Japanese escort closed in on them, looking very tough and aggressive. The Ammanites obviously found this persuasive because the leader came across to me indicating they would comply. I told him to withdraw his men out of range of the school. While he was doing so it dawned on me that I had no option, without losing face, but to march up to the school and talk to whoever was in it. The shots coming from the school had stopped since the Annamites had withdrawn, but nobody had shown themselves and there was nothing to indicate who the occupants were.

Telling Kemp, Klotz and the Japanese to stay where they were, I slowly walked down the road to the school, stopping at intervals and shouting 'Ne tirez pas, je suis officier anglais.' There was no response whatever. I continued in the direction of the school, not at all reassured to pass the bodies of two dead Annamites lying in the road. I shouted again near the school, but still got no reply. Slowly I started to climb the steps to the front door. On reaching the barricade in front of it I saw a number of men crouched behind, covering me with their rifles. Then at last someone spoke and a young officer in jungle green battledress with a French lieutenant's badges got up and introduced himself as Lieutenant Gausset. He had one Eurasian sergeant and ten Lao soldiers with him, two of whom were wounded.

When I asked him what was going on he replied that he was a Force 136 officer and had entered the town because he had heard that the Annamites had taken some French civilian hostages. As soon as they arrived they had been fired on by the Annamites and forced to shelter in the school. We appeared to have come just in time, for they were surrounded and outnumbered by the Annamites and had little chance of getting out of their predicament alive. They had done well to kill four Annamites for only two of their men wounded.

I took Gausset back to where the others were waiting, summoned the Annamite leaders and held a conference, at which the Annamites kept on holding up the dead bodies, one a very bloody one, for my inspection. I told them to take them away. In the end we came to a satisfactory solution. Gausset and his nine fit soldiers returned to where they wanted to be in the mountains, while we took the wounded soldiers with us. In addition I made the Annamites hand over all seven French civilians. One was a man, two were women, and four were children, all quite terrified. Then, leaving the Annamite leaders looking very glum with their four bodies, we drove back to Thakhek well pleased with our results.

Two weeks later I was in Mukdahan, taking over a number of ships on the Mekong river from the Japanese, when a telegram came from Kemp saying that Klotz had been murdered and would I come at once. I drove off immediately and arrived at Nakhon Phanom in time to meet a number of French women, many of them in tears, coming away from François Klotz's funeral. Kemp was with them, clearly under heavy strain. We both went back to his house where, speaking with great emotion, he told me the story.

The previous day he and François had crossed the Mekong to Thakhek in order to collect a car and drive out to see Tavernier about some medical supplies. 'Reece came with us.' I knew that Tavernier was one of the French Force 136 officers operating in the Thakhek area, but had not heard of Reece before, 'Who's Reece?' I asked; and Kemp replied, 'One of the officers with Banks.'

Major Banks and his mission were known to me. About two weeks previously they had been parachuted into Candle area without any reference to me and without my being officially informed. The mission consisted of a group of American officers and NCOs from the OSS based in China, and they had landed near Nong Khai. Winn had already reported to me on Banks's activities. Shortly after his arrival Banks had crossed the Mekong to Vientiane, where he had been extremely insulting to the French officers, whom he had attempted to order out of the town. Furthermore he had openly encouraged the Annamites against the French. I had already signalled to Calcutta complaining about his activities and had received a reply stating that he had no right to be in Siam, which came under SEAC (South East Asia Command), and they were taking the matter up with higher authority in SEAC. After fomenting trouble in Vientiane, Banks and his party had moved on to Thakhek, where he had announced to the Annamites that he intended to stop the 'French aggression' against them. He was now living in Thakhek in a house provided by Viet-Minh, the political organisation to which the Annamites belonged. Kemp had already met Banks and had given me his impressions of him, which were most unfavourable. He added that the other American officers were friendly, though somewhat overawed by Banks.

'We crossed in the governor's launch,' Kemp continued, 'and on reaching the Thakhek bank we were confronted by a platoon of armed Annamites.' As they disembarked, the leader, whom Kemp know as Delegate Tu, asked each of them his nationality. On being told he said 'The British and American officers can go – they are our allies – but the Frenchman remains our prisoner.' Kemp turned to Reece and said 'We can't leave Klotz here.' Then he told the Annamites they were all three allies, and all three stood together. 'Isn't that so?' he added, turning to Reece. Reece replied 'I guess we're neutral here', and sauntered off to prop himself against a nearby wall. Klotz and Kemp tried to walk back to the boat, but as they were doing so an Annamite crept up and shot Klotz in the back. Kemp dragged him back to the boat, where Klotz died in his arms. 'What did Reece do meanwhile?' I asked. 'Absolutely nothing,' Kemp replied, 'and he had been joined by some Americans in the meantime who also made no attempt to intervene.'

I was deeply upset by the death of François Klotz. He was one of the finest French officers that I had met, and he had become a friend of us all, especially of Kemp. I was horrified at the Americans' attitude and decided to cross the river to see Banks myself. I sent him a note to say I was coming and asked him to ensure that I had a safe welcome, for I had heard that the Annamites had posted notices in Thakhek stating that any French or British officers would be shot on sight. I told Kemp he mustn't come with me, as the Annamites were especially after his blood, and set off across the river alone.

Banks met me at the top of the steps on the waterfront and gave me a most effusive welcome, full of condolences for the death of Klotz. I took an immediate dislike to him. He had shifty eyes and would not look me in the face; he was nothing like the high-grade American OSS officers whom I counted as friends. In my diary I described him as 'a nasty bit of work'. 'Why,' I asked him, 'are you working with the Annamites?' 'All I want to do, Colonel,' he replied, 'is to avoid bloodshed.' I put it to him that he seemed to be doing this by giving all his support to the Communists. 'What's more,' I went on, 'I understand that you refer to the French officers as "bandits".' He strongly denied this. He could hardly have known that I had, at that moment, a letter in my pocket that Klotz had given me: it was written by Banks to a French officer and he had used that very word. So I knew he was a liar too. I returned across the river and at once sent an urgent signal to our head office in Ceylon asking that the removal of Banks and his mission be requested at once at the highest level. I should add here that on other occasions I met several of the American officers attached to Banks's mission. They were perfectly agreeable officers of a good type, and I would in no way connect them with Banks's – or Reece's – behaviour.

At the time it seemed inconceivable to us that the Americans were prepared to support the Communists against their former French and British allies. We assumed that either they were so naive that they did not realise they were Communists – in spite of ample evidence from red stars and clenched fist salutes – or American policy was so anti-colonial that they were prepared to help so-called liberation groups of whatever political colour.

Many years later I read *OSS* by R. Harris Smith.* His chapter 9 is titled 'Save England's Asiatic Colonies' and brings out clearly the anti-British feeling among the OSS in South-East Asia, especially in regard to Thailand and Indo-China. There is little doubt that the

*Published 1972 by the University of California Press.

American anti-colonial policy of helping the nationalist movements was responsible for the arming and financing of the Viet-Minh. They certainly achieved their aim of getting the French expelled from Indo-China, and the Dutch from the East Indies, but at what a price; it was this policy that resulted in the war in Vietnam.

Banks may well have been obeying superior orders to sabotage the French and British Force 136 efforts, but to all of us at the time his behaviour was despicable. It was ironic that the Viet-Minh, the political organisation of these Annamites, murdered the senior OSS officer in Saigon not long after this incident.

Later on, supply drops of arms were made to Kemp for him to smuggle across the river to Lieutenant Tavernier, the French Force 136 officer operating on the Thakhek side of the river. Tavernier and his loyal Lao soldiers did very good work, on one occasion attacking a house that was an Annamite HQ and killing fifteen. Kemp did an excellent job during this arms smuggling, at great risk to his life, and it is to his credit that the Annamites made no less than four unsuccessful attempts to assassinate him.

Early in November I drove to Nong Khai to visit Winn. He too had been having trouble with the Annamites and a state verging on anarchy existed in Vientiane, on the opposite bank of the river. At that time it was occupied by Chinese troops, who tolerated the Annamite guerrillas, and French Force 136 officers and their Lao soldiers led a precarious existence among them all. The French commander was Commandant Fabre, who had been operating in the area for over a year and had a number of French officers and about 500 Lao guerrillas under his command. Winn had established a close liaison with him and was receiving arms drops on his behalf. Winn had already been ambushed by the Annamites four times, and on the last occasion his jeep had been fired on, run off the road, and wrecked; Winn had broken his wrist, Fabre his shoulder, and a Lao sergeant suffered a broken leg. They had lain in a ditch for over two hours while the Annamites shot at them. Fortunately for the injured men, the Annamites had been too cowardly to press home their attack and had made off when friendly Laos appeared on the scene.

I wanted to meet Fabre and the Chinese officer in command, so we crossed the river in a steamer. Our party consisted of myself, Winn, Kemp, Lieutenant Larroue – a French Force 136 officer – and my own staff as bodyguard. As soon as we disembarked on the

Vientiane bank there was not a sign of life and we walked down deserted streets for our first call on Fabre. He was tall and quiet, but clearly a sick man who needed a rest; the strain under which he had been living for the past year, together with the ill effects of malaria and dysentery, showed on his features. He was one of those tough soldiers who would never give in. He drove himself hard, but in setting a fine example his health suffered. He was most indignant at his treatment by the Chinese and told me the story of his first contacts with them.

After the Chinese had arrived in Vientiane they asked Fabre and his officers to dinner at the French Residency. They all arrived, to find the French flag flying and a guard of honour drawn up outside. They were politely shown into a room, where they were met by six Chinese soldiers armed with Tommy guns, who removed their pistols, equipment, money and watches. They were then told to leave town or they would be arrested. Eventually Fabre obtained permission from the Chinese to stay in town alone with a wireless operator, but had to send his team ten miles away, having been instructed by his HQ to avoid incidents with the Chinese.

I went on to see the Chinese colonel and spent three hours with him. He was politely non-cooperative; we left having achieved nothing in our discussions and I failed to make any of my points. To this day I have no idea as to what command these Chinese troops belonged.

On leaving the Chinese we were warned that the Annamites had laid an ambush for us. We accordingly returned to the Chinese HQ and asked the colonel for an escort, which he gave us. We then reached the boat without incident, only to find the captain and engineer had been arrested by the Annamites; and so we sent off a Chinese patrol to find them. The patrol duly returned with the captain and the engineer, who told us that they had been tied up and beaten, and warned never to help the French or British again.

We returned to Nong Khai for an evening's entertaining. A macabre incident occurred just after we had finished dinner. I had given a Japanese sword to Winn's first-rate boatman as a reward for the very good work he had done in gun-running for us. We had our brandy beside us, and had just lit our cigars, when he came into the room with his sword in his hand dripping blood. He told us he had found a robber in Winn's store and had cut off his head. We went to look. He had.

I had a number of meetings with the Chinese, twice at Pakse and several times at Savannakhet, which was on the Mekong opposite Mukdahan. I found them polite but uncooperative, probably because their sympathies were with the Annamites rather than the French. I always suspected, for instance, that the Chinese tipped off a notorious member of the pro-Japanese Indian National Army, Debnatt Das, who was wanted for three murders. We knew he was in hiding in Savannakhet, being sheltered by an Annamite leader, but he was warned we were looking for him and disappeared.

I had to go to Bangkok on one or two occasions, and my first trip there was memorable for the adventures in our aircraft. I had, for some time, had an aeroplane for my own personal use; it had been sent to me by Wing-Commander Manop Souriya, known to all his friends as 'Nobby', who was in command of the Thai Air Force at Korat. It was a Mitsubishi advanced trainer, which cruised comfortably at 150 mph but was very temperamental. It arrived with a pilot officer with the ominous name of Prang.

Kemp and I were collected from Nakhon Phanom for our trip to Bangkok. We flew without incident to Udon, met Winn there, and then took off again. We were flying at about 5,000 feet to avoid some high, forested mountains when the engine stopped. We began to lose height and Prang started some feverish pumping. The engine spluttered and restarted, ran for about three minutes and did the same thing again. This performance was repeated five times in all, and at the end our height had dropped to 200 feet and we were skimming the tops of the trees. Kemp and I looked at each other resignedly. The next time really meant a crash. Luckily the engine finally behaved itself and we landed at Korat with a following wind – Prang dared not risk the extra circuit – and with such a bump that a wheel came off and the aircraft was wrecked. Luckily we were unhurt.

Nobby, our most stalwart ally in Korat, gave us both stiff drinks, which we needed by now to give us courage for our next hop on to Bangkok. He had fixed us up with another aircraft, which got us there with no more scares. Nobby was a marvellous character. He had been educated at West Point and done an attachment in England with the RAF. He was ready to help all comers and, if he thought it necessary, would break red tape to do so.

On our way back from Bangkok, Nobby lent us another Mitsubishi, which was a low-wing monoplane. I piloted this myself, with Kemp as my passenger; having held a pilot's licence before the war, I thought I'd renew my touch. However, after leaving Korat we hit a vulture and I found that I could not control the aircraft properly because the ailerons were jammed. I returned to Korat and brought the machine in as best I could. We found that the bird had caused considerable damage. A three-foot length of the metal wing had been bashed in to a depth of about nine inches, jamming the aileron wires. Nor was that my last flying escapade in Thailand. I had two further accidents, one of them in a Japanese bomber that overturned on landing and broke off a wing.

Following my first trip to Bangkok a number of visitors came to the Candle area. The first was Brigadier Wilson Brand, head of 207 Mission, whom I conducted round the whole area. We finished up at Korat, where the Thai general gave us an excellent dinner, after which we watched some Thai boxing finals. It looked a very dangerous sport: they not only used their feet to kick, but they hit with their elbows as well.

The time was slowly drawing near when my presence in Thailand would no longer be justified. In mid-October the French internees had all left Nakhon Phanom and had been sent down to Bangkok from Ubon by train – to the disgust of Kemp and Winn, both of whom had appropriated the best-looking French girls as cipherenes and were loath to lose them. A week after this all the Dutch left the camp at Ubon, less three drunks who missed the train and had to go the next day. Some of the girls in Ubon were very sad to see them go.

The guerrillas had long ceased to be my responsibility, and Pluto was left to wrestle with the disarming and disbanding of them. Before he did so, I made a grand tour of Candle area in which I visited all the different guerrilla groups. At each place the routine was roughly the same. First we had a big victory parade to celebrate our all too bloodless victory; then I would make a speech of thanks, someone would reply, and the guerrillas would give three 'Khios'. In the evening there would be a great feast, followed by singing and dancing, and to bed seldom alone. I was usually given a presentation cigarette box of Thai engraved silver on these occasions, suitably inscribed. One refers to me as 'Colonor Smiley' – I assume this to be a cross between a colonel and a governor; another refers to me as 'the brave and younger of the British Army'. By the time I had said all my farewells and arrived in Bangkok I was dead beat.

I spent three weeks in Bangkok as I was in no hurry to get home to England. Lord Wavell had written me a personal nomination for the Staff College, and I knew that I had plenty of time before the next course started. This period was one of the most enjoyable in my life. I spent the mornings writing reports, but the rest of the time was my own. Chin was there and I met many of his family and friends. Their hospitality was overwhelming. By day Chin took me sightseeing, or some lovely girl would take me shopping, and in the evenings there was always a party on a lavish scale.

Pluto and Cato were both in Bangkok, and we had several good parties together. Chat and Pun returned to their families in Bangkok, while poor Kong had to go to hospital suffering from tuberculosis. Other arrivals in Bangkok were Hare and his fiancée, Jill North. Moss also showed up, and most of the staff of the SCS from Calcutta.

I met a lot of old friends and made many new ones. Chin took me to meet the Regent (alias Ruth) in his palace, and I had a long talk with him, in which I was able to thank him for all he had done for me and for Pluto's and Cato's valuable help. He seemed a charming and intelligent man; it was tragic that later he became tarred with the Communist brush by Pibul.

Winn and I flew to Saigon for a couple of days where we saw Commandant Morlanne. He took us to General Leclerc, who thanked us for what we had done and told us that both of us, and Kemp as well, had been awarded the Croix de Guerre. Some months later we heard from the Foreign Office that we were not allowed to accept these decorations, because the dates of the citation were after the end of the war and so we did not qualify. We thought this a bit mean. Pluto told us that Ruth was going to decorate a number of BLOs who had worked in Thailand. Some high-ranking British officers were given Thai decorations – presumably by Pibul – but none went to anyone in Force 136 who had worked in Thailand during the war.

At this point I should mention the subsequent fate of my Thai friends. Chin Svasti, who was awarded the OBE for his services in SOE, left his voluntary exile in Virginia Water and returned to his own country, where he farmed fruit and vegetables until his death some years ago. Kong (Kris Tosayanonda), who received the MBE for his services, spent a considerable time in a sanatorium in Switzerland, at one moment being joined as a patient by Peter Kemp. Cured of his TB, he returned to Thailand to become a lieutenant-colonel in the Thai Police Force, later retiring to become a businessman. He too died some years ago. Chat and Pun both continued their careers as detectives in the Police Force; both were promoted.

Victor Jacques, who was awarded the CBE and DSO for his services in Thailand, returned there after the war. In 1952, while on holiday in London, he gave a dinner at the Special Forces Club for former members of the Siamese Country Section and their wives. Peter Pointon headed many guests. That was the last time I saw Jacques, for he died in 1955. His wartime activities in Thailand would have made excellent material for a book – it is a pity he did not write one himself.

John Hedley became a schoolmaster – his exploits with the Chindits were well recorded in John Master's bestseller *The Road past Mandalay*. He has also since died.

I kept in touch with the two former prisoners of war at Ubon, Colonel Philip Toosey and Sergeant Neave. Toosey's leadership while a prisoner of the Japanese was recognised by the award of the DSO. I lunched with him in Liverpool, where he was a leading personality in the business world, and he arranged for Neave, who also lived in the city, to meet me. Toosey, who received a knighthood for public services in Liverpool, has since died. For many years Neave ran the drill-hall for a local Territorial unit, but ill health finally forced him to retire. Like so many former prisoners of the Japanese, he suffered from delayed effects from his ill-treatment while a prisoner.

The story of Ruth is a sad one, from which neither the British nor the Americans emerge with any credit. At the end of the war Pibul was arrested and put on trial as a war criminal. The trial dragged on for months until the proceedings against him were dropped on the grounds that legislation for war crimes was retrospective and therefore invalid – although this argument did not hold good at the Nuremberg War Trials. Pibul was therefore released.

In November 1947, after Pibul's release, General Pulao and two of Pibul's former associates led a successful *coup d'état* against Ruth. Pibul was restored to power, while Ruth was smuggled out of the country with British help. He remained in exile for over a year, staying in Singapore, Macao and South China (before it was overrun by the Communists). In February 1949 he returned to Thailand and staged a counter-coup, but this failed and he fled to Singapore.

Pibul was then able to discredit Ruth and his associates by alleging that they held Communist sympathies and by implicating them in the mysterious death of the King. Both these charges were later proved to be groundless. In Singapore Ruth asked the British authorities for political asylum. This was refused. He then asked the Americans and they also refused. The British grounds for refusal were that Ruth was wanted in Thailand on a criminal charge – plotting the murder of the King. In my view this attitude was doubly iniquitous, since the charges were not substantiated and we owed a great debt to Ruth for all the help he had given the Allies during the war. He therefore had no alternative but to find asylum elsewhere; so he fled to China, where he already had friends. By then South China had been completely overrun by the Communists. After living there for several years he moved to Paris, where he died.

Several years later both Pibul and Pulao were removed from office by yet another of the coups which seem to be a feature of Thai politics. They were both expelled from the country; Pibul retired to a Buddhist monastery in Japan and Pulao went to Switzerland, where he died some years ago.

It distresses me to have to write what eventually happened to Pluto, for he was my closest Thai friend throughout the time I served in his country. As already related, he became a member of the first post-war government, headed by Ruth. I last saw him when he visited me at my home in London in 1948 accompanied by his wife and son; he was then on his way to New York as the Thai representative to the United Nations.

When Ruth's government was overthrown by Pibul, and Ruth's counter-coup had failed, Ruth, as I have already mentioned, fled eventually to China. Pluto remained in Thailand but, of course, out of office.

When Pibul returned to power, Pulao again became chief of police – the appointment he had held under the Japanese. He was in some way related to Pluto and, to keep Pluto from opposing the government too violently, he asked Pluto to stand for the House of Assembly and support the government. Pluto accepted this suggestion, as a means of being able to criticise the government constitutionally, sought election and was duly returned to the Assembly. With his very high ideals he found he could not stand idle while Pibul and Pulao pursued a policy based on totalitarian oppression, and he consistently opposed and criticised them in Assembly.

By the beginning of 1954 the government was becoming embarrassed by Pluto's policy of opposition; so Pibul, in collaboration with Pulao and his gangsters, decided to liquidate him. He was invited to dinner one night at the house of a police officer whom he knew. Two friends accompanied him, both of whom had been Free Thais in Force 136 during the war. They entered the house to be surrounded by a gang of police executioners, who seized them and strangled them to death on the spot. Their bodies were thrown into a truck and driven out to the jungle of Kanchanaburi, where petrol was poured over them and they were burnt. Three local villagers appeared on the scene at just the wrong moment. Two of them were murdered by the police as potentially incriminating witnesses, and their bodies were also burnt. The third managed to escape to tell the tale.

Some years later the ruling regime reopened the case, in response to strong public pressure, and the murderers were put on trial. The chief culprit, the senior police officer, committed suicide in jail. Two accomplices received life imprisonment, three others were exiled. The police officer who asked Pluto to dinner went into political exile in Malaya; two others went to Switzerland.

Cato, too, became a victim of Pibul and Pulao. He was arrested in February 1949 with three other ex-Force 136 Thais, immediately after the failure of Ruth's attempted coup. The government, unable to find any evidence of their guilt, decided to liquidate them as they were unable to put them on trial. They arranged for them to be moved from their place of detention in Bangkok, on the pretext that their lives were in jeopardy from political opponents. During the journey from Bangkok they stopped in the suburb of Bang Khen, where they were shot on the spot. Both the government and the police gave out a fabricated story that they had been shot by a gang of Communists from Malaya who had ambushed the convoy in an attempt to rescue them. Nobody was taken in by this, since it seemed odd that neither the escorting police nor any of the alleged attackers had suffered any casualties. So the government, again to appease the public demand for justice, put on trial the police officers who had shot them. They were found guilty and sentenced to life imprisonment.

In Thailand my three principal colleagues were Kemp, Winn and Collins. I have already written of Kemp and Collins. Winn did not receive any decorations for his work in Thailand (though I recommended, unsuccessfully, both Kemp and Winn for a well-merited Military Cross); but when he heard that his old regiment, the 8th Royal Irish Hussars, was being posted to Korea, he immediately rejoined it as a Reserve officer and proceeded to win both a Military Cross and a Croix de Guerre. This time he was allowed to keep it as it was awarded under the auspices of the United Nations. On the death of his father he succeeded to the title of Lord St Oswald and inherited Nostell Priory in Yorkshire. He became an active member of the House of Lords and held the political appointment of Under-Secretary of State, Ministry of Agriculture, in Harold Macmillan's Conservative government. He died in 1984.

PART FOUR

Albania Again

14
1949

I returned to England from the Far East in a troopship from Bombay, having in my charge Chin's two daughters, Ning and Noy, and their grandmother, Lady Nuang Buri. We docked at Tilbury in January 1946.

A spell of leave skiing in Switzerland was followed by a six-month course at the Staff College, Camberley. Many regular officers dropped a rank on returning to peacetime duties: I reverted to major, and on my course, as fellow students, were three brigadiers who had come down from being major-generals. My nomination by Lord Wavell ensured that I did not have to take an exam to pass in, and as I was courting at the time and spent most nights in London, returning in the early hours, I was perhaps lucky to pass out. My first staff appointment was as assistant military attaché in Warsaw, working under the British Ambassador, Bill Cavendish-Bentinck, later the Duke of Portland.

Warsaw was in ruins, having been bombed by both Germans and Russians as well as 'scorched-earthed' by the Germans when they withdrew. Life was never dull, if only on account of the fact that one was under constant surveillance from the UD, the Polish Secret Police, who were controlled by the NKVD. When driving, all service attachés were followed by a black Volkswagen; we were tailed wherever we went, whether on foot or by car. My room was also searched daily when I was living first in a hotel and then in a flat. We had no contact with the Poles other than those on the embassy staff, and social life was limited to parties within the diplomatic corps of friendly countries.

Before the day of the post-war elections embassy staff were sent to various towns as observers. I drove down to Lublin and counted eighteen bodies lying in the streets, members of the strongest opposition party – the Peasant Party. They were virtually eliminated before polling day and the Communists got in with a 99.9 per cent vote. I was not sorry to leave, though my departure was not voluntary. While in the town of Przemysl observing Polish and Russian troop movements towards the Carpathian mountains, where anti-Communist bands were still holding out, I was arrested by the security police. In spite of my diplomatic passport and a permit from the Ministry of the Interior giving me permission to be in the town, I was held for three days under interrogation without being allowed to contact the embassy. I was then released and escorted back to Warsaw. I suspect the real reason for my arrest was to stop me seeing the troop movements.

Shortly after this my interpreter at the embassy, Countess Maria Marinowska, was arrested and charged with spying. She was sentenced to fourteen years' hard labour. She was a gallant lady who had served in the Warsaw rising and was over sixty years old at the time of her arrest. I was expelled – declared *persona non grata* – before her trial. She died a few months after her release. Several of the military attachés who served in Warsaw after me were also declared *persona non grata*.

On returning I married Moy Scott and lived in London while I was seconded to MI6 for a year, working most of the time in the office in Broadway, near St James's tube station. As a staff officer in the War Planning Section I had an interesting job, for at that time there were proposals for the role of SOE in the last war to be taken over by the SAS in the next one. I worked closely with Brian Franks, then Colonel Commandant of the SAS, a delightful character who was subsequently managing director of the Hyde Park Hotel. I also spent some time on operations in the Mediterranean.

I then returned to my regiment in Germany, the First Household Cavalry Regiment having by now reverted to their original units – the Life Guards and the Royal Horse Guards (The Blues). I was second in command, an appointment I did not relish, so when approached by MI6 to find out if I was prepared to rejoin them for a special assignment, I readily agreed.

I was briefed for my new job by an old friend, Harold Perkins. He told me that the British and American governments had agreed to a joint operation to destabilise the regime of Enver Hoxha in Albania. The two governments, concerned at the spread of Communism from the east, wanted to stem its advance and had chosen Albania as their target. Our Foreign Secretary, Ernest Bevin, was very keen on the idea and in a short time Amery, McLean and Kemp were all involved, mainly in cooperating with the Free Albanian Committee that had been formed in London and New York. This committee included Abas Ermenji, Abas Kupi and Said Kryeziu.

My role was to go out to Malta to run a training establishment for Albanians, who would then be infiltrated into Albania. In the summer of 1949, with Moy, two young stepchildren and my son Xan, who was only a few weeks old, I took up residence in a large army quarter in Sleima, near Valetta.

As I had to have a cover for my activities, which were highly secret, I was appointed deputy chief of staff at Garrison HQ, Valetta, where I had a spacious office in the Castille, a lovely old building formerly belonging to the Knights of St John. However, my real work took place at Fort Benjimma built at the time of an expected invasion by Napoleon. It was ideally situated, on an isolated hilltop on the far side of Medina from Valetta. Not only was there accommodation for the Albanians and my British staff, but it was sufficiently far away from any village for any shots to be heard from our sub-machine-guns firing in the moat of the fort, which made a perfect range for small weapons.

My staff consisted of five officers and several NCOs, including 'Gunner' Collins who had been my radio operator in Thailand and was a good friend. He maintained a daily contact with our HQ in England which never failed. Moy, who had been in charge of the cipher office at East Africa HQ in the war, went on a refresher course in London before she came out with me and became my cipher clerk.

Our own security was a problem and resulted in our having to lead a double life. First, that of an Army married couple living a normal social life, which was quite extensive. I also had to play the part of a staff officer, checking in every morning at the Castille, collecting my mail and making myself conspicuous by chatting up various officers before finally driving up to the fort – about half an hour away.

Luckily summer hours did not require any office work in the afternoons, which I either spent in the fort or, four days a week, playing polo. Admiral Mountbatten was then serving in Malta as Flag Officer, Cruisers. He had volunteered to come down in rank from being the Supreme Commander in the Far East at the end of the war to resume his naval duties in his peacetime seniority. He was a very keen polo player and encouraged others to play, including his nephew Prince Philip who was serving in Malta as a naval officer, accompanied by his wife, then Princess Elizabeth, Duchess of Edinburgh.

Again in the interests of security, only three people in Malta knew officially what I was doing: Admiral Sir John Power, the commander-in-chief, his chief intelligence officer, and Colonel Bill Major. The latter was the MI5 representative in Malta and was of the greatest help to me. His Maltese sergeant of police, George, was a splendid man, invaluable at the customs when certain equipment had to be smuggled. Moy was very surprised on arrival when her baby was whisked away to a waiting police car. Bill Major was especially useful when any of the Albanians got involved with the military police. They wore British battledress with 'Pioneer Corps' shoulder titles but none could speak English. They were also devoted to gym shoes, which they insisted on wearing at all times, and to this the MPs did not take kindly. However, the quiet diplomacy of Bill Major usually got such matters sorted out.

The training went on all that summer, the operating of the wireless sets being the most important. We used the same B2 set that had been used by SOE in the war, but could not use batteries or charging engines as these would have been too heavy for man-packs. We therefore had to rely on a form of collapsible bicycle frame which a man had to pedal furiously to provide power during transmission. In the event it wasn't much good when used in Albania. Weapon training was carried out with pistols, Sten guns and grenades; minelaying and elementary demolition instruction was also given. Finally PT was an important factor. Most of these men had been recruited from refugee camps in Italy and were certainly not fit enough to carry a heavy pack up and down the mountain tracks of Albania. As well as PT they got plenty of swimming in a remote cove nearby.

These Albanians were selected by their leaders in the Free Albanian Committee. Abas Erminji, leader of the Balli Kombëtar visited Malta from time to time to see how his men were faring. Others were selected by Abas Kupi from his Legaliti movement. All these men were volunteers who were willing to risk their lives for their country against the hated Communist regime.

The first operation took place when I considered the men were sufficiently trained. This was the end of the summer 1949. The plan was to infiltrate groups of three or four men by sea at a selected point on the coast of Albania. The men themselves chose which group they would join, depending on what relationships they had made during the training. Some groups were formed on a tribal basis, some were of the same political party, some were blood relatives.

To get them to Albania by sea required two moves. First they were embarked at the dead of night on to a motor fishing vessel (MFV) manned by personnel of the Royal Navy, sworn to secrecy. The MFV sailed to a rendezvous in the Adriatic with a schooner called *The Stormie Seas*, manned by two British ex-Royal Naval officers and two ex-Royal Marine NCOs. The Albanians then had to be transferred from the MFV to the schooner. On a moonless night the schooner sailed as close to the coast as possible, then the men got into a rubber dinghy rowed by one of the ex-Royal Marines.

It was early October 1949 when the first men went ashore. The selected landing place was 'Seaview', the cove on the peninsula south of Valona from where I had left Albania in 1943. It was at a remote point in the cliffs from where a goat track led inland up a mountain covered with thick scrub. There was cover from aircraft and the track passed through no village nor near any houses until it reached the Valona-Himara road. From a study of recently taken air photographs I was able to confirm that there were no new buildings or tracks since I was last there.

The first nine men to be put ashore got ten miles inland before splitting into two groups. One group was immediately ambushed and three out of the four were killed. The other group made contact with villagers who told them that they must have been expected as there had been intense military activity in the area some days before they arrived. This group eventually made their way over the border into Greece to report their findings, having only sent a brief message on their radio to our signal station which had been set up in a large villa in Corfu. We were becoming increasingly concerned at the lack of radio contact.

Two landings were carried out, with a total of twenty-four men. All found evidence that they had been expected and it was lucky that only four were lost, the rest having made it back to Greece. I was extremely concerned that somehow there had been either a gross breach of security in Malta, or there was a traitor among us.

Once the teams had been put ashore, I moved with my family to

Greece, living in a house on the seashore at Glyfada, about half an hour from Athens. Again I had to have a military cover, so I was appointed G1 (Ops and I) with the British Military Mission, whose head, General Nigel Poett, was one of the two people in the know as to my true role. The other was Commander Pat Whinney, our MI6 man in the embassy. Again, too, Moy and I had to behave like a normal military couple, which involved quite a heavy social life.

Meanwhile I ran a safe house at Kifissia, a residential suburb of Athens where the Albanians who had crossed into Greece were accommodated. They had first been imprisoned by the Greeks, who have no love for the Albanians, and a great deal of my time was taken in liaising with the Greeks to get them released. During their debriefing all made the point that they were certain that they had been expected.

Once all the groups sent in by me had been accounted for, my role was over. Having spent about five months in Greece I returned to my regiment in Germany. While there I continually mulled over what reason there could have been for information of our operations from Malta getting to Enver Hoxha. It was not until 1963 that we had the solution, for it was then that Philby was uncovered as a Soviet spy. Later, in his book *My Silent World*, he admitted being the source of the information, which he passed on to Moscow and the Russians passed on to Hoxha. Philby had been the MI6 representative in Washington and had been the link between the British and the Americans. He therefore knew all the details of our planned operations down to the dates and places of our proposed landings. The news reached Hoxha in time for his security forces to prepare a reception.

After I returned to Germany the operations were continued, particularly by the Americans. Unhappily the Americans made the mistake of reinforcing failure and many brave and patriotic Albanians were sent to their deaths by parachuting into the hands of the waiting security troops, their wireless having been captured and the operator controlled by the Albanian security police (the Sigurimi).

It was a sad ending, but I did not think it was final. I wrote a book, *Albanian Assignment* (1984), in which this is the final paragraph: 'Today Albania has no friends, having fallen out with the Russians and Chinese. With hostile Greeks and Yugoslavs on their borders they are completely isolated and life there must be grim indeed. One can only hope that the day will come when Albania will be free. For one may be certain that so ancient, stubborn, courageous and freedom-loving a nation will not endure Communist domination for ever.' By 1992 my forecast proved correct.

15

1992

After returning to my regiment in Germany in 1950 I took over command. Our main role, as an armoured car unit, was patrolling the border with East Germany, occupied by Russian troops. When we returned to Windsor in 1952, of those who had marched out of the barracks in 1939 – the regiment had been abroad ever since – only two officers and thirteen men marched back, of whom I was one.

At home we had to perform various unorthodox duties such as providing men to work on stemming floods on the East Coast, driving cranes in the docks during a dock strike, and driving petrol tankers whose drivers were on strike. The soldiers completed these tasks in far less time then their civilian counterparts. But the highlight of 1952 was the Coronation. I was the commander of the sovereign's escort and had the honour of riding beside the State Coach just behind the Queen. I gave the order 'Sovereign's escort, walk march', which started the procession of some 12,000 people and the whole four-and-a-half-mile column moved off at the same time. We were engulfed in the continuous roar of the wildly cheering crowds intermingled with the strains of the National Anthem which every band struck up on the approach of the Queen in the State Coach.

In 1955, after three years in command, I was appointed military attaché, Stockholm, where the ambassador was Sir Robin Hankey, a particularly delightful boss. During this time I visited every unit in the Swedish Army and made many friends. We found the diplomatic social life and Swedish etiquette rather taxing.

At the end of my three-year tour I had intended to leave the Army and settle in Kenya. However, Julian Amery, then Under-Secretary of State for War, came out to Sweden and persuaded me to stay on in order to go out to Oman to command the Sultan's Armed

Forces, who were in need of reorganisation and training after a series of setbacks fighting rebellious tribes supported by Saudi arms and money.

I arrived by aeroplane in Oman in April 1958. It was only a fortnight since I had been driving my car on the sea in Sweden – the ice was over twenty feet thick – and towing my children on skis. The contrast in temperature was almost overwhelming.

I found myself faced with a difficult war, with rebels on the mountains mining the roads and shooting up oil company vehicles, then retiring to their high and inaccessible hideouts. The Jebel Akhdar (the Green Mountain) is a formidable affair, the range rising to 10,000 feet and with a distance round the base of over 800 miles. The rebellion came to an end with the capture of this feature in early 1959. I was unable to mount the assault with my Omani troops alone and was fortunate to obtain the help of a squadron of the Life Guards, two squadrons of SAS and air support from the RAF.

At the end of my three-year tour Bob Laycock, the adjutant when I first joined the Blues, now Major-General Sir Robert Laycock, colonel commandant of the SAS, asked me to take over command of the three SAS regiments. It sounded a job after my own heart, but I was embittered when the War Office refused to pay me as a brigadier. In Oman I had been commanding a force bigger than a brigade as a full colonel, the rank I had also held in Sweden, and I felt they were getting me on the cheap. Army pay was nothing like it is today – in Oman my pay was just £3,000 per year. I therefore declined the offer and handed in my resignation.

On returning home I had first to find a job, as we had changed our minds about settling in Kenya. A cousin of Moy's kindly lent us a border keep near Hawick as a home but it was difficult to earn a living in the area. After an abortive attempt to grow mushrooms I eventually became an inspector for the *Good Food Guide* for over a year. Then I was rung up one day by Billy McLean who asked me if I would like to come out with him to Arabia. I accepted at once and found I was going to work for the Saudis, my late opponents in the Oman. We saw Amir Feisal ibn Abdul Aziz, then Crown Prince and Prime Minister, who wanted me to go to the Yemen to visit the Imam and his royalist forces. They were engaged in a guerrilla war against the combined forces of Republican Yemenis, who had tried to depose the Imam with the help of an Egyptian army which had invaded the Yemen. It was Nasser's aim to remove the Imam, get control of the country and finally drive the British out of Aden.

I carried out a three-month tour of the royalist-held areas, which were mainly in the mountains, before returning to Riyadh to make my report. Among the various recommendations I made was the need for European mercenaries to train the wild tribesmen, who all carried rifles, in the use of heavier weapons, mines and radio. A number of mercenaries were recruited by Ahmed Shami, the royalist Foreign Minister, and McLean and Amery asked David Stirling if he could find any ex-SAS personnel to help. Stirling recommended a former commanding officer, Jim Johnson, who gave up his job at Lloyd's to take on the role of finding volunteers.

A few months later various of my recommendations had been put into effect. After further visits to the royalist leaders, mostly amirs (princes) of the royal family, King Feisal, who had succeeded his half-brother to the throne, and Amir Sultan ibn Abdul Aziz, the Minister of Defence, asked me to take command of the mercenaries. These numbered about forty-five at any one time, about half being French, Belgian or Swiss, while the other half were SAS who had been recruited by Johnson. With the agreement of the leaders of the mercenaries, I accepted.

In the years 1963 to 1967 I made thirteen trips to Arabia, each lasting from two to six months. During this time the Egyptians, with up to 80,000 troops, failed to dislodge the Imam and his loyal mountain tribes from their strongholds in the High Yemen. Finally, when another war was started with the Israelis, Nasser had a face-saving excuse for withdrawing his troops.

Before this occurred there was disagreement between McLean and Amery on the one hand and Johnson on the other. The former considered Johnson's role was to organise the recruitment and administration of the mercenaries from an office in London. Johnson considered he should consult the Saudis who were, after all, paying for the mercenaries. McLean disagreed, taking the view that he was the one to keep personal contact with King Feisal and Amir Sultan; he was well experienced in dealing with Arabs – something that needed, above all, tact and good manners.

Things came to a head when Johnson, frustrated at the lack of firm directives from Amir Sultan and his failure to enter into a contract to ensure the future employment of the SAS men, was tactless in his dealings with the Foreign Minister, who complained to McLean that he had been insulted by Johnson's rude manner. This caused a split in relations. Though I saw both points of view, my loyalty was to my two great friends. I therefore gave up work with the mercenaries.

The Saudis then sponsored a compromise truce whereby a coalition government was formed of republicans and royalists, but the Imam and the royal family had to leave the country as one of the conditions. This ended my Arabian activities, which I eventually retold in *Arabian Assignment* (1975).

I retired to Spain in 1968 where we built a house in the Alicante province. There I occupied myself for the next twenty years cultivating orchards of almonds, olives and carobs. As old age caught up I preferred not to trust myself to the Spanish health system, so we returned to England, where we bought a house in Castle Cary in Somerset.

Meanwhile, Albania had suffered since 1945 under the Communist dictator Enver Hoxha. The country was in a state of economic ruin, up to 20,000 political prisoners were being held in concentration camps or prisons, the population was suffering severe hardship, without freedom of speech or religion, and prevented from travelling abroad. Only foreigners from other Communist countries were granted visas to visit Albania. This was the situation when Enver Hoxha died in 1985.

His place as President was taken by Ramiz Alia, also a hard-line Communist. However, in 1990 the population grew increasingly rebellious, having become aware of the events sweeping Eastern Europe in 1989 and 1990. There were demonstrations in the larger cities which were brutally repressed; when 5,000 stormed the German embassy asking for permits to emigrate, many were shot and killed. But Ramiz Alia felt obliged to introduce some more liberal reforms, the most important of which was a law permitting other political parties to stand at the next election in February 1991 – though even this did not prevent further demonstrations in which statues of Enver Hoxha were toppled.

The election duly took place, with the Communists doing all they could to stifle the opposition, of which the Democratic Party was the biggest. The Democrats were denied access to television, radio and the rest of the media. They had no transport to visit the country villages as only the Communists had the use of cars. One of the

Democratic candidates was shot by the Sigurimi (Secret Police) in broad daylight as he was making a speech in Scutari. The Communists issued extra rations of bread to the villages and used every dirty trick possible before polling day.

The Communists won sixty per cent of the seats, the Democrats forty. With this result the Communists were forced to form a coalition government; for although most of the Communist vote came from the country peasants, for reasons already given, all the big towns voted overwhelmingly for the Democrats. The two leaders of the Democratic Party were Sali Berisha, the chairman, and Gramoz Pashko, the deputy chairman, both of whom won seats in the new elected parliament. In the coalition government Gramoz Pashko became Deputy Prime Minister and Economy Minister.

In the autumn of 1991 Julian Amery asked me to lunch. Among his guests were Gramoz Pashko and his attractive wife, Alan Hare and Richard Bassett, a journalist and author who specialised in Balkan affairs. At the lunch Pashko, who spoke excellent English, told me he had a message for me from his mother, who was a wartime partisan to whom she alleged I had promised a pair of boots! He also told us that Sali Berisha was going to ask us all to Albania as the guests of the Democratic Party. An invitation soon followed.

In October Amery, Hare and myself left for Albania, staying the first night with our ambassador in Rome, Sir Stephen Egerton, in his beautiful residence, the Villa Wolkonsky. The following day we were joined for our onward flight by Richard Bassett. As we crossed the coast of Albania my thoughts went back forty-eight years to the time we left in the dead of night by MTB, with a price on our heads, the relief of going tinged with sadness at leaving our loyal friends behind.

At Shijak, the airport of Tirana, we were met by Sali Berisha and a welcoming committee of the Democratic Party. We were allowed to bypass customs and passport control and were driven in a convoy of three Mercedes limousines to Tirana. The countryside appeared to be covered with giant mushrooms. These were the concrete pill-boxes that pockmarked the entire terrain and were facing every direction. Greece, Yugoslavia, Britain, America and Russia had all been pilloried as likely aggressors, but the best explanation that I heard on the trip was that the bunkers had been built by the Communists 'against themselves'. They must certainly have enhanced the sense of paranoia inculcated by Enver Hoxha in the people. As for the money he must have wasted on building these eyesores, they are said to have cost enough to have paid for the housing of a third of the population of three million.

On the way to Tirana we passed very few cars, one or two broken down lorries and a number of horse-drawn carts. In Tirana itself there was very little traffic but there were a great number of people. Most seemed to be strolling about with no apparent aim; groups stood around talking and a number were squatting on the pavements. There appeared to be no shops, bars or restaurants. We were put up in a villa that had previously been occupied by a high official of the Communist Party. The villa next to ours was occupied by Hoxha's widow, who was under house arrest. Later she was imprisoned, still an unrepentant Communist hard-liner. Throughout our stay in Albania we were always accommodated for the night in a luxury villa, usually one previously occupied by Enver Hoxha, who had had his own villa in every big town in the country. These villas were built with money raised by taxing the people. As a result of the recent reforms, all their privileged occupants had been kicked out and they were now being used as official guest houses. This made living more congenial than being put in one of the only two hotels in Tirana, of which the pre-war Italian built Dajiti was the better and the high-block Tirana Hotel the other. Neither were up to the standards of a European hotel.

On our first evening Sali Berisha gave a dinner party for us which included Democratic Party ministers in the government. In a speech he made it clear that the reason we had been asked to Albania was to thank us for all the help the British had given Albania during the Second World War. This clearly discredited Enver Hoxha and gave the lie to his speeches and writings in which he had maintained that it was only the Russians who had helped Albania and that the British help was negligible. History would have to be rewritten, for this had been taught in the schools. Sali Berisha later told us that interpreters and transport would be put at our disposal and we would be free to go anywhere in Albania we wished.

Our first request was to visit our old HQ and DZ at Bixha, where Amery, Hare and myself had all parachuted in and where I had set up the HQ in 1943. The next day we were flown up in a thirty-year-old Chinese helicopter, accompanied by Perikla Teta, the Minister of

Defence, and senior Army officers – at least we assumed they were senior, although they wore no badges of rank and addressed each other as 'Comrade'. We landed on the plateau not far from our old HQ (though the shepherd's hut had gone) and were surprised to find a group of soldiers with Communist red star badges awaiting us who had set up a tent with a barbecue lunch, with no shortage of wine and *raki*.

In the middle of lunch a figure approached carrying a white stick, seemingly blind and escorted by two soldiers. Emotions ran high when it turned out to be Sheqir Trimi, our former interpreter, whom we had been compelled to abandon to what we feared would be certain death when we left Albania in 1944. In the event he survived, but his punishment for the crime of working for the British was seventeen years' hard labour, of which five were spent in solitary confinement. His hardships had left him almost blind and he was now living in a village not far from Bixha. This meeting was re-corded by Nicholas Shakespeare, a journalist who accompanied us, in an article in the *Daily Telegraph*, which had a picture of Sheqir and me embracing.

The plain at Bixha had little changed and was just as beautiful – beech forests on the mountainside, sheep grazing and a stream flow-ing, but as in the rest of the country the ubiquitous pillboxes quite spoilt the scenery. It was a memorable and nostalgic occasion.

The next day we asked to visit the notorious prison at Burrel. We had been told that all political prisoners had been released, but we wanted to see for ourselves. British journalists had already visited the concentration camp at Gradishte where they found that the gates were open, all guards gone, but former prisoners still there. Their families had either been killed or gone into exile, and their homes had been taken over. They therefore had nowhere to live but in the old camp, though they were free to leave it.

Burrel had the reputation of being the most severe of all the prisons, with brutal guards and many executions. The mayor of Burrel accompanied us to the jail, which was grim in the extreme. A number of doors had to be unlocked before we could enter the courtyard, where we noticed recent fillings of plaster on the wall; these were clearly to eradicate the bullet marks and bloodstains of the executions. We were allowed to question any of the prisoners and they confirmed that the political prisoners had been released, though they complained about the severity of their sentences for petty crimes. One man alleged he was doing seven years' hard labour for stealing the equivalent of fifty pence.

On our return journey we stopped at Kruja, sited on a mountainside and dominated by a castle. Here we found a member of the Kupi family, who told us that as yet the government had not allowed the Legaliti party to operate. Kruja was King Zog's home town and many of the inhabitants were of his tribe and strong Zogist supporters.

Before leaving on a tour of the south of Albania we attended a congress of about 1,000 delegates from the Democratic Party, including some from Kossovo and Macedonia. Julian Amery made a speech which was received with great acclamation, during which he mentioned Hare's and my names. We were seated at the back of the hall and our minders made us stand up, whereupon all the delegates rose, turned towards us and gave us a standing ovation, much to our embarrassment. It was unbelievable to think that we were getting such a welcome after the dark clouds under which we had left Albania all those years ago.

I had been told by Lord Bethell* that on a visit to Albania he had been to the Enver Hoxha Museum. He was amazed to see a board headed 'War Criminals' under which were photographs of McLean, Amery and Smiley. Naturally I had asked to see my mugshot but was told that the museum had been looted and wrecked at the time of the anti-Hoxha demonstrations when all his statues were smashed.

We paid a visit to the Heroes' Cemetery on a hill outside Tirana where we saw Hoxha's tomb, guarded by four soldiers, and the tombs of several of the Communist leaders whom I had known in 1943, including Myslim Peza, Kahreman Ylli and Baba Faja. We wondered how much longer these tombs would be allowed to be honoured.

Our tour of the southern half of the country lasted several days, during which we stayed in all the major towns. It was sad to see the countryside so empty, and so many people in the towns and villages with nothing to do; there was a pall of poverty everywhere, with people ill-clothed – many of them barefoot – and far from healthy-looking. They were not starving, but malnutrition was rife and

*Author of *The Great Betrayal*, Hodder & Stoughton, 1984.

I never saw a fat person throughout the trip. In no town did we see any shops or coffee houses, though wayside groups were selling onions, tomatoes and water melons. We did find an outdoor market in Korça, which not only sold the usual vegetables but clothes as well; these were black market, smuggled from Greece.

During our travels we saw very few private cars. Chinese bicycles were common but the usual transport was by double-carriage buses or lorries, in the back of which twenty or thirty would be crammed. Many were broken down and spare parts were unobtainable. Horse-drawn carts were common, though many of the horses were lame, and in the country there were numbers of mules and donkeys, with the occasional ox-drawn waggon.

Apart from the mountainous scenery, with lakes and rivers, Albania has a lot to offer the tourist in the future. Roman remains at Appollonia and Butrinto, and castles in many towns such as Gjinokaster and Berat are well worth a visit; there are wonderful beaches, too, for swimmers and wind-surfers, and possible marinas for yachtsmen. Obviously the tourists could not be attracted without considerable investment, as the hotels were in a deplorable state. Some, such as the one in which I stayed at Kukes, were built on excellent sites, with superb views, but the good points ended there. The plumbing did not work at all so there was no water for baths or even shaving – for this I used mineral water. Lavatories were blocked; had there been water neither the bath nor the wash basin had plugs. My room had four electric light bulbs, of which only one worked. Rooms were dirty and service non-existent. Even in the hotels where there were maids or waiters they had the same surly attitude I had experienced in Communist Russia and China. Never a smile nor any offer to help.

Before foreign tourists can be expected to enjoy their visits, hotel managers and staff will have to be highly trained by qualified hoteliers. Roads will have to be improved, for many were badly potholed. Medical facilities were sorely sub-standard, for though doctors and nurses tried their best, they were greatly handicapped by lack of medical supplies. I visited a hospital in Sarande where I saw some pathetic babies, short not of care but of essential medicines and drugs. The surgeon to whom I spoke could only carry out one operation a day as he had so few sutures for wound stitching.

During our tour it was sad to see things that spoilt the beauty of the country. Row upon row of tree-stumps lined the roads, all cut about one metre from the ground. Previously most roads had been lined with black poplars to give shade to travellers and their animals. Now they had all been cut down for fuel, and when I asked one of the ministers if this could be forbidden by law he replied that they had to have the wood to cook and keep warm in winter and there was no other source of fuel. Even Elbasan, a lovely town as I had seen it (through binoculars) in the war, now had a heavy pall of smoke hanging over it, belched from a vast steel or chemical plant built by the Chinese a short distance away.

As our party drove in a convoy of limousines, with an escort of the dreaded Sigurimi, now under the control of our Democratic Party friends and there to protect us from bandits, not to spy on us, I saw more of Albania in two weeks than I had done in two years during the war. Then we had walked or ridden mules along narrow mountain tracks, as the roads, along which we were driving now, were under the control of the Germans or Italians who occupied the major towns.

My request to visit scenes of some of my wartime activities was also granted. On the way south from Korça we stopped near Barmash at the point in the road where, with a Ballist çeta, I had ambushed a German convoy. In Korça, while we were having coffee with the mayor in the town hall, a very old man, supported by two relatives, staggered into the room to speak to us. He looked on the point of death, but he held forth on the iniquities of the Hoxha regime and all that he had suffered. It transpired that he had been a member of the çeta in the Barmash incident and was able to remember details of it. Happy at having had his say with the mayor, he left. We all felt he had only a few days to live.

Our party was also taken to the bridge at Gjoles, which I had blown up during the war, and souvenir photographs were taken. The last time I photographed the bridge, after its demolition, a German soldier shot at me. He appears in the photograph in the act of shooting.

While in Tirana we made inquiries about the whereabouts of the grave of our wartime comrade Lieutenant-Colonel Arthur Nicholls, GC, for we knew his body had been moved from its original grave and we wanted to find the site of the new one. Nobody could tell us. However, during our final talk with Sali Berisha he said he wanted to build a memorial to all the British who were killed or died in Albania during the war, and that he would ask us out again to discuss this project.

On returning to England I was told by Ihsan Toptani that there had been a British war cemetery in Tirana. Nobody had mentioned this while we were there. I contacted the Commonwealth War Graves Commission and they confirmed it, sending me two photographs of the cemetery. These I took out on my next visit to Albania in July 1992, for Sali Berisha had asked me out again, and the question of the cemetery in Tirana was raised. As one of the photographs I had with me included a building I could recognise, I was able to pinpoint the site. There was no sign of graves or any monument. I told Sali Berisha this and he ordered his senior military adviser, Colonel Çobrani, to investigate. Çobrani soon discovered that the graves had been moved, but it was not clear precisely where. There were three possible areas. As I write investigations continue. The President meanwhile was outraged that Hoxha must have ordered the removal of the cemetery, which the Commonwealth War Graves Commission confirmed as having fifty-two graves, including that of Arthur Nicholls. One must assume that Hoxha's motive was to remove any signs that he had received help from the British during the war. Fifty-two dead British servicemen were rather a serious contradiction to his claims.

Since my visit at the end of 1991 big political changes had taken place. Sali Berisha had pulled his Democratic Party members out of the coalition and forced another election in March 1992. This time the Democrats won 62 per cent of the popular vote and 92 out of the 140 seats in the Albanian parliament. The Albanian Communist Party, changing its name to the Albanian Socialist Party, won 25 per cent of the vote and only 38 of the seats, the remaining ten seats going to other parties. Sali Berisha was elected President of Albania.

As the President's guest I was given complete freedom to go wherever I asked and to talk with any of his ministers. As before, I was accompanied by Richard Bassett. Together we met most of the ministers and leading officials, as well as many senior Army officers. Although most of these Democratic Party ministers were new in their appointments, having replaced the Communists, many of the rank and file remained in their previous jobs to serve their new masters.

Although the President had dismissed all the Communist chiefs, he drew some adverse criticism for being too lenient towards them. A very few were imprisoned, mainly on charges of corruption; leaders such as Ramiz Alia were at first allowed to move about freely, though later he was confined to house arrest. The strongest protests came from those who had been political prisoners, some for over forty years of hard labour and brutal treatment. These people felt that those responsible should have been tried for crimes against human rights and punished accordingly, some even executed. The President insisted, however, that his policy was one of reconciliation and not of revenge. One should also bear in mind that not only Sali Berisha and Gramoz Pashko but many members of the Democratic Party had started their political careers as Communists. They had eventually become disgusted with Enver Hoxha's policies and after his death split from the party as reformists.

As I had spent most of my previous visit in the south of Albania, this time I asked if I could go to the north, especially those areas with a common frontier with Kossovo. We drove to Kukes accompanied by two senior Army officers – by now they had been given ranks and wore badges, though so far no one had been appointed higher than colonel. I was also very glad to see that the red Communist star in the soldiers' caps had been replaced by the Albanian double-headed eagle. We drove down the road from Kukes towards Prizren in Kossovo and stopped at the customs house on the frontier. From there I could see the posts marking the frontier which ran north to Montenegro and south to Macedonia. Except where the roads ran through passes, the whole area was extremely mountainous.

Kossovo was a former autonomous Serbian province of Yugoslavia populated by over 1,500,000 Albanians and 200,000 Serbs. During and since Tito's time the Serbs have ruthlessly suppressed the Albanians and there were riots in 1968, 1981 and 1989 which the Serbs put down with great brutality, killing hundreds of Albanians. In 1991 Albania recognised the Republic of Kossovo diplomatically but this is strongly opposed by the Serbs.

Although the Albanians have lived in Kossovo for over 1,000 years, the Serbs claim the land is theirs as a result of a historic battle in 1389 when the Serbs were defeated by the Turks at a place known as The Field of the Black Birds. For the next 500 years the country was occupied by the Turks, but it is not easy for the Albanians to understand why this should give the Serbs the right to claim Kossovo as theirs. They add that the Albanians also fought against the Turks in this battle. As I write the Serbs are carrying out a policy of 'ethnic cleansing' in other provinces of Yugoslavia. Unless the United Nations can stop this it is almost certain that the Serbs will carry out the same policy in Kossovo.

If this occurs it is hardly likely that Albania will stand by without taking action. There is bound to be a serious refugee problem, for thousands of Albanians will flee from their homes rather than be massacred. The Albanian Army when I visited various units gave me the impression that it was not in a fit state to take on the Serbian-controlled Yugoslavia with its modern weapons. Their equipment is, by present-day standards, quite obsolete. With Soviet T34 and T54 tanks of Second World War vintage and artillery provided by the Chinese in the 1950s, the conscript Albanian soldiers, lacking modern equipment, have little but their courage if a war breaks out. They desperately need help in both training and modern weapons. Regrettably the British do not seem keen to do this, mainly for reasons of economy. The Italians and the Turks appear to be the most likely sources of military aid.

During my visit I saw many more cars on the road than last time, many bought by entrepreneurs who buy the cars in Germany or Italy, drive them back and sell them at a good profit. Also in evidence are Italian army lorries driven by armed Italian soldiers. I passed one convoy of over twenty lorries carrying food supplies to outlying villages and towns.

At least Britain is giving some help through charitable organisations such as the Red Cross, as well as through individual efforts, and medical help is already having a good effect. However, to rescue Albania from the chaos left by forty-seven years of Communist rule, not only is hard cash needed but specialists in industry, agriculture and many other occupations to train the Albanians themselves. They have enough agriculture to become self-supporting, and with their oil, chrome and other mineral exports, could build up reserves of currency.

Albania will have to go through hard times before this is achieved and one can only hope that President Sali Berisha can carry out the necessary reforms. The old Communists are still there, already making propaganda that under Communist rule things were better than they are today. Nevertheless I do not think Albanians will ever give up the freedom that has come with democracy, and though the preservation of law and order is a problem, nobody wishes to see it imposed by the Sigurimi as in the past.

Index

Abel Smith, Col Sir Henry, 10
Abu Simbel (Egypt), temple of, 35
Abu Kemal (Syria), 51-2
Aden, 19, 196
Ajax, HMS, 38
Akyab (Burma), 130
Al Kadhimain (Iraq), 45
Albanian Assignment, book by
    author, 192
Alexander of Tunis, Field-Marshal
    Earl, 99, 121
Alexandria (Egypt), 34, 41, 66, 70
Alia, Ramiz, Albanian Communist
    President, 197, 205
Alicante (Spain), 148
Alipore (India), 148
Allen, Maj W., 14
Alpini, 93
Amery, Capt Julian, later Lord, 101,
    103-7, 109-12, 117, 129-30, 189,
    194, 196, 198-9, 201
Annamite Communists, 166,
    168-78
Arab Legion, 42-4, 46
Arabian Assignment, book by author,
    197
Aranitas, Ramiz, Albanian
    commissar, 86
'Ascot', *see* Ban Non Han
Ashwell, Maj P., 147
Asslan, author's Albanian body-
    guard, 103
Assuan (Egypt), dam, 35
Assyrian troops, 40
Atbara, River, 26, 29
Athens, 192
Az Zib (Palestine), 20

Baghdad, 40, 43, 48, 56, 60, 118
Bajraktar, Muharrem, Albanian
    chieftain, 79
Baker Street, London, SOE HQ,
    115-16
Balli Kombëtar, 88, 90, 190
Ballists, 92-3, 96-7, 100, 102, 105, 107
Ban Han (Thailand), 136, 155
Ban Non Han (Thailand), codename
    'Ascot', 132, 142-3, 145
Ban Tao Ngoi (Thailand), codename
    'Kempton', 138, 141
Bang Khem (Thailand), 183
Bangalore (India), 119
Bangkok, 116, 123, 125, 130, 135,
    143-5, 149, 151, 158-61, 168,
    178-80, 183
Banks, Maj, American OSS, 173-6
Bardhok, Albanian Zogist guerrilla,
    104, 106
Bari (Italy), 96-7, 99, 105-7, 111-12,
    124
Barmash (Albania), 203
Basra (Iraq), 40
Bassett, Richard, writer on Balkans,
    198, 204
Bastar (Albania), 106; Mount, 103
Beirut, 17
Belgrade, 101
Bell, Sgt, radio operator, 90
Bengal, Bay of, 141
Benjimma, fort (Malta), 189
Berane (Yugoslavia), 104
Berat (Albania), 96, 202
Berbera (Somaliland), 19
Berisha, Dr Sali, Albanian President,
    198-9, 203-6

Berlin, 44
Bethell, Lord, MEP, 201
Bevin, Rt Hon Ernest, Foreign
 Secretary, 188
Bir Hacheim (Libya), 62, 67
Bixha (Albania), 94, 101, 199, 200
Black Watch, 19, 25
Blackburn, Sqn Ldr J., 80
Blathwayt, Maj C., 153
Blue Nile, river, 26
Boneng (French Indo-China), 171
Boutagy, Emil, 18
Boutagy, Roy, 18, 41, 77
Boyle, Maj R., 25, 33, 38
Breene, Maj A., 99
'Brillig', Thai codename, 116
Brindisi (Italy), 102
Bumçi, Bishop of Mirdite (Albania),
 111
Buri, Lady Nuang, 187
Burrel (Albania), 200
Butka, Safet, 88-9

Cairo, 16-17, 19, 23, 25, 66, 68, 70, 73,
 77-8, 80, 96, 99-101, 112, 115,
 117-18
Calcutta, 116, 122-3, 125, 127-8, 130,
 135, 143-53, 155, 174, 180
Camberley, Staff College, 180,
 187
'Candle', operation codename, 126,
 129, 138, 141, 143, 149-50, 152-3,
 164, 167, 173, 179
Carmel, Mount (Palestine), 12, 77
Carpathian Mountains, 188
Carton de Wiart, Lt-Gen Sir A., 117
Caserta (Italy), 112
Casey, Rt Hon Richard, Governor of
 Bengal, 149
Cassano, Sqn Ldr A., 44
Castelorizzo, island, 39
Castille, garrison HQ (Malta), 189
Castle Cary (Somerset), 197
'Cato 'see Daurong Chamrong
Caucasian Division, Russian, 58
Cavalry Division, 1st, 8, 41

Cavendish-Bentinck, Hon W., HM
 Ambassador Warsaw, 187
Cecil Hotel (Alexandria), 66
Chakrabandhu, Prince Karawik,
 124
Chamberlain, Rt Hon Neville, Prime
 Minister, 7
Chanteclair, night club (Cyprus), 69
'Chat', see Sudisakdi
Cheda, Maj, Japanese Army, 158,
 161, 164
Chelga Hills (Abyssinia), 33
Chesshire, Maj J., 95
'Chin', see Svasti
Chunking (China), 117, 168
Church of Scotland, canteen vans,
 64
Claridge's, hotel (London), 100
Clarke, Maj-Gen J., 41
Çobrani, Col, Albanian, 204
Collins, Sgt W. ('Gunner'), 122-3,
 132-6, 138, 140-2, 145-6, 149, 152,
 155, 159, 183, 189
Colombo (Ceylon), 119-20, 123
Combined Military Hospital, No. 1,
 Calcutta, 143
Commandos, 19, 22-3, 39, 46; No. 51
 (Middle East), 33; No. 52 (Middle
 East), 23, 32
Commonwealth War Graves Com-
 mission, 204
Cook, Capt J., 81
Corfu, 191
Cosson, Cdr A. de, RN, 112
'Coupling', operation codename, 126,
 128, 152-3
Crawley, Canon, Dean of Windsor, 8
Crespigny, Brig-Gen Sir R. de
 (Crawley), 10

Daily Telegraph, 200
Dajti Hotel (Tirana), 199
Dani, Ramiz, 104-6, 112
Darby, Tpr, 9
Dass, Debnatt, Indian Nat. Army
 criminal, 178

Daurong, Chamrong (codename 'Cato'), 134, 140, 146, 149, 160, 180, 183
Davies, Brig 'Trotsky', 95, 100, 102
Davis, Cpl, radio operator, 105-7
de Gaulle, Gen Charles, 19
Dead Sea, 61
Delhi, 118, 123
Democratic Party, Albania, 197-9, 201, 203-5
Derna (Libya), 79, 80
Detcharat, Adul (codename 'Pulao'), 117, 144, 181-3
Dibra (Albania), 104
Dilwara, SS (troopship), 11
Dimbleby, Richard, 59
Dine, Fiqri, 110
Dine, Skender (Koço Tashko), 85-6, 91
Dishnica, Dr Ymer, 85
Djibuti (Somaliland), 19
Dodecanese Islands, 25
Dolpur House, Delhi, 118
Dover, 10
Drin, River (Albania), 110-11
Drymades (Greece), 82, 84
Duffy, Lt Garry, RE, 79, 81, 84
Dukati (Albania), 97
Dume, Petrit, Albanian partisan leader, 88-9
Dunkirk, 11
Durazzo (Durrës) (Albania), 102, 104, 107-8

'E' Force, 120
EAM, 82, 84
Eden, Rt Hon Anthony, Foreign Secretary, 100, 104, 107, 111-12, 116
EDES, 82, 84
Edinburgh, Duke of (Prince Philip), 190
Edinburgh, Duchess of (Princess Elizabeth), 190
Egerton, Sir Stephen, HM Ambassador Rome, 198

El Adem (Egypt), 67
El Alamein (Egypt), 70-2
El Qassasin (Egypt), 69
ELAS, 82
Elbason (Albania), 78, 92-3, 203
Elmaz, Albanian interpreter, 79
Emmaus (Palestine), 60
Emwas, monastery (Palestine), 60
Erbil (Iraq), 49
Ermenji, Prof Abas, 90, 96, 189, 190
Eton College, 124
Euphrates, River, 43
Evans, Maj-Gen E., 164
Evans, Dr Horace, later Lord, 6
Eyre, Capt J., 107

Fabre, Commandant, French Force 136, 176-7
Faja, Baba (Baba Mustafa), 78, 94, 201
Famagusta (Cyprus), 69
Fanny, author's mule, 96
Fawzi al Qawukchi, 52, 56
Feisal, Amir ibn Abdul Aziz, Crown Prince, Prime Minister, later King of Saudi Arabia, 195, 196
Ferguson, Col A., 46, 74
Fergusson, Brig Bernard, later Lord Ballantrae, 39
Field, Maj G., 88, 97-8
Fielding, Maj A (Xan), 99, 100, 112, 120, 123
Firth, Maj C., 9
Fleming, Col P., 119
Flood, Raider, 30-1
Flood-Paddock, Tpr, 56
Force 136, 116, 118-20, 123-6, 147, 149, 151, 153, 168, 176, 180
Foreign Legion, French, 24
Foul Island (Burma), 129
Fournier, Lt E., French Force 136, 168
Fowler, Saddle-Cpl, 54
Franco, Italian officer, 111
Franks, Col B., Commandant SAS, 188
Frasheri, Midhat, 110

Fuller, Maj Sir Gerard, 44, 55, 59, 69

Gallabat (Sudan), 25-6, 33-5
Ganges, River, 130
Gausset, Lt, French Force 136, 173
Gaza (Palestine), 18
Gazala (Libya) 62
Gedaref (Sudan), 25-6, 33-4
Geneifa (Egypt), 22-3, 35
George, Maltese police sgt, 190
Gerard Leigh, Col W.H., 16-17, 53
George VI, King, 8
Geraldine, Queen (of Albania), 102
Gezira Club, Cairo, 60
Gezira Island, 99
Gilan (Persia), 58
Gjinokaster (Albania), 84, 202
Gjoles, bridge (Albania), 104, 111, 203
Glen, Lt-Cdr Sir Alexander RN, 98
Glubb Pasha, 42, 47
Glyfada (Greece), 192
'Goldfish '(codeword), 152-3, 155-6
Gondar (Abyssinia), 29, 33
Gooch, Col Sir Eric, 50, 74
Gopal, Ram, Indian dancer, 119
Gordon, Maj M., 31
Gorgopotamus viaduct (Greece), 81
Gradishte (Albania), 200
Graham, Maj-Gen Sir Miles, 14
Grant-Taylor, Capt, 79
Great Betrayal, The, book by Lord Bethell, 201
Grenadier Guards, 123
Greys, The Royal Scots, 8, 39, 78
'Grin', author's codename, 143
Griswold, Maj A., OSS, 156
Grivas, Col G., 69
Grobba, Dr, German Minister Baghdad, 48-50
'Gunner', see Collins
Gurkhas, 48 120, 128; 1/5 Royal, 58

H4, pumping station (Jordan), 41-2, 56, 118

H5, pumping station (Jordan), 41
Habbaniya (Iraq), 40-3, 48, 51, 56, 60, 118
Habforce, 41
Haifa (Palestine), 12, 17, 20, 41, 77
Haile Selassie, Emperor of Abyssinia, 27
Hamada, Lt-Gen, Japanese Army, 164
Hands, Sqn Ldr A., 88
Harding, Maj-Gen Sir John, later Lord, 71
Hankey, Sir Robin, later Lord, HM Ambassador Stockholm, 194
Hare, Maj Hon A., 95-6, 102-5, 117-19, 123, 180, 188-9, 201
Harrison, Sgt, Scots Guards, 29-31, 33
Harrow School, 124
Hasluck, Mrs Margaret, 78-9, 94
Hassan, Veli, Albanian interpreter, 103-4, 111
Hawtreys, school, 123
Hebron (Palestine), 60
'Hector', see Jacques
Hedley, Maj J., 165-6, 181
Hervey-Bathurst, Maj B., 123, 127, 130, 149
Heston, landing ground (Thailand), 138-9, 141, 145, 149
Hibberdine, Capt J., 103-4
Higland Light Infantry, 25
Himara (Albania), 97, 191
Hirata, Lt-Gen, Japanese Army, 164-5
Hitler, Adolf, 59
Hoey, Millie, of Bag of Nails, 6
Holliday, Maj, OSS, 136-7, 149
Homs (Syria), 52
Hopkinson, Lt-Cdr, RNR ('Hoppy'), 123
Horrocks, Lt-Gen Sir Brian, 71
Hoseda, Lt, Japanese Army, 161, 170-1
Hosumi, Col, Japanese commadant of Ubon, 164, 170

Household Cavalry Regiment, 1st, 8, 13, 20, 32, 38-40, 57, 65, 68, 71, 73, 118, 188
Houston, USS, 160
Hoxha, Enver, Communist Albanian President, 87, 89-90, 94, 96, 102, 105, 107, 111-12, 188, 192, 197, 199, 204
Hoxha, Kadri, Albanian commissar, 94
Hudson, Maj ('Soapy'), 126, 128, 151-3, 156
Hussars, 8th Royal Irish, 184; 11th, 70-1
Hyde Park Barracks, 3
Hyde Park Hotel, 188

Igumenitsa (Greece), 82
Indian Lancers, 13th, 58
Iraq Levies, 40
Irrawaddy, River (Burma), 129, 131
Ismalia (Egypt), 18, 25
Italian Brigade, 24th Colonial, 33

Jacques, Brig Victor ('Hector'), 125, 130, 144, 151, 181
Jaipur, Maharajah of, 41
Jannina (Greece), 80, 82
Jebel Akhdar (Oman), 195
'Jedburghs', 121
Jenkins, Sgt G., 88, 90, 94, 102-4, 111-12
Jericho (Palestine), 61
Jerusalem, 16, 60
Jessore (India), 127, 129-30
Jin, Chinese girl in Ubon, 162
Johnson, Lt-Col J., SAS, 197-7
Jones, Sgt, 88, 90, 102-3, 112

K3, pumping station (Iraq), 41, 56
Kabrit (Egypt), 78
Kameshle (Syria), 50
Kandy (Ceylon), 120, 123, 125
Karkur (Palestine), 17
Kashgar (China), 120
Kassala (Sudan), 25, 33-5

Kazaks, 109
Keble, Brig C., 78
Kelcyre, Ali, 110
Kelham House (Notts), 9
Kemp, Maj P., 88, 90, 101-2, 117-18, 150-3, 155, 158, 166-9, 170-6, 178-9, 180, 182-4, 189
Kempai Tai, Japanese Security Police, 144
Kempton, *see* Ban Tao Ngoi
Keren (Somaliland), 34
Kermanshah (Persia), 58
Keyes, Lt-Col G., VC, 39
Khartoum (Sudan), 25
'Khem', *see* Ungpakorn
Khon Kaen (Thailand), 147, 151
Khor Gumsa (Abyssinia), 29, 30
Kifissia (Greece), 192
King David Hotel, Jerusalem, 61
Kirkuk (Iraq), 41, 57
Klotz, Lt F., French Force 136, 168-70, 172-5
Klugman, Capt J., 107
Knightsbridge, Battle of (Egypt), 68
Kola, Halit, Albanian interpreter, 103, 108, 110-11
'Kong', *see* Tosayanonda
Konitza (Greece), 84
Korat (Thailand), 126, 152, 156, 178-9
Korça (Koritza) (Albania), 84-5, 88, 92, 202-3
Koreans, prison guards, 158-9, 161; comfort girls, 167
Kossovo (Yugoslavia), 101, 201, 205-6
Kozelli, Sulo, partisan leader, 85
Krujë (Albania), 201; mountain range, 104
Kryeziu, Said, 106-7, 111-12, 189
Kukes (Albania), 202, 205
Kunming (China), 116
Kupi, Maj Abas, 79, 102-12, 189, 190; family, 201

Labinot (Albania), 93-4, 96
Larroue, Lt, French Force 136, 176
Laos, 168, 173, 176

Latrun, monastery (Palestine), 60-1
Lavinia, Mount (Ceylon), 115
Lawson, Sgt, radio operator
  ('Spider'), 151-3
Laycock, Maj-Gen Sir Robert, 5, 36,
  195
Layforce, 36, 38
Leclerc, Gen, 180
Lees, Maj R., Gordons, 159
Legentilhomme, Gen, 19
Legaliti, Albanian monarchist party,
  190
Leigh Fermor, Maj P., 99, 100, 112
Leopold, King, of Belgium, 3
Lesh (Alessio) (Albania), 111
Leshnjë (Albania), 86-7
Leskovik (Albania), 85, 88
Lewis, Capt J. SAS, 39
Life Guards, The, 188, 195
Liverpool, 181
Llenjë, 91-2
LNÇ (Levizje Nacional Çlirimtare),
  84, 87, 94, 102, 105, 107
Loey (Thailand), 147
Lublin (Poland), 187
Lutyens, Sir Edwin, 118
Lyon, Maj M., 107

Macao, 181
Macedonia, 92, 201, 205
Mackenzie, Colin, 124
McLean, Lt-Col N. ('Billy'), 18-19,
  34, 74, 77-9, 81-2, 84-7, 90-2, 94-8,
  100-1, 103-12, 117-20, 123, 126,
  189, 195-7, 201
Macmillan, Rt Hon Harold, later Earl
  of Stockton, 112, 184
McTaggart's Wall, 20
McTavish, RSM, Argylls, 155, 159
Mafraq (Jordan), 56
Mahasarakham (Thailand), 134, 138,
  140
Major, Lt-Col W., 190
Mal i Bardhe (Albania), 110
Marie Céleste, Soeur, French nun, 171
Marinowska, Countess Maria, 188

Marku Gjin, Albanian partisan
  leader, 86, 96
Marseilles, 11-12
Martenesh (Albania), 94
Mashaida (Iraq), 47
Maskelyne, Capt J., 79
Mati, River (Albania), 111
Matsukull (Albania), 105
ME 25, School of Jungle Warfare
  (Ceylon), 119, 121, 125, 142
Mekong, River, 126, 129, 132, 142,
  152, 166, 168, 171, 173-4, 178
Mersa Matruh (Egypt), 61-2
Messenger, Charles, 39
Messervy, Gen Sir Frank, 67
Metemma (Abyssinia), 25-6, 33, 35
MI6, 188, 192
Micklethwaite, Maj G., 81-2
Military Mission 207 (Thailand),
  165
'Millie', see Huey
MO4, 77-8
Mokër (Albania), 91
Montenegro, 111, 205
Montfort (Palestine), 21
Montgomery, Field-Marshal
  Viscount, 71
Morlanne, Commandant, French
  Force 136, 180
Morton, Tpr, 1 HCR, 43
Moshpina (Greece), 82
Moss, Capt W., 99, 100, 112, 120, 180
Mosul (Iraq), 43, 48-9, 51
Mountbatten, Adm Earl, 116, 125-6,
  189
Mukaj (Albania), 107
Mukdahan (Thailand), 144, 152-3,
  157, 166, 173, 178
Munzetti, Capt (Italian), 98
Murray-Smith, Maj A., 62, 64-5
Musgrave, Col, 120
Myers, Brig E., 81

Naarn (Thailand), landing strip, 147
Nakajima, Capt, Japanese Army,
  169-71

Nakon Phanom (Thailand), 142, 144, 152-3, 155, 168-70, 173, 178-9; governor of, 153, 171
Nakon Sawan (Thailand), 116
Nasser, President (of Egypt), 196
Nathanya (Palestine), 19
Nazareth (Palestine), 56
Neave, Sgt, Gordons, 159, 181
Neel, Sqn-Ldr A., RAF, 88
Newark (Notts), 9, 10
Nicholls, Lt-Col A., GC, 95, 102, 203-4
Nile, River, 35
NKVD, 187
Non Han (Thailand), 147, 151
Nong Khai (Thailand), 126, 144, 152-3, 174, 176-7; governor of, 153
Noo, Thai 'White', 147
Noon, Thai 'White', 147
North, Jill (later Hon Mrs Alan Hare), 180
North Somerset Yeomanry, 10
Nosi, Fred, Albanian interpreter, 102
Nostell Priory (Yorks), 184
Novikov, Gen, Russian Army, 58

Ohrid, Lake (Albania), 91-2
OSS, Office of Strategic Services, USA, 116, 120, 126, 136, 168, 174-5
Otter, Cpl, radio operator, 103, 105

Pai Tak Pass (Persia), 60
Pakse (French Indo-China), 178
Palmer, Lt-Col A., 95
Palmyra (Syria), 52-4, 56
Panarit (Albania), 90
Panomyong, Pridi (Luang Pradit), codename 'Ruth', 116-17, 124-5, 134-5, 140, 143-4, 146-7, 160, 180-1
Pashko, Gramoz, Albanian Democrat, Deputy Prime Minister, 198, 205
Pepys, Col A., 65
Perkins, Harold, 188
Permet (Albania), 88
Pettini, Sgt, 104

Peza, Maj Myslim, 79, 94, 201
Philby, Kim, 192
Philae, temple (Egypt), 35
Phillips, Capt T., Norfolk Regt, 160, 162
Phillips, Cpl, RASC, 159
Pibul, see Songkram
'Pluto', see Sirikhandra
Po, U Tin (Burmese), 123
Poett, Gen Sir Nigel, 192
Pogradec (Albania), 91-2
Pointon, Maj P., 123, 130, 181
Port Said (Egypt), 25, 69
Port Sudan (Sudan), 25
Pot, Col Prom, Thai, 154, 165
Prajadhipok, King, of Siam, 115, 117
Prang, Pilot Offr, Thai Air Force, 178
Prapussorn, Chinese girl in Ubon, 162
Pratt, Capt Lord R., 71
Prevesi, Gen Prenk, Albanian C-in-C, 110
Przemyz (Poland), 188
Pulao, see Decharat
'Pun', see Sintavi

Qattara Depression (Egypt), 70-2
Quayle, Maj A., later Sir Anthony, 101
Qum (Persia), 58

Rambai Barni, Queen of Siam, 115, 117
Rangoon, 148, 151
RAPWI, 157
Ras en Naquara (Palestine), 21
Rashid Ali, 40, 48, 52
Rasmee, see Chakrabandhu
Ratcliffe, Cpl of Horse J., 43-4
Red Cross, British, 206
Reece, OSS officer, 173-5
Reeve, Tpr, 53 Resolution, HMS, 19
Reta, Albanian bodyguard, 86
Rhodes, 25, 36, 39
Rhona, SS, horse transport, 12
Rifles, 60th, 62
Ritz Hotel, London, 100

Riyadh (Saudi Arabia), 196
Rodonit, Cape (Albania), 106
Romanon, monastery (Greece), 81-2
Rommel, Field-Marshal Erwin, 39, 67
Rotunda Segnali (Libya), 64-5
Rowanduz (Iraq), 49
Royal Horse Guards (The Blues), 3-8,
    9, 143, 188
Royal Marines, 191
Royal Tank Regiment, No 101, 62-5
Royals, The (1st Royal Dragoons), 8,
    62-5
'Ruth', see Panomyong

Saigon (French Indo-China), 176, 180
St Cyr, French militray academy, 27
Salween, River (Burma), 129, 131
Sakon Nakon (Thailand), 129, 132,
    134, 136-7, 144, 152-3; governor of,
    153
Santa Maria, monastery (Albania), 91
Sandhurst, Royal Military College, 3,
    19, 118
Sarafand (Palestine), 56
Sarande (Albania), 202
SAS (Special Air Service), 39, 78, 188,
    195-6
Savannakhet (French Indo-China),
    166, 178
Scots Guards, 29
Scott, Lt D., RN, 98
Scutari (Skodra) (Albania), 110-11,
    198
SEAC (South East Asia Command),
    174
'Seaview '(Albania), 98, 101, 103, 191
Selborne, Lord, 100
Sennar (Sudan), 26, 58
Sensui, Maj, Japanee Army, 167
Serafis, Maj, EAM, 82
Seymour, Maj G., 88, 102, 104, 107
Shah of Persia, 56, 59
Shakespeare, Nicholas,
    writer/journalist, 200
Shami, Ahmed al, Yemeni Royalist
    Foreign Minister, 196

Shanter, author's horse, 40
Shearer, Brig J., DMI, 19
Shehu, Mehmet, Albanian commissar
    and Prime Minister, 87-9
Shen Naum, monastery (Macedonia),
    92
Shëngjergj (Albania), 102, 105
Shengjin (Albania), 111
Shepheard's Hotel (Cairo), 60
Shepr (Albania), 96-7
Shijak, airport (Albania), 198
Shkumbini, River (Albania), 93
Shtab, general staff of LNÇ, 94, 96
Shtylla (Albania), 87-8, 90
Sigurimi, Albanian Security Police,
    198, 203, 207
Simcox, Maj A., 122
Simla (India), 149-50
Sinai Desert (Palestine), 118
Singapore, 181-2
Sintavi, Santa (codename 'Pun'),
    122-3, 125, 130-3, 136, 138, 142-3,
    145-6, 149, 159, 180-1
Sirikhanda, Nai Tieng (codename
    'Pluto'), 132, 134-7, 140-2, 144-5,
    149, 151-3, 155-6, 167, 180-1
Sittaung, River (Burma), 131
Sleima (Malta), 189
Slim, Field-Marshal Viscount, 58
Smiley, Mrs David (Moyra, née
    Montagu Douglas Scott), 188-90,
    192, 195
Smiley, Xan, 189
Smith, Lt, FBI, 79
Smith, Capt V., 105
Smithforce, 62, 64-5, 68-70
Smyth, Maj E., RAMC, 154-5
SOE (Special Operations Executive),
    77, 99, 107, 126, 145, 180, 188, 190
Somaliland Camel Corps, 18-19
Songkram, Field-Marshal Pibul, Thai
    Army, 116, 134, 160, 180-3
Souriya, Wing-Cdr ('Nobby'), Thai
    Air Force, 178
Spahiu, Bedri, Albanian partisan
    commissar, 84, 97

Spears Mission, 64
Special Forces Club, 181
Speed, Brig J., 14
'Spider', *see* Lawson
Stirling, Lt-Col (later Sir) David, 39,
 78, 196
Stone, Capt L., RAMC, 155
Stormie Seas, The, caique, 191
Struga (Albania), 93
Sudan Defence Force, 27
Sudisakdi, Sudhi (codename 'Chat'),
 122-3, 125, 130-3, 138, 142-3, 145-6,
 149, 159, 180-1
Suez (Egypt), 19; Canal, 17, 22
Sultan, Amir ibn Abdul Aziz, Saudi
 Minister of Defence, 196
Sultan's Armed Forces (SAF), Oman,
 194
Summers, Cpl-Maj, 71
Sunderbunds (India), 131
Svasti, Ning, daughter of Chin, 187
Svasti, Noy, daughter of Chin, 187
Svasti, Prince Subha ('Chin'), 115,
 117, 124-5, 128, 135, 180, 187

T, pipeline (Tripoli, Syria), 52
T1, T2, pumping stations (Iraq),
 52
T3, pumping station (Syria), 52-3
Taji (Iraq), 44, 47
Tajiks, 109
Tamara, Nina, 119
Tara, house in Cairo, 99, 100, 112,
 117, 121
Tarnowska, Countess Sophie, 99,
 112, 117
Tavernier, Capt, French Force 136,
 173, 176
Taylor, Lt J., USN, 103-4
Tehran, 58-9
Tel Aviv (Palestine), 20
Tel el Kebir (Egypt), 35, 69, 74
Teta, Perikla, Albanian Minister of
 Defence, 199
Thakhek (French Indo-China), 152,
 168-76

Thomas, Sgt, RAOC, camp
 interpreter, 159, 170
Tigris, River, 57
Tilbury, docks (London), 187
Tilman, Maj W., 88, 96
Tirana (Albania), 102, 104, 111,
 198-9, 203-4; Hotel, 199; River, 104
Tito (Josep Broz), 104, 205
Tobruk (Libya), 62, 64-5, 68
Tom, Albanian interpreter, 91-2
Toosey, Lt-Col P., RA, 156-9, 164,
 181
Toptani, Ihsan, 103, 106, 110-12, 204
Toriani, Gen (Italian), 92
Tosayanonda, Kris (codename
 'Kong'), 132, 135-6, 141, 145, 155,
 159, 180
Toy, Winn's Thai interpreter, 151
Trimi, Sheqir, Albanian interpreter,
 103, 111, 200
Tripoli (Syria), 41
Tu, delegate, Annamite Communist,
 174
Tulkarm (Palestine), 12-13. 17-20
Turkestan, soldiers, 108-10
Tut, U Tin, Burmese politician, 123

Ubon (Thailand), 126, 145, 152-9,
 161-2, 164-7, 170, 179; governor of,
 160
UD, Polish Security Police, 187
Udon (Thailand), 126, 136, 144,
 152-3, 155
Ungpakorn, Puey (codename
 'Khem'), 116
Uzbegs, 109

Valetta (Malta), 189
Valona (Vlorë) (Albania), 88, 96-7,
 191
Velijë (Albania), 111
Viceregal Lodge, Simla, 150
Viceroy's House, Delhi, 118-19
Vientiane (French Indo-China), 152,
 176-7
Viet-Minh, 174, 176

Villa Wolkonsky, Rome, 198
Vinçani, Nexhip, Albanian partisan
 leader, 85, 88, 90
Virginia Water (Surrey), 115, 124, 180
Visani (Greece), 82, 84
Vithkuq (Albania), 85, 88
Voskopoj (Albania), 85, 90

Wadi Halfa (Sudan), 35
Warsaw, 187-8
Watrous, E., 107
Wavell, Archie John (later 2nd Earl),
 118
Wavell, Field-Marshal Earl, 19, 25, 180
Wavell, Countess, 149
Westminster, Duke of, private
 regiment, 44
Whinney, Cdr P., RN, 192
'Whites', codename for Thais, 116,
 128
Williamson, Cpl, Black Watch, radio
 operator, 79, 81, 84, 86, 94
Wilson, Field-Marshal Sir Henry
 ('Jumbo'), 112

Wilson-Brand, Brig, 179
Wiltshire Yeomanry, 58
Windsor (Berkshire), 4, 7-8, 194
Windsor Annexe, hotel, Haifa, 18, 41,
 77
Winn, Maj Hon R., later Lord St
 Oswald, 99, 120, 149-53, 158, 167,
 170, 174, 177, 179-80, 183-4
Woolwich, Royal Military Academy,
 115; Arsenal, 9

Xhibër (Albania), 103

Yasatorn (Thailand), 153
Ylli, Kahreman, Albanian partisan
 commissar, 96, 201
Young, Lt-Col George, RE, 25, 33, 38

Zaloshnjë, mountains (Albania), 86
Zervas, Gen, EDES, 82
Zog, King, of Albania, 102, 104, 201
Zog Bridge (Albania), 111
Zoggists, 90, 92, 100, 102, 105, 109
Zogolli, glade of (Albania), 105